The Stilling of the Storm
Studies in Early Palestinian Judaic Traditions

The Stilling of the Storm

Studies in Early Palestinian Judaic Traditions

Roger David Aus

International Studies in Formative Christianity and Judaism
Global Publications, Binghamton University
2000

Library of Congress in Publication Data

Roger David Aus, *The Stilling of the Storm: Studies in Early Palestinian Judaic Traditions*

ISBN 1-586840-19-3

Published and Distributed by:
International Studies in Formative Christianity and Judaism
Global Publications, Binghamton University
State University of New York at Binghamton
Binghamton, New York, USA 13902-6000
Phone: (607) 777-4495 or 777-6104; Fax: (607) 777-6132
E-mail: pmorewed@binghamton.edu
http://ssips.binghamton.edu

Dedication

In deep gratitude to Wayne Meeks, teacher, friend and critic, upon his retirement from Yale University after a long and distinguished career of teaching the New Testament,

and

Peter von der Osten-Sacken, professor of New Testament and director of Humboldt University's "Institut Kirche und Judentum" in Berlin, friend and critic, who has instilled knowledge of, and great respect for, Christianity's "mother religion" in thousands of theological students and others.

TABLE OF CONTENTS

CHAPTER TWO

Jesus' Calling the First Four Disciples
in Mark 1:16–20
and
Judaic Traditions on Elijah's Calling Elisha as his Disciple
in 1 Kgs 19:19–21

CHAPTER THREE

The Road to Emmaus
(Luke 24:13–35)

Preface

Jesus' stilling of the storm on the Sea of Galilee in Mark 4:35-41 par. is one of the most vivid narratives in the Gospels. In Chapter One I make concrete proposals as to the major influences on it of Palestinian Judaic traditions concerning the prophet Jonah, also caught in a violent storm which was stilled (Jonah One). The pre-Markan Semitic account was also influenced in a minor way by the incident of the Roman emperor Julius Caesar's unsuccessful attempt to cross the Adriatic Sea in a severe storm in 48 BCE.

In Chapter Two I describe the influence of Palestinian Judaic traditions regarding Elijah's calling Elisha as his disciple in 1 Kgs 19:19-21 on Jesus' calling his first four disciples in Mark 1:16-20 par. In a related excursus on fishing in the Sea of Galilee with nets and the expression "fishers of people" in Mark 1:17 par., I call attention to numerous metaphorical usages of the term "fisherman" in Palestinian Judaic sources, some of them positive like Jesus' saying.

Chapter Three portrays the major influences Palestinian Judaic traditions on the prophet Elijah, after his ascension to heaven, exerted on the creation of the Semitic form of the Emmaus narrative in Luke 24:13-35. Another interesting result of this study is the localization of the site of the village Emmaus near Jerusalem. While not historical, the narrative of the resurrected Jesus' encounter with Cleopas and his companion on the road to Emmaus conveys major religious truths, which I spell out.

The bibliography at the end of this volume lists the many Judaic sources which have been employed in the above three chapters. In the main text and the footnotes only the standard abbreviations have been used. No index has been made of all the biblical and post-biblical passages cited, for its length would be inappropriately long. Nevertheless, an index of modern authors is included, primarily to indicate where I differ from many modern interpreters. I have attempted to dialogue with the most important secondary literature, yet also not to overburden the footnotes.

Many translations of the rabbinic sources I cite are my own, yet I have also gratefully employed those of Jacob Neusner and his students, as well as others'. New Testament scholars usually have little expertise in rabbinic Hebrew, not to speak of Aramaic, and they hesitate to employ rabbinic sources in part because of the vexing problem of dating them. Each individual Judaic tradition must be examined and evaluated on its own merits. Here the chaff must definitely be separated from the wheat. While this act of separation is often very difficult, the results can be truly rewarding.

Professor Peter von der Osten-Sacken of Berlin generously read all three chapters, as did Dr. Niko Oswald of the "Institut für Judaistik" at Berlin's Free University. Dr. Gottfried Reeg of that institution was kind enough to share with me bibliographical information on Judaic place-names. Professor Wayne Meeks of Yale University also read Chapter Three. The footnotes indicate the points at which I have incorporated any of their specific suggestions. My deep thanks also go to my son Jonathan Aus for typing and formatting the manuscript on his computer, especially because the final two chapters were handwritten. The Rev. Dr. Thomas Day of Berlin kindly proofread it. In conclusion, I would like to thank Professor Jacob Neusner for accepting this work in the *International Studies in Formative Christianity and Judaism*. It is my second volume in this fine series, and it is being published in the year I turn sixty, 2000 CE. It is my hope that the three studies will help to make modern Christians more appreciative of their deep, sustaining Jewish roots (Rom 11:18).

Roger David Aus
October 1999
Berlin, Germany

Chapter One

The Stilling of the Storm: Jesus, Jonah and Julius Caesar in Mark 4:35-41

Introduction

The narrative of Jesus' stilling a ferocious windstorm from a boat on the Sea of Galilee is found in Mark 4:35-41, Matt 8:18, 23-27, and Luke 8:22-25. In the following study I shall concentrate on the earliest version, that of Mark.[1]

A. Edersheim spoke of "a simplicity of language and a pictorial vividness of detail" in the narrative.[2] M. Dibelius also noted the author's "joy in lively and graphic description."[3] S. Johnson considered its style "almost poetic,"[4] and H. Holtzmann observed that the narrative has a distinctively "aesthetic character," indeed, it creates the impression of "a

---

[1] For recent secondary literature on the Markan narrative, cf. R. Gundry, *Mark. A Commentary on His Apology for the Cross* (Grand Rapids, Michigan: Eerdmans, 1993) 237-247; F. Neirynck et al., *The Gospel of Mark. A Cumulative Bibliography, 1950-1990* (Leuven: University Press, 1992) 580-581; and H. Humphrey, *A Bibliography for the Gospel of Mark. 1954-1980* (Studies in the Bible and Early Christianity 1; New York: Mellen, 1981) 63-64.

[2] *The Life and Times of Jesus the Messiah* (Grand Rapids, Michigan: Eerdmans, 1942; reprint of 1886²) 1.603.

[3] *From Tradition to Gospel* (New York: Scribner's, no date) 78.

[4] *The Gospel According to St Mark* (Black's; London: Black, 1960) 98. See also F. Hauck, *Das Evangelium des Markus (Synoptiker I)* (THKNT 2; Leipzig: Deichert, 1931) 62 for the description in "poetisch gehobener Sprache." Contrast the "simplicity" of Edersheim in n. 2, as well as V. Taylor's comment on the details of the story as "at once vivid and artless..." in his *The Gospel According to Mark* (New York: St Martin's, 1966) 272.

work of art."[5]   Finally, P. Carrington regards the scene as "one of the strongest in the Gospel."[6]

Despite many studies of the pericope in individual essays and in the commentaries, however, basic problems in the account remain unresolved, as the following questions indicate.   What does the phrase in 4:36 mean, "just as he was"?   The same verse notes that "other boats were with him (Jesus)," yet after this they strangely disappear, not to be mentioned again.   Would the structure of the narrative not be more logical if Jesus' questions in v 40, "Why are you afraid?   Have you still no faith?" came after the disciples' waking him and reproaching him with the words of v 38, "Teacher, do you not care that we are perishing?" What was the original language in which the narrative was composed, and where?   Finally, is the account historical, and if not, why was it composed?

The following analysis of Jesus' stilling the storm offers solutions to the above difficulties, as well as to others found in the narrative.   Above all, I propose that early Palestinian Judaic traditions on Jonah One strongly influenced the author of the original account (Section I.).   They were then supplemented in a minor way by the narrative of the Roman emperor Julius Caesar's unsuccessful attempt to cross the Adriatic Sea in a severe storm in 48 BCE (Section II.).   Section III. then deals with the extent of the original narrative and pre-Markan or Markan editing, Section IV. with the original language, provenance and date of the narrative, and Section V. with its historicity, purposes and genre.

---

[5] *Die Synoptiker* (Hand-Commentar zum Neuen Testament 1; Tübingen and Leipzig: Mohr / Siebeck, 1901³) 74.

[6] *According to Mark* (Cambridge: University Press, 1960) 116.

I. Early Palestinian Judaic Traditions on Jonah One, and Mark 4:35-41.

1. *Jonah and the Messiah Jesus.*

Most first century Palestinian Jewish Christians were probably acquainted with the "Q" or sayings tradition in the Gospels which has Jesus speak of the sign of Jonah (Matt 12:38-41 // Luke 11:29-30, 32).[7] It concludes with the words of the prophet from Nazareth: "Behold, something greater than Jonah is here!"[8] It is thus very understandable that after his Crucifixion and Resurrection, in a typically haggadic manner one of Jesus' followers composed a narrative which showed in a concrete way how his Lord, the Messiah, was indeed more than the prophet Jonah.[9]

One strand of Judaic interpretation on Jonah appears to have been messianic and thus capable of association with the Messiah Jesus. *Eliyyahu Rabbah* 18, like other passages,[10] identifies Jonah with the son of the widow (of Zarephath: 1 Kgs 17:17-24). Here Elijah labels him the

---

[7] Cf. also Matt 16:4. On Jonah in the NT, see the art. Ἰωνᾶς by J. Jeremias in *TDNT* 3.408-410.

[8] For Jesus as greater than Solomon, see Matt 12:42 and Luke 11:31; and for Jesus as greater than the Temple, Matt 12:6. In Matt 13:17 and Luke 10:24, Jesus states that *many prophets* desired to see and hear what his disciples now encounter in him. See also *b. Sanh.* 99a (Soncino 670) and *Ber.* 34b (Soncino 215) for all the prophets as prophesying only in respect to the days of the Messiah.

[9] Cf. J. Goldin's remark that "imaginative dramatization" is one of the "familiar devices of haggadic Midrash..." in *The Song at the Sea* (Philadelphia: The Jewish Publication Society, 1990; original New Haven: Yale University Press, 1971) 27.

[10] Cf. *Midr. Pss.* 26/7 on Ps 26:9 (Buber 220; Braude 1.363), which states that Jonah, "a completely righteous man," did not die but "while still alive, entered into his glory, into the Garden of Eden." On this, see also *Eccles. Rab.* 8:10 § 1 (Soncino 8.222). For Jonah as the son of the woman of Zarephath, see also *Gen. Rab.* Vayechi 98/11 on Gen 49:13, which also states that Jonah's home town, the Gath-hepher of 2 Kgs 14:25, is Gobebatha of Sepphoris (next to Jesus' home town of Nazareth; Theodor and Albeck 1261; Soncino 2.959, with notes 5 and 6); *y. Sukk.* 5:1, 55a (Neusner 17.116); *Pirq. R. El.* 33 (Eshkol 113; Friedlander 240); and *Yalquṭ Shem'oni* on Jonah 550 (German in Wünsche 238, in the name of R. Eliezer). See also *Lives of the Prophets* 10 on Jonah, cited below.

"Messiah ben Joseph."[11] In the same chapter, the latter is also associated with Elijah and the Messiah ben David.[12]

In the *Lives of the Prophets* 10 on Jonah, the author also states that after Jonah "had been cast forth by the sea monster (Jonah 2:11, Eng. 10), and had gone away to Nineveh and had returned ...," Elijah then "found the widow with her son...." When the latter died (1 Kgs 17:17–18), "God raised him again from the dead through Elijah...."[13] This writing was composed in a Semitic language, probably in the first part of the first century CE, and most probably in Palestine.[14]

Here in a very early Judaic source Jonah is also considered to be the son of the widow of Zarephath. The narrative assumes that the prophet was first raised from the dead when, after Jonah was in the fish's belly three days and nights (Jonah 2:1, Eng. 1:17), the Lord caused it to vomit him out upon dry land (2:11, Eng. 10).[15] When Jonah later died again, God raised him from the dead through Elijah.

If the Palestinian Jewish Christian who composed the narrative of Jesus' stilling the storm was aware of the above Judaic tradition on Jonah's being raised from the dead (twice!), it too may have encouraged him to apply Palestinian Judaic comment on Jonah One to his own Messiah, Jesus, whom God raised from the dead on Easter Sunday.

This may have been reinforced by an early Palestinian Jewish Christian comparison of Jonah's being in the belly of the large fish three days and three nights, and Jesus' being in the heart of the earth (the grave) so long, which is now reflected in Matt 12:40. A rabbinic tradition found in a number of sources states that God never leaves the righteous in distress (צרה) more than three days. To support this assertion, Jonah 2:1 and 11 as well as Hos 6:2 are cited, the latter concerning God's raising the dead.[16]

---

[11] Friedmann 97–98; Braude and Kapstein 257, with n. 59.

[12] Friedmann 96; Braude and Kapstein 254, with n. 52. I doubt that the Judaic attribution of messiahship to Jonah was influenced in a major way by Christianity. For this possibility, see L. Ginzberg, *The Legends of the Jews* 6.351, n. 38. This manner of thinking appears to be a trend in some modern scholarship on the formative period of early Judaism.

[13] *OTP* 2.392.

[14] Cf. the remarks by D. Hare in *OTP* 2.380–381.

[15] Cf. "the belly of Sheol" in 2:3 (Eng. 2) and "You brought up my life from the Pit" in 2:7 (Eng. 6).

[16] Cf. *Midr. Pss.* 22/5 (Buber 183; Braude 1.301–302); *Esth. Rab.* 9/2 on Esth 5:1 (Vilna edition, p. 28; Soncino 9.112); *Gen. Rab.* Vayera 56/1 on Gen 22:4 (Theodor and Albeck 595; Soncino 1.491); and Mikketz 91/7 on Gen 42:17

The church father Origen, who died ca. 251 CE,[17] also considered Jonah to be a predecessor of Jesus in regard to his preaching of repentance and his remaining three days and three nights in the belly of the whale (fish).[18] In respect to the latter and Jesus' Resurrection, Jerome, who died in Bethlehem in 420 CE,[19] maintained that Jonah *typus est Saluatoris*.[20] He applied this specifically to Matt 8:25 on the stilling of the storm.[21]

Origen and Jerome were among the very few early church fathers who knew and worked with Hebrew and were acquainted with Judaic traditions.[22]

2 Kgs 14:25 speaks of "His (God's) 'servant' Jonah the son of Amittai, the prophet, who was from Gath-hepher." The noun "servant" here is עבד in Hebrew. Very early Judaic tradition transferred the term to Jonah 1:9, which reads in the Hebrew: "And he (Jonah) said to them (the sailors in the ship in the midst of a ferocious windstorm): 'I am a Hebrew' – עִבְרִי אָנֹכִי ...." The definitely pre-Christian Septuagint interpreted the latter noun, however, as "the / a servant of the Lord," עבד י ' : Δοῦλος κυρίου ἐγώ εἰμι.[23] Here ר was read as ד, as frequently happened, and י was considered an abbreviation for יהוה.

(Theodor and Albeck 1129–1130; Soncino 2.843). In this respect see also *m. Ta'an.* 2:4, in regard to the Eighteen Prayer spoken daily: "After the sixth [benediction: 'A prayer of the afflicted when he is overwhelmed' – Ps 102:1, Eng. superscription] he says, 'He who answered Jonah in the belly of the fish will answer you and hear the sound of your cry this day. Blessed are You, O Lord, who answers prayer in a time of trouble'" (Neusner 309; Danby 196).

[17] W. Walker, *A History of the Christian Church* (New York: Scribner's, 1959) 74.

[18] Cf. the Greek in his "Contra Celsum" 7.57 in *Origenes Werke*, ed. P. Koetschau, 2.206–207.

[19] Walker, *A History* 159.

[20] See the preface to his commentary on Jonah in Latin, with a French translation, in Y.-M. Duval, *Jérôme. Commentaire sur Jonas* 161–162.

[21] Cf. the Latin in *S. Hieronymi Presbyteri Opera*. Pars I, Exegetica, 7: Commentariorum in Matheum, Liber IV, 52.

[22] Cf. Jerome's remark that "the Hebrews" say Jonah was the son of the widow of Zarephath, revived by the prophet Elijah, in the preface to his commentary on Jonah (Duval 164–165). There he also notes that "Geth" (Gath-hepher) was near Sepphoris (see n. 10 above with *Gen. Rab.* 98/11).

[23] The Prophets had already been translated into Greek at least by the end of the second century BCE. Cf. O. Eissfeldt, *The Old Testament. An Introduction* (Oxford: Blackwell, 1966) 703.

This interpretation of Jonah as "the / a servant of the Lord" recalls *the* servant of the Lord in the Hebrew Bible. Isa 52:13 – 53:12 became a major aid in Palestinian Jewish Christians' fathoming the suffering of their Messiah, Jesus, on the Cross.

Isa 53:10 for example states regarding the suffering servant: "You (the Lord) make his soul (נַפְשׁוֹ) an offering for sin...." In *Mek. R. Ish.* Pisḥa 1 on Exod 12:1, R. Nathan, a fourth generation Tanna,[24] maintains that Jonah embarked (in the ship to Tarshish) "only in order to cause himself to 'perish' in the sea," for which he quotes Jonah 1:12.[25] The Tannaitic commentary on Exodus continues by noting that "the patriarchs and the prophets gave 'their soul' (נַפְשָׁם) on behalf of Israel."[26]

Here Jonah is considered in a very positive light because of his willingness to offer his own life on behalf of others.[27] This motif may have aided Palestinian Jewish Christians in applying other Judaic traditions on Jonah One to their own suffering servant / Messiah, Jesus, when he also was pictured as having encountered a ferocious windstorm on the Sea of Galilee.

Finally, it was also thought that one of Jonah's future tasks was to capture and slaughter the fish Leviathan as food for the righteous at the messianic banquet.[28]

The above Judaic traditions on Jonah, if all or even only several were known to early Palestinian Jewish Christians, may have influenced the decision of one of them to describe his Messiah Jesus, who suffered on

---

[24] H. Strack and G. Stemberger, *Introduction to the Talmud and Midrash* 88.

[25] Lauterbach 1.10. The verb אָבַד, to perish, is of relevance to ἀπολλύμεθα in Mark 4:38. See below.

[26] *Ibid.*

[27] Cf. the remarks of G. Friedlander in *Pirkê de Rabbi Eliezer* 67–68, n. 10. See also W. Braude, who believes that "the idea of the suffering Messiah may be native Jewish tradition...." Cf. his *Pesikta Rabbati* 678, n. 5. In n. 2 on p. 685 he proposes that the idea "may" have arisen after the destruction of the Temple in 70 CE. In *Pesiq. R.* 36/1 (Friedmann 161b; Braude 678) the Messiah's name is "Ephraim." It can be explained as his being the "son of (ben) Joseph" (Gen 41:52). See Jonah as labeled "Messiah ben Joseph" in *Eliyyahu Rabbah* 18, quoted above. In *De Jona* 13 (54, p. 17) the author speaks of Jonah's self-sacrifice, and in 14 (59, p. 18, following an emendation) the prophet throws himself into the raging sea (cf. also 15 [60], p. 18: Out of concern for the survival of others, he finally surrenders his own salvation).

[28] Cf. *Pirq. R. El.* 10 (Eshkol 32; Friedlander 70, with n. 4) and other sources noted by L. Ginzberg, *The Legends* 6.350, n. 31; Matt 8:11; Luke 13:29; 14:15; Rev 19:9; and the materials cited in Str-B 4.1154–1159.

the Cross, with terms and motifs related to the calming of a ferocious windstorm on the sea by the prophet Jonah. Jesus' act on the Sea of Galilee was portrayed as more than the Hebrew prophet's. Wind and water obeyed his verbal command, for example, without the disciples' throwing him into the Sea, as the sailors did to Jonah in order to save their own lives (1:15).

2. The Jonah Midrash.

A. The Sources and Their Dating.

Although many different Judaic sources comment on the Book of Jonah,[29] those which are most important for the narrative of Jesus' stilling the storm deal with the stilling of the storm in Jonah One. They are now found in *Midrash Jonah*, which is available in several recensions;[30] *Pirqe de Rabbi Eliezer* 10;[31] *Tanhuma Vayiqra'* 8;[32] and *Yalqut Shem'oni* Jonah §§ 549-551.[33] There is also an extensive Hellenistic Jewish sermon originally in Greek by "Pseudo-Philo" called *De Jona*.[34]

---

[29] Cf. L. Ginzberg, *The Legends* 4.246-253 and 6.348-352; the art. "Jonah," "In Rabbinical Literature," by E. Hirsch in *JE* (1904) 7.226-227; and the art. "Jonah," "In the Aggadah," by E. Hallevy in *EJ* (1971) 10.173-174. G. Friedlander in *Pirkè de Rabbi Eliezer* 65-73 and 341-343 also cites numerous parallels. R. Bowers' short study, *The Legend of Jonah* (The Hague: Nijhoff, 1971), refers to Jonah traditions in the church fathers on pp. 20-32. M. Zlotowitz, *Yonah / Jonah. A New Translation with a Commentary Anthologized from Midrashic and Rabbinic Sources* (New York: Mesorah, 1980), has not been available to me.

[30] Cf. the text in A. Jellinek, *Bet ha-Midrasch* 1.96-105, and XIX-XX; a German translation by A. Wünsche is found in *Aus Israels Lehrhallen* 2.39-56. The second and much later section is from the Zohar. See the English translation by H. Sperling and M. Simon in *The Zohar* (London: Soncino, 1956) Haye Sarah in 2.3-4, Vayaqhel in 4.172-176, and Pequde in 4.285-287. Other versions of *Midrash Jonah* are found in J. Eisenstein, *Ozar Midrashim* 1.217-222, including part of the De Rossi MS on pp. 221-222. Ch. Horowitz, *Sammlung kleiner Midraschim* 1.11-23, has three recensions. S. Matlofsky of Jerusalem was so kind as to photocopy for me the first edition of *Midrash Jonah*, Prague 1595, in the Jewish National and University Library. See also Strack and Stemberger, *Introduction* 350, on *Midrash Jonah*.

[31] Eshkol 29-33; English in Friedlander 65-73. Cf. also the M. Higger edition in *Horeb* 8 (1944) 114-119. On *Pirqe de Rabbi Eliezer*, see Strack and Stemberger, *Introduction* 356-357.

[32] Eshkol 486-490. See Strack and Stemberger, *Introduction* 329-333.

[33] A German translation is offered by A. Wünsche, "Der Prophet Jona in der agadischen Deutung des Jalkut Schimoni" in *Vierteljahrschrift für Bibelkunde* 1 (1905) 235-255. On this compilation, see Strack and Stemberger, *Introduction*

While a number of the Hebrew and in part Aramaic traditions on Jonah One are patently Amoraic, many of them are also very early. The following sources attest this.

a) The Septuagint of Jonah 1:9 cited above is evidence of haggadic interpretation already in the second century BCE. The same is true for the humorous remark in LXX 1:5 that Jonah went down into the belly of the ship, fell asleep and "snored" (ἔρρεγχεν). The Hebrew instead states that he went down (ירד) into the hold of the ship, lay down "and was fast asleep" (וירדם, a word play).

b) 3 Macc 6:8 says that "Jonah, wasting away in the belly of a huge, sea-born monster, You, Father, watched over and restored unharmed to all his family." The latter is a haggadic addition to Jonah 2:11 (Eng. 10). This section of Third Maccabees is Egyptian and was also composed in the second century BCE.[35]

c) In the *Lives of the Prophets*, as noted above, chapter 10 deals with Jonah. It reveals many details regarding the prophet, his mother and Elijah which are not found in the Bible. As previously stated, the writing is most probably Palestinian, it is originally Semitic, and it derives from the first half of the first century CE.[36]

d) The Jewish historian Josephus, a native of Jerusalem whose mother tongue was Aramaic, finished his *Jewish Antiquities* in 93/94 CE.[37] In *Ant.* 9.208–214 he betrays knowledge of Palestinian haggadah on Jonah, noting for example that the boat with Jonah was en route to Tarsus in Cilicia; there were sailors, pilots and a shipmaster in it; Jonah tells them he is a prophet of the Most High God; he had entrusted his life to those in the ship; and he was cast up on the shore of the Euxine (Black) Sea. All of these details modify or supplement the Scriptural account, and it is very improbable that Josephus himself invented them. Instead, they point to Palestinian, perhaps even Jerusalem traditions on Jonah, at the latest from the time before 70 CE.

383–385. Jonah is also commented on in A. Greenup, *The Yalkut of R. Machbir bar Abba Mari* 3–28. On it, see Strack and Stemberger, *Introduction* 385–386.

[34] It has been translated from the Armenian into German by F. Siegert in *Drei hellenistische Predigten*. Siegert calls attention to the lack of any Christian influence; the place and date of composition are unfortunately unknown (p. 2). He believes *De Jona* was actually held as a sermon and has a missionary, universalistic character associated with the Day of Atonement (p. 7).

[35] Cf. G. Nickelsburg, *Jewish Literature Between the Bible and the Mishnah* 169–172.

[36] Cf. notes 13–14.

[37] Cf. *Vita* 7 and *Bell.* 1.3 on Jerusalem, *Ant.* 20.267 on the date, and *Bell.* 1.3 for (Aramaic).

e) Finally, early Tannaitic rabbis and anonymous statements by them are cited on Jonah One for example in *Mek.* Pisha 1 on Exod 12:1.[38] These early comments, together with the pre-Christian Judaic materials noted above, show that the early Tannaitic rabbis cited in *Midrash Jonah* are most probably genuine attributions.[39] Indeed, although the present form of the text is very late, many of the expressions and motifs which appear there are pre-Christian, as the following comparison with Mark 4:35–41 confirms.

B. General Recognition of the Relevance of Jonah One to Mark 4:35–41.

Ever since Origen, Jerome and other church fathers, a number of scholars commenting on the narrative of the stilling of the storm have noted the major relevance of Jonah One to it.

This has, however, been denied by commentators such as A. Edersheim,[40] J. Wellhausen,[41] V. Taylor,[42] W. Schmithals,[43] and S.

---

[38] Lauterbach 1.6–11 with Jonah 1:3–4 and 12, as well as 3:1. Shirata 5 on Exod 15:5 cites Jonah 2:4 and 6 (Lauterbach 2.38). An activity of Jonah's wife is described in Pisha 17 on Exod 13:9 (Lauterbach 1.154).

[39] I would also maintain this for *Pirq. R. El.* 10 on Jonah. Strack and Stemberger note for example that the work employs "a wealth of older tradition" and is often aware of the pseudepigrapha (*Introduction* 357). I am aware, however, of the problem of pseudonymous authorship at other places in the work.

In addition to the *Jonah Midrash* and Mark 4:35–41, another, third Judaic development of Jonah One also took place. Its earliest, very abbreviated form is now found in *t. Nid.* 5:17 (Zuckermandel / Liebermann 647; Neusner 6.220–221 – cf. his dots of omission between C. and D.). It deals with a Jewish boy who encounters a storm while on a ship in the Mediterranean Sea, and it quotes Jonah 1:5. The full incident is found in *y. Ber.* 9:1, 13b (Neusner – Zahavy 1.316; Horowitz 223), with allusions to Jonah 1:4, 5, 6 and 15, and similarities to the *Jonah Midrash* and to parts of Mark 4:35–41. Here, for example, God hears the boy's prayer, "and the sea became calm" (ושתק הים). P. Fiebig called attention to this narrative and the stilling of the storm in his *Rabbinische Wundergeschichten des neutestamentlichen Zeitalters* (Berlin: de Gruyter, 1933²) 23–24 for the Hebrew text, with a German translation in *Jüdische Wundergeschichten des neutestamentlichen Zeitalters* (Tübingen: Mohr, 1911) 61–62.

[40] *The Life and Times of Jesus the Messiah* (1886) 1.603, n. 1: "I cannot here perceive any kind of parallelism with the history of Jonah...."

[41] *Das Evangelium Marci* (Berlin: Reimer, 1903) 39: "unsere Geschichte ist nicht der Widerhall der Geschichte des Jonas."

[42] *The Gospel According to Mark* 273: "Strangely enough, the parallels with the story of Aeneas ... are quite as impressive...."

Lachs.[44] Nevertheless, the specific influences of the Jonah narrative were correctly perceived, for example, already in 1870 by G. Volkmar, who posited six similarities between LXX Jonah 1:2–16 and Mark 4:35–41.[45] He was followed by L. Goppelt in 1939, who suggested that LXX Jonah 1:4–6, 11 and 15–16 were relevant to the Markan version of the stilling of the storm.[46] Above all, it has been R. Pesch in recent times who has strongly argued for the relevance of Jonah, especially for the motif "Here is more than Jonah."[47]

With the exception of Pesch, all those scholars who have dealt with the relevance of Jonah One to Mark 4:35–41 have only employed the Septuagint. Pesch himself does not adduce *Judaic* comment on the first chapter of the prophetic book. Yet it is precisely here that most similarities occur. I shall now point to sixteen such similarities, which help to explain terminology, motifs and the structure of the Markan narrative of the stilling of the storm.

C. *Judaic Traditions on Jonah One as Reflected in Mark 4:35–41.*

M. Dibelius labeled Mark 4:35–41 a "tale" (German "Novelle").[48] He noted in regard to this genre "the desire of Christians to relate many great deeds of their Saviour which would proclaim His epiphany; and the tendency of folk-tradition to narrate current stories as if they were about some well-known and famous 'hero.' Such a transference may at times have taken place as an unconscious process. Jewish-Christian

---

[43] *Das Evangelium nach Markus. Kapitel 1–9,1* (ÖTKNT 2/1; Gütersloh, Mohn; Würzburg: Echter, 1979) 256: borrowings from Jonah are only of a prosaic nature.

[44] In *A Rabbinic Commentary on the New Testament. The Gospels of Matthew, Mark and Luke* (Hoboken, New Jersey: KTAV, 1987) 160 on Matt 8:24, he states: "The setting harks back to Jonah 1.4–5, but here the similarity ends."

[45] *Die Evangelien oder Marcus und die Synopsis der kanonischen und ausserkanonischen Evangelien nach dem ältesten Text mit historisch-exegetischem Commentar* (Leipzig: Fues, 1870) 308.

[46] Cf. his *Typos. Die typologische Deutung des Alten Testaments im Neuen* (Gütersloh: Bertelsmann, 1939) n. 5 on pp. 84–85. He also emphasizes regarding the Markan version: "Here there is truly more than Jonah" (p. 85). J. Jeremias in his art. Ἰωνᾶς in *TDNT* 3.408 had also stated: "There are also echoes of Jonah (1:3, 4, 5, 6, 10, 11, 12, 16) in the story of the stilling of the storm (Mk. 4:35–41 par.)." The German original appeared in 1938.

[47] *Das Markusevangelium. 1. Teil* (HTKNT 2; Freiburg: Herder, 1984⁴) 267–277. Cf. especially p. 269, and his article on Jonah One cited in n. 25 on p. 273.

[48] *From Tradition to Gospel* 71.

narrators would make Jesus the hero of well-known legends of prophets or rabbis."[49]

I suggest that a Palestinian Jewish Christian made Jesus the hero of the incident of the stilling of the storm, a creative process which transferred numerous aspects of the well-known legend of the prophet Jonah, based on Jonah One, to him. The following sections attest such a transfer.

1.   *The Mediterranean "Sea" and the "Sea" of Galilee.*

a)   All fifteen occurrences of the word "sea" (θάλασσα) in Mark 1–7 deal with the Sea of Galilee,[50] called so in 1:16 and 7:31.[51] While Luke correctly labels this body of fresh water a "lake" (λίμνη),[52] the Hebrew designation, םָי, means both a saline sea and a freshwater lake.[53] In the Hebrew Bible the Sea of Galilee is called the Sea of Chinnereth in Num 34:11 and Josh 13:27; the Sea of Chinneroth in 12:3; and simply "sea" in Deut 33:23.[54]

In Mark 4:35 Jesus says to (the disciples): "Let us go across to the other side." "Of the Sea" is assumed, and it is specifically mentioned as θάλασσα in vv 39 and 41. The broader setting is that of 4:1, where Jesus begins to teach "beside the Sea," from a boat "on the Sea." Then, after the incident of the stilling of the storm, Jesus and the disciples are represented as having come "to the other (east) side of the Sea, to the country of the Gerasenes" (5:1). Thus both within the narrative of 4:35–41 and the Markan context before and afterwards, the Sea plays a dominant role.

b)   In the narrative of the calming of the sea in Jonah One, the prophet is described as boarding a ship at Joppa in order to travel with it to Tarshish on the edge of the Mediterranean Sea. The term "sea" (םָי) occurs eleven times in the chapter's sixteen verses, which also describe a

---

[49] *Ibid.*, 100.

[50] Cf. 1:16; 2:13; 3:7; 4:1 twice, 39, 41; 5:1, 13 twice, 21; 6:47–49; 7:31. A general usage for "sea" is found in 9:42 and 11:23.

[51] In John 21:1 it is called the Sea of Tiberias, and in 6:1 the Sea of Galilee, of Tiberias.

[52] Cf. 5:1, Lake Gennesaret, 2; 8:22–23, 33.

[53] BDB 410–411.

[54] The RSV has here "the lake," the NRSV "the west."

ferocious windstorm there. All of them are translated in the LXX with θάλασσα, as in Mark 4:39 and 41.

One standard method of Judaic exegesis is called *gezerah shawah*. It is the second of the seven rules of Hillel, and also the second of the thirteen rules of R. Ishmael. It draws an analogy from the same expression used in two different places in Scripture.[55] I suggest that, in a similar way, the Palestinian Jewish Christian author of Mark 4:35–41 borrowed terminology, motifs and even part of his structure from the Hebrew text of Jonah One in part because of the catchword "Sea" (םָי). He transferred Judaic traditions on this chapter to his own narrative of a sea storm on the "Sea" (םָי) of Galilee. Throughout this study, I shall argue for a Semitic background to Mark 4:35–41, which originally employed the Hebrew םָי or the Aramaic אָמַּי.[56]

2. *Jesus' Crossing to the Other Side of the Sea, and Jonah's Crossing to the Other Side of the Sea.*

a) The phrase "on that day" in Mark 4:35 is a later editorial addition. It was made, probably by Mark himself, when he inserted the narrative of the stilling of the storm after Jesus' long day of teaching in parables beside the Sea (4:1–34). Although I believe the phrase "when evening had come" to be original (see Section II. 3 below), it is now incompatible with 5:1–20, the healing of the Gerasene demoniac on the "other (east) side of the Sea" (v 1). This, including thc people's reaction to the miracle, certainly did not take place in the dark. Mark's remark in 5:21, that Jesus then again crossed in the boat to the other side, is also redactional. It gets Jesus back to Capernaum, where he then can heal Jairus' daughter.

The original narrative of the stilling of the storm probably began in Mark 4:35 so: "Jesus was once at the Sea of Galilee. When it became evening / late...."

Verse 35 states of Jesus: "And he says to them (the disciples): 'Let us go across to the other side' (διέλθωμεν εἰς τὸ πέραν)." The verb διέρχομαι is only found here and in 10:25 in Mark. It basically means "go through, pass through," but also "pass through and reach, arrive at."[57] In 1 Cor 10:1 Paul employs it with διά of "'passing' through the (Red - Reed) Sea." Luke says in Acts 18:27 that Apollos wished to "cross" (διελθεῖν – the Aegean Sea from Ephesus) to (εἰς) Achaia. This

---

[55] Strack and Stemberger, *Introduction* 21 and 24.

[56] Jastrow, *A Dictionary* 579.

[57] LSJ 425–426, with 5.

usage with εἰς is also found in Mark 4:35. BAGD 194.2 simply translate here with: "go over...to the other side."

The Greek term πέραν is an adverb of place, employed here as a noun with τό in the sense of "the shore or land on the other side."[58] After Jesus stills the storm in Mark 4:35-41, Mark also states in 5:1 that "they came to the (land on the) 'other side' of the Sea" (of Galilee).[59]

Here in 4:35 Jesus speaks to the disciples, taking the initiative for the journey across the Sea to its other side. This motif of crossing over to the other side of the sea primarily derives from Jonah One and its Judaic interpretation.

b) In Jonah 1:2 the Lord instructs the prophet to go to Nineveh, the immoral[60] Assyrian city on the Tigris River to the northeast of Israel. Jonah refuses and instead attempts to flee to the far west, to Tarshish, which is mentioned three times in v 3. To do so, he boards a ship at Joppa heading for Tarshish, usually identified with Tarsis or Tartessos, a Phoenician settlement on the western coast of Spain at the mouth of the Guadalquivir River.[61]

The *Jonah Midrash* at this point states that when Jonah got to Joppa, the ship in which he wanted to embark was already a two days' journey away. Therefore God brought a windstorm (רוּחַ סְעָרָה) upon the sea and returned the vessel to Joppa.[62] Thus the severe windstorm mentioned in Jonah 1:4-16 was actually considered to be the second such tempest.

---

[58] BAGD 643.

[59] *Ibid.*, which I slightly modify.

[60] Cf. Nah 1:1 and the city's sins in chapter three.

[61] Cf. A. Deissler, *Zwölf Propheten II* (Die Neue Echter Bibel; Würzburg: Echter Verlag, 1984) 155; J. Smart, "The Book of Jonah" in *IB* (1956) 6.879; J. Bewer, *Haggai, Zechariah, Malachi and Jonah* (ICC 30; Edinburgh: Clark, 1951) 29; L. Allen, *The Books of Joel, Obadiah, Jonah and Micah* (NICOT; Grand Rapids, Michigan: Eerdmans, 1976) 204, n. 10; and A. Weiser, *Das Buch der zwölf Kleinen Propheten* (ATD 24; Göttingen: Vandenhoeck & Ruprecht, 1974⁶) 218 (who mistakenly has the east coast of Spain). H. W. Wolff appears to favor this identification in his *Dodekapropheten 3, Obadja und Jona* (BKAT 14/3; Neukirchen-Vluyn: Neukirchener, 1977) 78. A two-year round trip from Israel to Spain is presupposed in *m. B. Bat.* 3:2 (Danby 369; see also *b. B. Bat.* 38a in Soncino 167, with n. 9). I analyze rabbinic and other Judaic sources on Tarshish in "Paul's Travel Plans to Spain and the 'Full Number of the Gentiles' of Rom. XI 25" in *NovT* 21 (1979) 232–262.

[62] Cf. *Pirq. R. El.* 10 in Eshkol 30 and parallels. Higger in 8.115 has "a mighty storm" (סער גדול) here.

Jonah then negotiated with the sailors.[63] The *Jonah Midrash* at this point states:

> He said to them, "We will go with you in the ship / boat." They said to him, "Behold, we are going to the coastlands of the sea, to Tarshish." He said to them, "We will go with you."[64]

Then the midrash notes that they had "passed" or "crossed" (פֵרְשׁ)[65] the sea for a journey of one day when the ferocious storm of Jonah 1:4 took place, with ships / boats "passing by" (עבר) and returning.[66]

Three things are worth noting here in regard to Mark 4:35. First, "He said to them" (אמר להם), i.e. to the ship's sailors, provided the basis for "He says to them" (λέγει αὐτοῖς), i.e. to the disciples in the boat in v 35. Secondly, "We will go" (נבוא)[67] can also mean "Let us go." It provided the basis for Jesus' saying "Let us go" (διέλθωμεν) in v 35. Thirdly, the sailors' telling Jonah from their ship, "Behold, we are going 'to the coastlands of the sea,' to Tarshish,"[68] provided the basis for "to the other side" (εἰς τὸ πέραν – of the Sea of Galilee) in v 35. If one did not have 4:1 in mind, with Jesus' entering a boat and sitting in it on the Sea of Galilee, one would gain the impression from v 36 (without the editorial "and having dismissed the crowd") that the disciples were in their boat and took Jesus, on land, with them after he spoke v 35b. The basis for this is the dialogue in the *Jonah Midrash* between Jonah on land at Joppa and the sailors in their ship / boat, docked there.

It should also be noted in this regard that the *Targum* omits all three instances of "Tarshish" in Jonah 1:3, substituting "the sea" for it.[69] The Judaic tradition behind this substitution may also have made it easier for the Palestinian Jewish Christian who composed the narrative of Jesus' stilling the storm to change "to the coastlands of the sea" from the *Jonah Midrash* to the phrase "to the other side" in Mark 4:35.

---

[63] Jonah 1:5 labels these men הַמַּלָּחִים. For the rare noun מַלָּח, cf. BDB 572.

[64] Cf. Higger 8.115 and parallels.

[65] Jastrow, *A Dictionary* 1242, 2).

[66] Cf. n. 64.

[67] Cf. Higger 8.115, n. 42, with MS א. It is also found in the Vienna MS of Abraham Epstein (Friedlander 66–67).

[68] Higger 8.115, Eshkol 30. Friedlander translates "to the islands of the sea," which is also possible.

[69] Levine 39, English 49; Sperber 3.436. In *De Jona* 7 (24, p. 14) the sailors do not name the "place" to which they are sailing.

"To the coastlands of the sea" in Hebrew is לְאִיֵּי הַיָּם. The Hebrew אִי means "coast, region." The plural אִיִּים is "coast, border, region." The phrase אִיֵּי הַיָּם can mean "coastlands," as in Isa 11:11, 24:15, etc.[70] "To the coast / border of the sea" would then mean "to the other side of the sea." This is expressed in Mark 4:35 by the Greek εἰς τὸ πέραν, as noted above. I suggest that the Palestinian Jewish Christian author of 4:35-41, paraphrasing the *Jonah Midrash* at this point, employed something like הָעֵבֶר here, "to the other side."[71] A strong argument for this proposal is that the root עבר always stands behind εἰς τὸ πέραν in the Septuagint, as in Deut 30:13, "Who will go across to the other side of the sea for us?"[72]

3.   *The Sailors in Their Ship / Boat, and the Disciples in Their Boat.*

a)   There is no reason not to think that the twelve disciples are meant by "He says to 'them'" in Mark 4:35.   They alone are also addressed by Jesus with the words, "Let us go across to the other side." The Markan editorial phrase "And having dismissed the crowd" refers back to the "very large crowd" in v 1.   Then "they (the disciples) take him along as he was in the boat, and other boats were with him" (v 36). This presents the disciples as having their own boat, into which they take Jesus.[73]   When a great windstorm arises and the boat begins to fill with water from the waves, they wake Jesus, who had gone to sleep in the stern, and reproach him for not caring if they perish (vv 37-39).   After Jesus rebukes the wind and calms the sea, he asks them why they are afraid and have no faith (v 40).   The pericope then ends by the disciples' being filled with awe and asking each other who could perform such a miracle (v 41).

Throughout the narrative the disciples are portrayed as sailors with their own boat (πλοῖον – vv 36, 37 [twice]).   It is they who take Jesus along.   Since a sail cannot be used during a ferocious storm, it is assumed

---

[70] BDB 15-16. It can also mean "islands."

[71] See the Hebrew New Testament of Delitzsch, who has here (p. 68): נַעַבְרָה הָעֵבֶר.   On the noun עֵבֶר, cf. BDB 719, and Jastrow 1040: "border, bank, side."   If the Evangelist Mark did not add "when evening had come," as I suggest below, it may have been ערב in Hebrew, a word play.   Both Delitzsch and the United Bible Societies' Hebrew New Testament (p. 99) employ the root here.

[72] Cf. the other instances in Hatch-Redpath 119-120.

[73] Cf. the remark of J. Wellhausen in *Das Evangelium Marci* 39 regarding the original setting: "Jesus is here on land and is taken into the ship ... by the disciples."

that the disciples are rowing while Jesus lies sleeping on a headrest or pillow in the stern.

The Palestinian Jewish Christian author of the narrative knew that at least four of the disciples were experienced fishermen on the Sea of Galilee. Mark 1:16 for example has Simon and his brother Andrew cast a net in the Sea, and James and John, the sons of Zebedee, mend the nets in their own boat in v 19.[74] This enabled the narrator of the stilling of the storm to more easily characterize the disciples as sailors with their own boat.[75]

Since it has been maintained that all the twelve disciples plus Jesus would not have fit into a typical boat of the time on the Sea of Galilee,[76] it should be noted here that a boat from the first century BCE to the first century CE was discovered during low water in the Sea of Galilee south of Kibbutz Ginosar in January of 1986. S. Wachsmann notes that "The craft was primarily used for fishing; however, it no doubt also served to transport passengers and supplies...." Its hull was almost nine meters long. Wachsmann also remarks: "At least fifteen men, inclusive of crew, were able to sail at once in a boat of this class...." He also estimates regarding Josephus' boat fleet used as a ruse on the Sea of Galilee at the time of the Jewish-Roman War: "each boat would have carried 16–17 men, including the crew."[77]

---

[74] Luke 5:3 maintains that Simon also owned a boat. In John 21:2–3, seven of the disciples go fishing in a boat on the Sea of Tiberias after Jesus' Resurrection. It should also be noted that Matt 16:17 labels Simon "bar Jonah," i.e. the father of Simon and his brother Andrew was named "Jonah."   There is no reason to question the authenticity of this tradition. If it was also known to the Palestinian Jewish Christian author of Mark 4:35–41, it too may have encouraged him to apply Judaic traditions on Jonah One to his narrative. Two disciples on board the boat on the Sea of Galilee were sons of Jonah.

[75] Cf. the statement by W. Wuellner in his art. "Fishermen (NT)" in *IDBSup* (1976) 338: "The use of ships for fishing led to the equating of fishermen with sailors...."

[76] Cf. F. Hauck, *Das Evangelium des Markus (Synoptiker I)* 62: "Die Fahrzeuge auf dem See waren klein (Jsph B III, 523; Dalm: Orte 161f); schwerlich könnten die Zwölf mit Jesus in e i n e m Platz haben. So kann ein Teil der Jünger in den begleitenden Booten gedacht sein." See also W. Grundmann, *Das Evangelium nach Markus* (THKNT 2; Berlin: Evangelische Verlagsanstalt, 1977⁷) 138, with n. 17, and J. Gnilka, *Das Evangelium nach Markus (Mk 1 – 8,26)* (EKKNT 2/1; Zurich, Benziger; Neukirchen-Vluyn: Neukirchener, 1978) 193.

[77] Cf. S. Wachsmann, ed., *The Excavations of an Ancient Boat in the Sea of Galilee (Lake Kinneret)* ('Atiqot, English Series 19; Jerusalem: Israel Antiquities Authority, 1990) 1, 132, 41, 134 and 120 respectively. On the latter, see also 120, n. 9, and Josephus, *Bell.* 2.635 (230 boats on the Sea) – 641.

It thus seems that the twelve disciples and Jesus could indeed have found enough room in a fishing boat of the time, also used for transport. The disciples in their boat, however, are modeled on the sailors and their ship / boat in Jonah One.

b) In the narrative of Jonah's causing the sea to become calm in Jonah One, the prophet boards a "ship" (אֳנִיָּה) in v 3. This term is repeated in vv 4 and 5.[78] The vessel is also labeled a סְפִינָה in v 5, which means it is covered over or has a deck.[79] The latter is of relevance to the background of Jesus' sleeping in the stern of the boat in Mark 4:38 as found in Jonah One (see below, section 8). Jonah's ship is thought of as a freighter, propelled forward both by sails and oars.[80] The sailors' "rowing" in the storm is specifically mentioned in 1:13.

The Septuagint translates all four occurrences of אניה and ספינה in Jonah One with πλοῖον, as in the three occurrences of the Greek term in Mark 4:36–37. Recognizing the background of the narrative in the Jonah story, the Hellenistic Jewish Christian translator of the Semitic original of Mark 4:35–41 later logically employed πλοῖον, as in the Septuagint of Jonah One.

Jonah 1:5 mentions "the sailors" (הַמַּלָּחִים) of the ship, a rare term.[81] In Aramaic, the verb מלח can mean "to row."[82] The "captain" of the vessel in v 6 is רַב הַחֹבֵל, i.e. head "sailor." A חֹבֵל is one who pulls "rope," חֶבֶל, on board a ship.[83] It too is a rare expression in the Hebrew Bible.[84] In Jonah 1:10, 13 and 16 the sailors are simply referred to as "the men."

As will become more and more apparent in the course of this study, the sailors of the ship in which Jonah sleeps, and for which a severe windstorm occurs, are the basis for the portrayal of the disciples as the sailors or rowers of the boat in which Jesus also sleeps during a severe windstorm.

---

[78] BDB 58. Cf. also the ships of Tarshish in 2 Chr 9:21 and 20:36.

[79] BDB 706.

[80] Cf. Wolff, *Dodekapropheten 3*, 79, for examples of such a ship.

[81] Elsewhere it is only found in Ezek 27:9, 27 and 29. Cf. also Jastrow, *A Dictionary* 788.

[82] Jastrow, *ibid.*

[83] Cf. a ship's "tackle" in Isa 33:23.

[84] BDB 287. It occurs elsewhere only in Ezek 27:8 and 27–29. The NRSV translates it here as "pilot."

4.   *As He Was.*

a) Mark 4:36 states: "And having dismissed the crowd, they (the disciples) take him along 'as he was' in the boat, and other boats were with him." The expression "as he was" (ὡς ἦν) has greatly puzzled the commentators. It apparently puzzled Matthew (8:23) and Luke (8:22) too, for both simply omitted it. Numerous suggestions as to its meaning have been made.

A frequent explanation is that "as he was" intentionally refers back to 4:1's "he got into a boat and sat in it on the sea."[85] Another is that it means the disciples took Jesus along without stopping for further preparations.[86] A related proposal is that it signifies "without delay."[87] Two commentators interpret the phrase to mean Jesus' tiredness, preparing for his sleeping in v 38.[88] As noted above, J. Wellhausen suggests that the original setting had Jesus on land, who is then taken by the disciples "into" the boat. He interprets ἐν τῷ πλοίῳ as εἰς τὸ πλοῖον.[89] While I agree that this proposed setting is basically correct, I see no compelling reason to change "in the boat" with the dative, as it is.

Rather, the puzzling expression ὡς ἦν means "alone." S. Johnson says almost the same when he notes that it presumably means "without

---

[85] Cf. for example R. Bultmann, *A History of the Synoptic Tradition* (New York: Harper & Row, 1963) 215, and E. Klostermann, *Das Markusevangelium* (HNT 3; Tübingen: Mohr / Siebeck, 1950) 46, for it as a redactional addition; Pesch, *Das Markusevangelium* 270 for it as a pre-Markan redactional remark; and Schmithals, *Markus* 255.

[86] Cf. A. Edersheim, *The Life and Times* 599: "probably without refreshment of food, or even preparation of it for the journey"; H. Meyer, *Kritisch exegetisches Handbuch über die Evangelien des Markus und Lukas* (Göttingen: Vandenhoeck & Ruprecht, 1846²) 49: "ohne mit weiterer Zurüstung sich aufzuhalten."

[87] Cf. E. Lohmeyer, *Das Evangelium des Markus* (Meyer's, 1/2; Göttingen: Vandenhoeck & Ruprecht, 1963) 90, who notes 4 Kgdms 7:7 and Luc., *As.* 24; he points out the strangeness of the phrase, coming just after Jesus had given the order to depart. See also E. Gould, *The Gospel According to St. Mark* (ICC 32; Edinburgh: Clark, 1955) 84: "without further delay or preparation"; V. Taylor, *Mark* 273: "without going ashore"; and M. Hooker, *The Gospel According to St Mark* (London: Black, 1991) 139: it "presumably means 'without disembarking.'"

[88] Cf. G. Wohlenberg, *Das Evangelium des Markus* (Kommentar zum Neuen Testament, 2; Leipzig: Deichert, 1930³) 145: "müde und matt, der Ruhe bedürftig, der Stille begehrend..."; and A. Schlatter, *Markus. Der Evangelist für die Griechen* (Stuttgart: Calwer, 1935) 110: it prepares for the notice that Jesus slept during the crossing.

[89] *Das Evangelium Marci* 39.   Mark 5:30 has Jesus turn around "in the crowd" (BAGD 301, 2.a.α. on ἐπιστρέφω), which Wellhausen apparently thinks should be: "having turned around to the crowd" with εἰς and the accusative.

other companions."[90] It too derives from Judaic interpretation of Jonah One.

b) It is seldom noted that Jonah is presented as the only passenger on board the cargo ship or freighter going from Joppa to Tarshish in the Mediterranean Sea in Jonah One. The captain only speaks with Jonah in 1:6, and the sailors are only concerned with him (vv 7–16). He is alone on board with the crew.

Judaic tradition on 1:3 also emphasizes that Jonah is alone. The *Jonah Midrash* as found in *Pirq. R. El.* 10, for example, says that Jonah does not want both Israel and the nations of the world to call him a lying prophet. He therefore seeks to escape to a place where God's glory is not mentioned. Since this is the case, however, in the heavens and on the earth, Jonah decides: "Behold, I will flee 'by myself' (לִי) to a place where His glory is not mentioned. Jonah went down to Joppa, but he did not find there a ship in which to embark. The ship in which Jonah was to embark was a two days' journey away from Joppa." God then employs a windstorm to bring it back to Joppa, and Jonah departs in it.[91]

The Venice edition of *Pirqe de Rabbi Eliezer* also reads here לִי, as above.[92] Higger at this point has the third person singular: "Jonah went down 'by himself' (לוֹ) to Joppa."[93] *Yalquṭ Makhiri* here reads: "I will go 'by myself' (לִי) outside the Land (of Israel) to a place where the Shekinah is not revealed."[94]

I therefore suggest that Judaic tradition on Jonah's desire to go "by himself" or "alone" in a boat / ship to the other side of the Mediterranean Sea provided the basis for the Semitic original behind ὡς ἦν in Mark 4:36. In Hebrew it could have been לְבַדּוֹ, "by himself," "alone."[95] The Hellenistic Jewish Christian translator of the narrative then paraphrased this with "as he was," ὡς ἦν.

---

[90] *The Gospel According to St Mark* 36.

[91] Eshkol 30.

[92] C. Horowitz 44 (cf. his non-published edition of this rabbinic work, as described in Strack and Stemberger, *Introduction* 357). In his *Pirḳê de Rabbi Eliezer* 66, n. 4, Friedlander also remarks: "In the first edition the word (לִים) 'to the sea' is replaced by (לִי) 'for myself.'" See also Eisenstein 218.

[93] 8.115, n. 36, with MS Casanatense I. VII. 15 as "he went down by himself (לוֹ) to (לְ) Joppa," while the main text has אֶל, "to" Joppa.

[94] Greenup 4–5.

[95] BDB 94 on בָּדַד, II., and Jastrow, *A Dictionary* 138 on בַּד III.

The above suggestion becomes much more probable when one considers that its background in Judaic tradition is found directly before mention of the "other boats" which accompany Jonah's boat. I now turn to these.

5.   *Other Boats.*

a)   Conclusive evidence of the dependence of the original narrative behind Mark 4:35–41 on the *Jonah Midrash* is shown at v 36, where after the mention of "as he (Jesus) was" the statement is made: "and 'other boats' (ἄλλα πλοῖα) were with him." Nowhere else do they appear again, and their strange occurrence most probably caused both Matthew (8:23) and Luke (8:22) to omit them at this point. Here too the commentators have been very puzzled, offering the most varied suggestions.

E. Lohmeyer thought the Evangelist Mark added the other boats in order to hold "those who were about him (Jesus) with the twelve" in Mark 4:10. Originally the sentence read: "But there were no other boats with him." Mark then omitted the negation.[96] As noted above, F. Hauck considered boats on the Sea of Galilee so small that others were needed to hold all of Jesus' disciples.[97] R. Bultmann estimates that the mention of the "other boats" is old, but it "has been rendered unintelligible by the editing."[98] E. Schweizer asks whether those in the other boats at an earlier stage were witnesses of the miracle of Jesus' stilling the storm, but no longer function so.[99] V. Taylor thinks the other boats simply "dispersed in the following storm, for we hear no more of them."[100] M.-J. Lagrange posits that they were fishing boats which went out with Jesus' boat to fish during the night; they were then brought back by the storm or dispersed.[101] G. Wohlenberg considers the people in the other boats to be from the other (eastern) shore; they had been over on the

---

[96] *Das Evangelium des Markus* 90. See also J. Gnilka, *Das Evangelium nach Markus (Mk 1 – 8,26)* 193.

[97] *Das Evangelium des Markus (Synoptiker I)* 62.   See also Grundmann, *Das Evangelium nach Markus* 138, with n. 17.

[98] *The History* 215.

[99] *Das Evangelium nach Markus* (NTD 1; Göttingen: Vandenhoeck & Ruprecht, 1983) 54.

[100] *The Gospel According to Mark* 273.

[101] *Évangile selon Saint Marc* (Ebib; Paris: Librairie Lecoffre, 1929, reprint 1966) 123.

western shore in order to hear Jesus.[1] R. Gundry thinks the other boats show the positive results of Jesus' preaching and hold other disciples. Mark introduces them in v 36 "as a pointer to Jesus' magnetism...."[2] G. Theissen believes they are an example of Mark's strongly condensing an older story he had from tradition. They may earlier have illustrated a threatening situation by having gone down in the storm.[3] R. Pesch labels the "other boats" a "splinter of tradition" which cannot be explained with certainty. For him they most probably go back to the pre-Markan redaction of the collection of miracle stories, which imagines disciples in the accompanying boats.[4]

The above broad spectrum of opinions in regard to the identity or function of the "other boats" in 4:36 shows how puzzling they have been. I propose that they are indeed a "splinter of tradition" and derive from the *Jonah Midrash* just before the ferocious storm.

b) Jonah 1:3 states that the prophet went down to Joppa, found a ship going to Tarshish, and paid שְׂכָרָהּ. The RSV translates the latter as "the fare," the NRSV as "his fare." Literally, however, it is "her (the ship's) fare."[5] In *b. Ned.* 38a R. Yoḥanan (bar Nappaḥa), a second generation Palestinian Amora,[6] therefore comments on Jonah at this point: "He paid for the hire of the whole ship."[7] This too gives the impression that Jonah was alone on the cargo ship or freighter with only the crew also on board.

---

[1] *Das Evangelium des Markus* 145.

[2] *Mark* 238.

[3] *Urchristliche Wundergeschichten.* Ein Beitrag zur formgeschichtlichen Erforschung der synoptischen Evangelien (SNT 8; Gütersloh: Mohn, 1974) 180. On the latter point, see also D. Lührmann, *Das Markusevangelium* (HNT 3; Tübingen: Mohr / Siebeck, 1987) 96.

[4] *Das Markusevangelium* 270. He also mentions several other views. His pupil R. Kratz in *Rettungswunder.* Motif-, traditions- und formkritische Aufarbeitung einer biblischen Gattung (Europäische Hochschulschriften 23/123; Frankfurt am Main: Lang, 1979) 205, also lists a number of opinions. Kratz thinks the other boats were added by a later redactor, whether in a pre-Markan stage or by Mark himself (207).

[5] Cf. BDB 969, 3., on the noun as "passage-money, fare" here.

[6] Strack and Stemberger, *Introduction* 94–95.

[7] Soncino 119–120. R. Romanus then names the sum: 4000 gold denarii. This material then entered the *Jonah Midrash* in its various forms. *Midrash Jonah* in the first printed edition of Prague, and in Jellinek 1.97 has ´ ר for the second authority, an abbreviation of Rabbi or Judah the Prince, a fourth generation Tanna (Strack and Stemberger, *Introduction* 89–90).

At this point *Midrash Jonah* remarks: They had been traveling for one day on the sea when "the Holy One, blessed be He, stirred up the sea upon them by means of a wind storm (רוּחַ סְעָרָה). And 'all the ships' which were in the sea passed by (עוֹברוֹת) and came back peacefully. For it is written: 'but *the* ship threatened to break up' (Jonah 1:4), but not 'the other ones' (הָאֲחֵרוֹת) which were in the sea."[8]

Here early Judaic tradition interpreted "ship" with the definite article in Jonah 1:4 to mean that only the ship of Jonah became involved in the ferocious storm.   The "other ships" were not affected.   One of Eisenstein's versions of the text of *Midrash Jonah* reads at this point: "but not the 'other boats' (אֳנִיוֹת אֲחֵרוֹת) which were in the sea."[9] *Yalquṭ Shem'oni* § 550 on Jonah also notes here: "They were crossing the sea when a windstorm came upon them. At their right and at their left 'all the boats' (כָּל הָאֳנִיוֹת) were passing by and coming back peacefully and silently. Only that ship (Jonah's) was in great distress: 'And it threatened to break up' (Jonah 1:4)."[10] *Pirq. R. El.* 10 at this point reads: " 'And all the rest of the boats' (וּשְׁאָר כָּל הָאֳנִיוֹת) were passing by and coming back peacefully and silently," etc.[11]

These "other boats" are never heard of again in the *Jonah Midrash* because they are a haggadic development related to "*the* ship" in Jonah 1:4. They are the basis for the "other boats" (ἄλλα πλοῖα) which were with Jesus in Mark 4:36. These too are never alluded to again in the narrative. The Palestinian Jewish Christian who composed what is now found in Mark 4:35–41 here retained a motif from the major source of his account, the *Jonah Midrash*. His first hearers would have understood the allusion and appreciated it as part of his narrative artistry.

The above early Judaic tradition from the *Jonah Midrash* may also explain why "the" and not "a" or "their" boat is mentioned just before this in Mark 4:36. The disciples "take him (Jesus) along as he was ἐν τῷ πλοίῳ." They could just as well have taken him along in "a" boat, just as

---

[8] Jellinek 1.97. The first printed edition of Prague reads the same here.

[9] *Ozar Midrashim* 1.219, second (left) column.

[10] Cf. the Hebrew text in Wünsche, *Vierteljahrschrift* 1.237, and his German translation on p. 242.

[11] Higger 8.115. One MS (cf. n. 51) has "the way of." This is also found in Eshkol 30, and in the Abraham Epstein MS (Friedlander 67). In *De Jona* 12 (52, p. 17), however, the sailors tell Jonah that with skill he can transfer to "another ship" which he meets. The large fish which swallows the prophet is meant (16 [63], p. 19).

Jesus in 4:1 gets into "a" boat and sits in it on the Sea of Galilee.[12] "The" boat thus ultimately may also derive from the emphasis in Judaic tradition on "the" ship / boat in Jonah 1:4. It is the only one of many which threatens to break up in the ferocious windstorm.

6. A Great Windstorm.

a) Mark 4:37 states that a "great windstorm" arose on the Sea of Galilee, causing the waves to beat into the boat with Jesus and the disciples. The result was that the boat was already filling up with water or swamping. The "great windstorm" here is λαῖλαψ μεγάλη ἀνέμου. A "storm" (λαῖλαψ) occurs in the four Gospels only here, with its parallel in Luke 8:23. The wind is mentioned again in Mark 4:39 (twice) and 41, this threefold repetition emphasizing its importance. The "great" storm of wind is also contrasted to the "great" (μεγάλη) calm in v 39. Both nouns, storm and calm, are governed by the verb γίνομαι.

The expression "a great windstorm" also derives from Jonah One and its Judaic interpretation.

b) Jonah 1:4 relates that the Lord hurled "a great wind" (רוּחַ-גְּדוֹלָה) upon the sea, and there was "a great storm" (סַעַר-גָּדוֹל) on the sea. In v 11 the cognate verb סָעַר is employed for the sea's growing more and more "tempestuous." Verse 12 has this "great storm" as before, and the verb form reoccurs in v 13. The storm's effect on the water is underlined by the sea's ceasing from its "raging" in v 15.

The verb סָעַר means to storm or rage. The noun סַעַר is a storm or tempest. The related סְעָרָה[13] is found in Ps 107:25 together with רוּחַ as "the stormy wind."[14]

The Greek λαῖλαψ translates סַעַר at LXX Jer 32 (Heb. 25):32, and סְעָרָה at Job 38:1. The Septuagint, however, does not employ λαῖλαψ for סַעַר in Jonah 1:4, but rather κλύδων, which literally means wave or billow. Here it is used in the collective sense of "rough water,"[15] and it is repeated in vv 11–12. The Septuagint has πνεῦμα for רוּחַ in 1:4, and it omits "great" with it.

---

[12] To my knowledge only A. Edersheim in *The Life and Times* 599, n. 1, calls attention to the significance of the definite article here. Yet he thinks it implies "a well-known boat which always bore Him." Edersheim was well acquainted with Judaic sources and had a feeling for Hebrew and Aramaic nuances.

[13] Cf. BDB 704 on all three.

[14] Ps 107:23-32, with the Lord's making the storm be still and hushing the waves, is correctly alluded to by the commentators as also relevant to Mark 4:35–41.

[15] LSJ 962.

The above shows that the Hellenistic Jewish Christian translator of the original Semitic version of Mark 4:35–41, who certainly recognized a major part of its background in Jonah One, was not dependant on the LXX at this point. He employed neither κλύδων for סער, nor πνεῦμα for רוח. Rather, for the first he used λαῖλαψ, as in two other passages in the LXX, and for the second ἄνεμος, as almost always in the LXX.[16]

The "great storm of wind" on the Sea of Galilee in Mark 4:37 is based on the "great wind" and "great storm" on the Mediterranean Sea in Jonah One, which are also commented upon in Judaic tradition. Two examples are the following.

R. Huna (b. Abin), a fourth generation Palestinian Amora,[17] maintained: "In three instances did a wind go forth of unmeasured force, which was capable of destroying the world...." One of these times was in the days of Jonah, as in 1:4 : "But the Lord hurled a great wind upon the sea."[18]

R. Yehudah bar Simon, Huna's frequent interlocutor,[19] then added regarding this wind: "the one in the case of Jonah was for that ship only...."[20]

While these comments in their present form are Amoraic, they reflect earlier Judaic tradition on "the" ship in Jonah 1:4, which implied that others were also there.

As noted in section 5. above, the *Jonah Midrash* as found in *Pirq. R. El.* 10 says that although the ship in which Jonah wanted to embark at Joppa had already proceeded a two days' journey, God brought "a great storm" (סער גדול) upon it and caused it to return to Joppa. Then when Jonah boarded it and they had been traveling for one day, "a great storm" (סער גדול) came upon the sea at their right and their left. All the rest of the ships were passing by and returning peacefully in the silence

---

[16] On the latter, see the concordance of Hatch-Redpath 86–87.

[17] Strack and Stemberger, *Introduction* 103. He taught at Tiberias on the Sea of Galilee.

[18] The "unmeasured force" may be reflected in Josephus, *Ant.* 9.209, where the Jewish historian from Jerusalem speaks of a "most severe storm," and of "winds" in 210.

[19] *Introduction* 103.

[20] Cf. *Lev. Rab.* Thazria 15/1 on Lev 13:2 (Soncino 4.188). Parallels are found in *Gen. Rab.* Bereshit 24/4, which also quotes Jonah 2:8 (Soncino 1.200–201, with n. 2); *Eccles. Rab.* 1:6 § 1 (Soncino 8.18–19); and *y. Ber.* 9:2, 13d (Neusner / Zahavy 1.326). The latter deals with what one says when encountering (storm) "winds": "Blessed is He whose power and might fill the world." In the first three rabbinic sources, which also deal with Isa 57:16, the messianic king is mentioned.

of the sea. Yet the ship in which Jonah had embarked was in great distress and "threatened to break up," as it is written, "And the Lord hurled a great wind upon the sea," etc. (Jonah 1:4).[21] For the second "great storm" above, the Eshkol edition has: "a windstorm" (רוּחַ סְעָרָה).[22] *Midrash Jonah* at this point reads: סיער... ברוח סערה.[23]

The above examples suffice to show that the "great storm of wind" in Mark 4:37, mentioned in connection with the "other boats" at the end of v 36, derives from Jonah 1:4 and its Judaic interpretation.

7. The Danger of the Boat's "Sinking."

a) Mark 4:37 relates that after a great windstorm arose on the Sea of Galilee, the waves beat into the boat "so that the boat was already 'filling up / being swamped.'" The latter verb is γεμίζεσθαι, the passive of γεμίζω.[24] Except for Luke 14:23, this is the only occurrence of the passive form in the Gospels.[25] Matthew rewrites the sentence into "so that the boat 'was being covered' (passive of καλύπτω) by the waves" (8:24), and Luke into "and 'they were being filled up' (passive of συμπληρόω) and were in danger" (8:23).

This motif of the boat's "filling up / being swamped" by a severe windstorm also derives from Judaic tradition on Jonah's ship.[26]

b) In his retelling of the Jonah narrative, Josephus in the first century CE notes that Jonah found a boat (πλοῖον) in Joppa and embarked in it, sailing for Tarsus of Cilicia. "However, a most severe storm arose. The vessel in danger of 'sinking,' the sailors and the pilots and even the commander were making prayers and (promises of) thank-offerings if they could survive the sea" (*Ant.* 9.209).

The verb "to sink" here is καταδύνω, meaning to go down, sink; of ships, to be sunk.[27] Later on in the same account, Josephus notes that

---

[21] Cf. Higger 8.115–116, with the relevant notes.

[22] P. 30.

[23] Cf. Jellinek 1.97.

[24] BAGD 153.

[25] Cf. the unexpectedly large catch of fish, filling up two boats so that they (began to) "sink" (passive of βυθίζω), also on the Sea of Galilee / Lake Gennesaret, in Luke 5:7. This deals, however, with the call of Simon Peter and his partners James and John, the sons of Zebedee.

[26] Cf. the similar motif in regard to Julius Caesar's boat in a severe stormwind below in II.7.

[27] LSJ 890.

"the vessel was about 'to sink'" (9.212). The passive of βαπτίζω is employed here, meaning for ships to "sink."[28]

This double emphasis on Jonah's boat as about to "sink," (thus having filled with water), is therefore very early. Like many other aspects of Josephus' account, it belongs to Palestinian haggadic interpretation of Jonah One. It forms the main background to the boat containing Jesus and the disciples as "filling up / being swamped" in Mark 4:37.

8. *In the Stern.*

a) Mark 4:38 states that "he (Jesus) was now in the 'stern,' sleeping upon the headrest / pillow." The term "stern" here is πρύμνη, which occurs only here in the Gospels.[29] Both Matthew and Luke omit it at this point.

It too has its basis in the Jonah narrative in Jonah One.

b) When Jonah's ship threatened to break up (Jonah 1:4), the sailors became afraid, and each cried to his (pagan) god. Then they lightened the ship by throwing its cargo overboard. "And Jonah went down to the 'hold' of the ship, lay down and fell into deep sleep" (v 5).

The Hebrew for "hold" here is the dual of יְרֵכָה or יַרְכָה, meaning "extreme parts, recesses." In regard to a building it can mean the extreme or hind part.[30] The *Targum* of 1:5 reads: "the bottom portion of the ship" (אַרְעִית שְׂדָא דִבְאִלְפָּא).[31] The LXX translates verse five as Jonah's going down "into the κοιλία of the boat," which also means "hold."[32] The translator certainly intended a comparison with Jonah's later landing in the "belly" (κοιλία) of the fish in 2:1–2, which then became for him the "belly of Hades" (v 3).

---

[28] LSJ 305.

[29] BAGD 724; see also LSJ 1542. Cf. also Acts 27:29 (and 31). It is lacking in the LXX. Philo in *Op.* 88 defines it as "the hindmost place in the ship," to which the pilot goes.

[30] BDB 438. It is only used in Jonah 1:5 of a ship. In rabbinic Hebrew יָרֵךְ can mean "side" (Jastrow, *A Dictionary* 597,2).

[31] Sperber 3.436. Cf. also Levine 40. On p. 60 he translates "below the mast of the ship," which must be a mistake, for on p. 49 he has "below the deck of the ship."

[32] LSJ 966, with their reference to κοῖλος as "hollow" or "hold" of a ship.

The word for "ship" in Jonah 1:5 is סְפִינָה, the only occurrence of the noun in the Hebrew Bible. From the root סָפַן, to cover,[33] it means a ship with a deck.[34] That is, Jonah went down into the cargo ship's hold, which was covered by a deck.

When the Palestinian Jewish Christian who composed Mark 4:35–41 described Jesus as being in the "stern" and sleeping there in v 38, he borrowed this imagery from Jonah 1:5 and modified it to suit the circumstances on the Sea of Galilee. J. Staffy notes for example in regard to the ancient boat discovered in 1986 near Kibbutz Ginosar: "Undoubtedly, it had a deck in the stern...."[35] S. Wachsmann remarks that for the fishing boats of that era "a large stern deck was necessary for laying out and spreading the net." He states concerning Jesus' sleeping in that place: "the area beneath this deck would have been the most sheltered place in the boat."[36] That is, fishing boats on the Sea of Galilee at about the time of Jesus also had a "deck," even if it was on a much smaller scale than that of the cargo ship with a deck in which Jonah traveled.

The term "hold" in Jonah 1:5, the dual יַרְכְּתַיִם, was not employed in rabbinic Hebrew or Aramaic. One expression used, however, was אֲחוֹרִים, the plural of אָחוֹר, back or hind-part.[37] In his special study *Nautica Talmudica*, D. Sperber says *y. 'Erub.* 5:8, 23a with אחורי ספינה should be translated as "stern" (of a covered ship).[38] If this is correct, as

---

[33] For both, see BDB 706.

[34] Cf. also Wolff, *Dodekapropheten 3*, p. 83, n. 5d, and p. 89.

[35] *The Excavations* 41. As noted above (p. 16), the bottom of the boat was almost nine meters long.

[36] *Ibid.*, 111. High storm waves would have first splashed onto the rowers and others in front at the prow. Cf. also Wachsmann's statement on p. 133: "A large stern deck was added to permit the use of the seine net; it also served as the station of the helmsman." The latter was stationed above the deck. In his study *The Sea of Galilee and its Fishermen in the New Testament* (Kibbutz Ein Gev: Tourist Department and Kinnereth Sailing Co., 1989), the experienced Sea of Galilee fisherman M. Nun also describes the seine or dragnet as being arranged "on the 'table' of the stern of the boat" (16; cf. also p. 19).

[37] Jastrow, *A Dictionary* 39.

[38] Cf. his p. 152 (Leiden: Brill, 1986). Neusner in 12.172 has "the outer sides of a ship," following Jastrow 39,1), as in *b. Pesah.* 17b. In modern Hebrew אָחוֹר can also mean stern. See R. Alcalay, *The Complete Hebrew-English Dictionary* 58. The term יְרֵכָה, both in the singular and the plural, is also again used for the stern (p. 963).

seems probable,[39] the Palestinian Jewish Christian author of the Semitic behind πρύμνη in Mark 4:38 probably employed אחורים or אחור at this point. It expressed Jesus' being in the stern or back part of the boat just as Jonah was in the hold or remotest part of the ship.

Finally, it was a part of the author's narrative artistry to employ the above expression after the "other" (אחרות) boats in v 36.

9. Sleeping.

a) Mark 4:38 states that Jesus was in the stern of the boat, "sleeping" upon the headrest or pillow. The Greek for sleeping here is καθεύδω. Together with the parallel in Matt 8:24, it is the only place in the Gospels where Jesus sleeps.

Jesus' "sleeping" in the stern of a boat is also based on Jonah One and its Judaic interpretation.

b) While the sailors during a ferocious windstorm were jettisoning the ship's cargo in order to lighten it, Jonah had gone down into the hold, lain down and "fallen fast asleep" (Jonah 1:5). The latter is the niphal of רדם, to fall into heavy sleep.[40] As pointed out above, the LXX at this point humorously has: "he slept and 'snored.'" *Targum Jonathan* simply states: "he lay down and slept."[41]

In his *Ant.* 9.209, Josephus reveals early haggadic interpretation by noting that Jonah, "when he had covered himself completely, threw himself down."[42] The first expression is the aorist active of συγκαλύπτω, which can mean cover or veil completely. With "head," κεφαλή, it can mean to cover one's face / head.[43] If head is implied in Josephus' phrase, this may be one reason Jesus in Mark 4:38 was in the stern of the boat, sleeping upon the προσκεφάλαιον, a *head*rest / pillow / cushion located there (see below).

The *Jonah Midrash* at this point remarks that "Jonah in the distress of his soul 'was overcome' (נרדם) and 'was sleeping by himself / alone'

---

[39] Cf. the plural construct אֲחוֹרֵי of אָחוֹר as "hinder part," and אָחוֹר as "the hinder side, back part" (BDB 30), as well as 438 on ירכה in regard to a long building: "extreme or hinder part."

[40] BDB 922.

[41] Sperber 3.436; Levine 40 and 49.

[42] The pluperfect of βάλλω occurs here. It may simply mean that Jonah "lay down." Cf. LSJ 304 and 305, III., including an example with "lie down and sleep."

[43] LSJ 1662.

(וִישָׁן לוֹ)."[44] This emphasizes, as in Jonah 1:5, that Jonah like Jesus was the only one on board who was sleeping during the ferocious windstorm.

The *Jonah Midrash* continues by having the ship's captain come to Jonah and say: "Behold, we are standing between life and death, and you 'slumber and sleep'?"[45] The Hebrew text of Jonah 1:6 has here: "What are you doing sound asleep?" (NRSV). The niphal of the verb רדם is employed here, as in v 5.

The above double emphasis on Jonah's sound sleeping alone in the hold of a ship while a ferocious windstorm takes place provided the basis for Jesus' sleeping alone in the stern of a boat, also while a ferocious windstorm takes place (Mark 4:38).

A major difference, however, prevails between Jonah's and Jesus' motivation for sleeping. Jonah's "anguish of soul"[46] is due to his reluctance as a prophet to preach the message of repentance to the wicked city of Nineveh. Therefore he wants to flee as far as possible from the presence of the Lord, to the far west, to Tarshish (Jonah 1:1–3). Judaic tradition expands this by maintaining that Jonah had already had two unsuccessful endeavors in regard to Israel and Jerusalem, and the people ended up by calling him a lying prophet. Fearing that the nations, for example Nineveh, would more easily repent and God would then become very angry with Israel, and that the nations would also call him a lying prophet, he chose to flee as far as possible.[47] This was the background of his "anguish of soul."

Jesus, in contrast, is presented in Mark 4:38 as sleeping, undisturbed by the terrible storm about him. He is not afraid because, in contrast to the disciples, he has "faith" (v 40). The church father Jerome commented on Jonah 1:5 by stating that in contrast to Jesus' sleep, the prophet's was *non securitatis, sed maeroris*, "not of security but of sadness."[48] Here too

---

[44] *Pirq. R. El.* 10 in Higger 8.116. On the niphal of רדם in rabbinic Hebrew as "to be overcome by sleep," cf. Jastrow, *A Dictionary* 1453.

[45] *Pirq. R. El.* 10 in Higger, *ibid.* I employ the English of Friedlander here (*Pirkê de Rabbi Eliezer* 68).

[46] Cf. Jonah 2:3 for Jonah's "anguish / distress" (צרה), and 1:14; 2:6 and 8; and 4:3 and 8 for his "soul" (נפש).

[47] Cf. the beginning of *Pirq. R. El.* 10 in Higger 8.114–115.

[48] Cf. his *Commentariorum in Ionam Prophetam*, ed. Duval, as Jérôme. *Commentaire sur Jonas* (SC 323, p. 190). See also Jerome's commentary on Matt 8:24 in *S. Hieronymi Presbyteri Opera*. Pars I, Opera Exegetica 7. Commentariorum in Matheum, Liber IV, p. 52, as well as the Vulgate on Jonah 1:6, *quid tu sopore deprimeris*.

Jerome betrays his knowledge of Judaic traditions. The first Palestinian Jewish Christian hearers of Mark 4:35–41, acquainted with the *Jonah Midrash* from its use in the afternoon service on the annual Day of Atonement (see below), would have appreciated the contrast in motivation for Jesus' and Jonah's sleep at this point.

The προσκεφάλαιον on which Jesus slept in the stern of the boat may also derive from Judaic tradition on Jonah's sleeping in the hold of his ship. It is a cushion for the "head," or pillow.[49] The term occurs only here in the NT, with Matthew and Luke omitting it.[50]

As noted above, in his retelling of the Jonah story Josephus may allude to something like this. If "head" is assumed, as in many instances with συγκαλύπτω, the native of Jerusalem may mean that Jonah "covered (his head)" and lay down (*Ant.* 9.209). If so, a pillow was intended.

Knowledge of ancient fishing boats in Palestine may, however, be of more help here. Fishing or seine nets[51] were employed on the Sea of Galilee, being let out from on top of the stern deck of a boat.[52] Beforehand, when still dry, they probably were stored under the same deck.

In *y. Beṣa* 5:1, 62d it is stated regarding nets[53] spread out in the sun to dry on a Sabbath: "It is normally forbidden to touch them [but] take account of using them as headrests under your heads."[54] "Using them as headrests" translates מיתגגין here. The verb derives from the root גגי, גנה, which means to cover, be covered,[55] as in the συγκαλύπτω of Josephus above. The Aramaic גני, גנא means to lie down, to sleep.[56] The *Beṣa* passage thus has the basic meaning of reclining or sleeping on a (dry) fishing net, with the latter positioned under one's head. This may explain Jesus' sleeping in the stern of a (fishing) boat upon a cushion or

---

[49] LSJ 1516.

[50] Cf. also BAGD 715–716 for other references.

[51] On the seine net (חֵרֶם, Jastrow, *A Dictionary* 504), cf. the quotation from S. Lieberman in D. Sperber, *Nautica Talmudica* 34, as well as S. Krauss, *Talmudische Archäologie* 2.145–146. See Matt 13:47–48 for its also being thrown into the sea and later drawn ashore. M. Nun in *The Sea of Galilee* describes it on pp. 16–21.

[52] Cf. S. Wachsmann, *The Excavations* 111, and M. Nun, *The Sea of Galilee* 16.

[53] See Jastrow, *A Dictionary* 822–823 on מצדתא.

[54] Neusner 18.109.

[55] Jastrow, *A Dictionary* 259.

[56] *Ibid.*

pillow for his head. He is pictured as employing an unused, dry net
stored under the stern deck.

S. Wachsmann suggests another possibility. He thinks the definite
article in τὸ προσκεφάλαιον "indicates that it was part of the boat
equipment. This may have been a sandbag, used for ballast." Such
sandbags "served to trim the boat when under sail; when not in service,
they were stored beneath the stern deck where they could be used as
pillows."[57]

Whether it was a fishing net, sandbag or other type of headrest /
pillow / cushion, the προσκεφάλαιον employed by Jesus when he slept
in the stern of the boat in the midst of a ferocious windstorm is definitely
a further haggadic embellishment of the narrative's basis in Jonah 1:5.
There Jonah was fast asleep in the hold of his ship, also in the midst of a
ferocious windstorm. The LXX already modified this to say the prophet
"snored." Jesus' "headrest" or "pillow" was a similar haggadic addition.

10. (Approaching and) Waking Someone.

a) In Mark 4:38 Jesus is portrayed as being in the stern of the boat,
sleeping upon the headrest / pillow / cushion. Then "they wake" him
and reproach him for this type of behavior in an extremely dangerous
situation.

The Greek ἐγείρουσιν, the present third person plural of ἐγείρω, is
employed here: to wake or rouse a sleeping person.[58] At 8:25 Matthew
converts this into the past tense, ἤγειραν, and Luke at 8:24 has the aorist
of διεγείρω, also meaning to wake up or rouse someone who is
sleeping.[59] Both Matthew and Luke preface their verbs for waking with
προσελθόντες, "when they had approached him...." Either this is
accidental similar rewriting of the Markan text, or these two Evangelists
were aware of a similar version of the narrative in their respective
Christian communities. The latter is more probable, as will now be
shown.

b) After Jonah went down into the hold of the ship, lay down and
fell fast asleep (Jonah 1:5), the captain "approached" him and spoke to
him (v 6). The Hebrew for "approached" is וַיִּקְרַב, from קָרַב, to come

[57] *The Excavations* 111–112.

[58] BAGD 214.

[59] *Ibid.*, 193–194. In the Synoptics the verb only occurs here and in Mark 4:39 (on
this, see below).

near, approach.[60]   The usual translation for this in the LXX is προσέρχομαι, as in Jonah 1:6 – προσῆλθεν.

Since "approached" is found in both Matt 8:25 and Luke 8:24, and it is lacking in their "Vorlage," Mark 4:38, this appears to be the only point in their retelling of Mark's version of the stilling of the storm where, independently of each other, they reveal influence from the Jonah narrative, specifically from 1:6.

Neither in the MT nor in the LXX does the captain "wake" Jonah before speaking to him. It is simply assumed. Nor is the motif found in the *Jonah Midrash*, although there Jonah does not answer the captain, but "them."[61]   That is, the sailors are thought of as also accompanying the captain to speak with Jonah, which they then do (1:8–9).   Like the disciples in the boat with Jesus, only then do they tell Jonah to "arise" (קוּם) and call upon his god (1:6).   It is probable that the Palestinian Jewish Christian author of Mark 4:35–41 was struck by the strangeness of the captain's or the sailors' not "waking" Jonah from his deep sleep before they spoke to him.   He thus remedied this in his own account by having the disciples "wake" Jesus before addressing him.

A word play was probably involved in the Semitic of the disciples' "waking" Jesus in Mark 4:38 and his "bestirring himself" in v 39.   In Hebrew the first could have been וַיְעִירוּ אוֹתוֹ, the hiphil of עוּר[62] : "And they waked him."

Then the disciples half reproachfully asked Jesus why he was not concerned about their being about to perish.   Verse 39 begins with the aorist passive participle of διεγείρω : διεγερθείς.   The verb in the active means to "wake up, arouse" someone sleeping, and in the passive, as here, to "awaken."[63]   Yet Jesus has just been awakened and spoken to in v 38.   It is illogical that he should only awaken or wake up later.   At 8:28 Matthew sensed the difficulty involved and smoothed over the text by employing the simple form ἐγερθείς.   The passive intransitive of ἐγείρω

---

[60] BDB 897.

[61] Cf. for example Higger 8.116 on *Pirq. R. El.* 10.

[62] BDB 734–735, with the hiphil in Zech 4:1, connected to sleep.   Other passages with sleep are Ps 44:24 (Eng. 23); Cant 5:2; and Job 14:12.   See also Jastrow, *A Dictionary* 1057–1058 for this verb in rabbinic Hebrew and Aramaic, including many examples with sleep.

[63] BAGD 194.

here means to "rise, get up."[64] Having risen, Jesus then rebuked the wind.

I therefore suggest that the Semitic behind διεγερθείς in Mark 4:39 was the hithpolel or nithpolel of the same verb as in v 38, עוּר. In Hebrew it could have been הִתְעוֹרֵר or נִתְעוֹרֵר, with the meaning of "to be waked up"; "to bestir oneself," i.e. become active.[65] The United Bible Societies' Hebrew New Testament has the hithpolel form here.[66]

This means that Jesus does not begin to "wake up" as in the Greek of v 39, which as pointed out above is illogical, for the disciples have already spoken to him. Instead, he begins to "bestir himself" or "become active," rebuking the wind. It was a part of the narrative art of the Palestinian Jewish Christian who first formulated 4:35–41 to employ such a word play with the root עוּר. Unfortunately, this was lost when a Hellenistic Jewish Christian translated the account into Greek.[67]

11. Teacher.

a) After Jesus goes to the stern and falls asleep on the headrest / pillow, the disciples "wake him and say to him: 'Teacher / Rabbi, don't you care that we are perishing?'" (Mark 4:38).

The Greek for "Teacher / Rabbi" here is the vocative διδάσκαλε, the first of twelve occurrences of the noun in the Gospel of Mark. Ten of these are the same form. BAGD correctly state that this form of address corresponds to the title רַב or רַבִּי, rabbi.[68] It too derives from chapter one of the Jonah narrative.

b) After Jonah had lain down and was fast asleep in the hold of the ship, a ferocious windstorm came up, and the "captain" of the vessel went to Jonah and said to him: "What are you doing fast asleep?" (Jonah 1:6) Here it is simply assumed that he awakens Jonah before addressing him. Mark 4:38 spells out this "awakening" with the verb ἐγείρουσιν of

---

[64] BAGD 215, 2.b. See the United Bible Societies' Hebrew New Testament here (p. 21), as well as Delitzsch (p. 13), both with the root קוּם. Luke at 8:24 retains the Markan διεγερθείς.

[65] Jastrow, *A Dictionary* 1057. The Aramaic is the same (1058).

[66] P. 100. Delitzsch employs the biblical niphal form on p. 68, possible also in rabbinic Hebrew.

[67] This may also account for the variant forms διεγείραντες and διεγείρουσιν in some MSS at v 38. They attempted to reproduce the word play.

[68] P. 191.

the disciples. There is no "captain" in their boat, so "they" (i.e., some of them) awaken Jesus.

The Hebrew for "captain" in Jonah 1:6 is רַב הַחֹבֵל. *Targum Jonathan* is similar: רַב סַפָּנַיָּא.[69] A חֹבֵל is a sailor, and רַב הַחֹבֵל employs the collective form to mean "captain."[70] In rabbinic Hebrew רַב can also mean "teacher."[71]

I suggest that the Palestinian Jewish Christian narrator of Mark 4:35–41 not only knew of Judaic haggadic traditions on Jonah One. He was also well acquainted with the Hebrew text itself. He therefore borrowed the רַב from "'chief' sailor" (captain) and applied it to Jesus: רַב. This is made possible by what the disciples now say to Jesus, for it is based on what the captain or chief sailor said to Jonah.

12. *"Don't You Care That We're Perishing?"*

a) In Mark 4:38, when a ferocious windstorm causes the boat to begin to swamp, the disciples awaken Jesus, who is sleeping on a headrest in the stern, and say to him: "Teacher, 'don't you care' that we are perishing?" Matthew in 8:25 paraphrases the first part of this as "Save, Lord!" Luke 8:24 simply has "Master, master!" (ἐπιστάτα twice).

The Greek for the first phrase in Mark 4:38, "don't you care," is οὐ μέλει σοι. The verb μέλω in the active means "care for, take an interest in." The third person singular followed by ὅτι connotes: "someone is concerned that...."[72] A reproach similar to that of the disciples is found in Martha's remarks regarding Mary in Luke 10:40 : "Lord, 'do you not care that' my sister has left me to serve alone? Tell her then to help me!"[73]

In regard to the second half of the question found in Mark 4:38, it should be noted that the middle form of ἀπόλλυμι means to "perish, die."[74] It most frequently translates the Hebrew אבד in the LXX.[75]

---

[69] Sperber 3.436; Levine 40.   Cf. Jastrow, *A Dictionary* 1015 on סְפָנָא as sailor.

[70] BDB 287.   The Hebrew חֶבֶל is cord or rope, so חֹבֵל is a puller of (ship) ropes, a sailor (*ibid.*, 286).

[71] Jastrow, *A Dictionary* 1438,2).   Since it also means "chief," it could easily be borrowed from the phrase " 'chief' of the sailors."

[72] LSJ 1100; BAGD 500.   The same construction is found in Mark 12:14, where some of the Pharisees and Herodians also address Jesus as "Teacher" and admit that he "cares" for no man.   Here, however, the phrase means that Jesus gives no preference to the rich or learned, those who have a better position than others.

[73] Cf. also John 10:13, where the hireling "cares" nothing for the sheep.

[74] BAGD 95, 2.a.α., with a similar example from Arrian.

The entire phrase "Don't you care that we're perishing?" also derives from Judaic tradition regarding Jonah 1:6, which also includes the term רב.

b) Jonah 1:6 has the captain of the ship, speaking on behalf of all the sailors on board, state: "What are you doing sound asleep? Get up, call on your god! Perhaps the god 'will spare us a thought' so that we do not 'perish'" (NRSV). For the first verb the RSV has: "will give a thought to us."   I suggest that the two expressions in single quotation marks provided the basis for the question, "Don't you care that we're perishing?" in Mark 4:38.

The verb עָשַׁת in Jonah 1:6, in the hithpael, only occurs here in the MT. It basically means to "think," to "give a thought to."[76] It is hard to define it more precisely.[77]   This is why the LXX at this point has διασώζω, to save.[78] *Targum Jonathan* reads here: "there will be mercy ... upon us."[79]

In one version of the *Jonah Midrash*, יִתְעַשֵׁת ... לָנוּ is elaborated into the captain's telling Jonah: "Have we not heard that the god of the Hebrews is great? Rise, call upon your god! Perhaps he 'will cause us to become careless / without care' according to all the miracles he did for you (pl.) at the Reed Sea."[80] This is the Hebrew ישלוה לנו, as is still found in MS ג of *Pirq. R. El.* 10. The verb שלו means to rest, to be at ease, to "be careless."[81]

---

[75] Hatch-Redpath 136–138.

[76] BDB 799. The related noun עַשְׁתוּת, occurring only in Job 12:5, means "thought." A similar noun, עֶשְׁתֹּן, is also connected to "perishing" (אבד) in Ps 146:4. The Aramaic verb עֲשִׁית, to "think, plan," is only found in Dan 6:4 (BDB 1108). See also the related phrase with חשׁב in Ps 40:18 (Eng. 17): "The Lord takes thought for me."   The Vulgate of Jonah 1:6 has: "if God will perhaps 'reconsider / think it over' (*recogitet*) in regard to us...."

[77] Cf. J. Sasson, *Jonah* (AB 24B; New York: Doubleday, 1990) 104: "a precise translation cannot be established."   The verb is not found in rabbinic Hebrew. In Aramaic it means to make strong, harden, forge, and only in another verb form to "plan" or "devise" (Jastrow, *A Dictionary* 1128).   H. Ginsberg in "Lexicographical Notes," *Hebräische Wortforschung*.   Festschrift zum 80. Geburtstag von Walter Baumgartner (Supp. *VT* 16; Leiden: Brill, 1967) 82 argues for the Hebrew's meaning "will be gracious to us."

[78] Cf. again Matt 8:25 with σώζω.

[79] For רחם, see Sperber 3.436 and Levine 40.

[80] Higger 8.116. The main text has: "Perhaps he will do for us according to...."

[81] Jastrow, *A Dictionary* 1578. Cf. the related noun שֶׁלוּ, a synonym of "without care."

I suggest that this expression from Judaic tradition, as well as the Hebrew "give thought to us" in the MT of Jonah 1:6, are the basis for the Semitic background of οὐ μέλει σοι ὅτι in Mark 4:38, "Don't you 'care' that ...?" In Hebrew, it could be the phrase הֲלֹא אִכְפַּת לְךָ שֶׁ.[82] The noun אִכְפַּת means burden, "care," solicitude, and many statements in Judaic sources express one's care or lack of it for someone or something.[83] Thus the above Hebrew phrase means: "Don't you care" that..., or "Are you not concerned" that..., as in the Greek text of Mark 4:38.

The second half of the disciples' reproach to Jesus, "Don't you care that 'we are perishing' (ἀπολλύμεθα), is also based on the captain's words to Jonah in the ship in Jonah 1:6, "that we do not perish" (וְלֹא נֹאבֵד). The motif is reinforced by the sailors' words in v 14: "We beseech you, O Lord, let us not 'perish' for this man's life...!"[84]

The Hebrew אָבַד means to "perish."[85] The *Targum* of 1:6 is literal: וְלָא נֵיבַד.[86] The LXX has καὶ μὴ ἀπολώμεθα, "lest we perish." As noted above, ἀπόλλυμι is the usual translation of אָבַד in the LXX.

In the *Jonah Midrash* the captain tells Jonah to arise and call upon his god. "Perhaps he 'will cause us to become careless / without care'...." Just before this the captain also states with reproach: "Behold, we are standing between life and death, and you are slumbering and sleeping...."[87] To "stand between life and death" paraphrases the Hebrew of Jonah 1:6, "lest we perish."

---

[82] Cf. the United Bible Societies' Hebrew New Testament on this verse (p. 100) for the expression as also employed in modern Hebrew. Delitzsch uses דְּאָגָ (p. 68), which, however, is rather anxiety, anxious care, sorrow (BDB 178, and Jastrow, *A Dictionary* 275). In *De Jona* 9 (35-37, p. 14) there is a long speech of the captain directed to Jonah, including: "Man, you're sleeping and don't care about anything?"

[83] Jastrow, *A Dictionary* 65; it is always followed by לְ. Cf. for example *b. Ber.* 19a (Soncino 113); *Ḥag.* 22a (Soncino 140); *Keth.* 14b (Soncino 79); *Giṭ.* 32a (Soncino 132); and *Qidd.* 11a (Soncino 42); *Sifre* Num. 131 (Horowitz 171; Kuhn 511); and *Sifre* Deut. Debarim 16 on Deut 1:16 (Finkelstein 26; Hammer 40).

[84] Cf. the same Hebrew term also in 3:9 and 4:10.

[85] BDB 1. Cf. Jastrow, *A Dictionary* 2,1): to be lost, perish.

[86] Sperber 3.436; Levine 40.

[87] Cf. *Pirq. R. El.* 10 in Higger 8.116; *Midrash Jonah*, without "slumbering," in Jellinek 1.97; and *Yalquṭ Shem'oni* on Jonah § 550, with only "slumber," in Wünsche, *Vierteljahrschrift* 1.237, and the German on p. 242.

It is thus very probable that וּלְ אֹ נֹאבֵד in Jonah 1:6 is also the basis of the Semitic background of ἀπολλύμεθα in Mark 4:38.[88]

13. The Wind Ceased, and There Was a Great Calm.

a) Having risen, Jesus rebuked the wind and commanded the sea: "Be calm! Be silent!" Then "the wind ceased, and there was a great calm (NRSV: a dead calm)" (Mark 4:39). I shall deal with the first part of this verse in section 14. below. Here the second part will be analyzed.

The verb κοπάζω is employed at this point for the wind's "ceasing." In the NT it occurs only here and in the narrative of Jesus' walking on the Sea of Galilee (Mark 6:51 // Matt 14:32).[89] It means to grow weary, abate, stop, rest, "cease." A passage in Herodotus also has the wind as "ceasing."[90]

The noun γαλήνη occurs in the NT only here and in the parallel passages in Matt 8:26 and Luke 8:24. It means a "calm" or "stillness" of the sea.[91] It occurs both in Josephus and in Philo. Thinking of fleeing the besieged city of Jotapata in Galilee at the time of the Jewish-Roman War, Josephus thought it would be unworthy "to leap in the storm from the vessel on which he had embarked in a 'calm.'"[92] While this figurative usage of γαλήνη by Josephus is the only occurrence in his writings, the contemporary of Jesus, Philo of Alexandria, employed the noun frequently in such a sense, usually also contrasted to a storm or storm winds.[93] Since the noun was used as a loanword in rabbinic Hebrew (גַּלְנֵי),[94] the Palestinian Jewish Christian author of Mark 4:35–41 may

---

[88] In his Hebrew New Testament (p. 68), Delitzsch also has כִּי-נֹאבֵד.

[89] Matt 8:26 omits the verb, and Luke 8:24 substitutes the middle of παύω in the plural for both the wind and the raging waves.

[90] LSJ 978 and BAGD 443, who both cite Herodotus 7.191.

[91] LCJ 336, and BAGD 150, who cite Appian, "Civil Wars" 4.115: "But the wind suddenly failing, the rest drifted about in a dead 'calm' on the sea..." (trans. H. White in the LCL edition of Appian's *Roman History*). Cf. the cognate verb γαληνίζω, used in the active of calming or stilling waves or winds, and in the intransitive of becoming calm (LSJ *ibid.*).

[92] *Bell.* 3.195 in the LCL translation of H. Thackeray.

[93] Cf. *Op.* 63; *Sac.* 16,90; *Post.* 22; *Gig.* 51; *Deus* 129; *Cong.* 93; *Som.* 2.166; *Mos.* 1.41; and *Spec. Leg.* 1.224.

[94] Cf. Jastrow, *A Dictionary* 249; Krauss, *Griechische und lateinische Lehnwörter* 2.177; and Sperber, *Nautica Talmudica* 138.

have intentionally contrasted it to the raging "waves" in v 37, Hebrew plural גַּלִּין.[95]

Both the wind's "ceasing" and there being a great "calm," however, derive from Jonah One and Judaic traditions on it.

b) The "'great' (μεγάλη) calm" of Mark 4:39 corresponds by contrast to the "'great' wind" (רוּחַ־גְּדוֹלָה) of Jonah 1:4, mentioned together with a "'great' tempest" (סַעַר־גָּדוֹל, also in v 12).

The Palestinian Jewish Christian author of Mark 4:35–41 borrowed his Semitic term for "cease" (later translated by a Hellenistic Jewish Christian as κοπάζω) in v 39 from Jonah 1:11–12. Both verses deal with the sea's becoming calm or quieting down for the sailors in Jonah's ship. The Hebrew employs שָׁתַק, to be quiet, silent.[96] Ps 107:30, also after a windstorm at sea which was "stilled" (v 29), notes that those in the ships were now glad because "they had quiet."

The LXX of Jonah 1:11–12 translates both occurrences of שָׁתַק as κοπάζω, as in Mark 4:39.[97]

The sailors' wish for the sea to quiet or calm down in Jonah 1:11–12 is realized in v 15. After they threw the prophet into the water, "the sea 'ceased' from its raging." The Hebrew for "cease" here is עָמַד.[98]

This great emphasis on the windstorm's dying down, the raging sea's quieting down or ceasing in Jonah 1:11–15, is also reflected in the *Jonah Midrash* and expanded there. The comment is divided into two portions.

aa) Although the ship in which Jonah was to embark was already a two days' journey away from Joppa, God brought upon it a "windstorm" (רוּחַ סְעָרָה) in the sea and returned it to Joppa.[99] When Jonah then did embark in it and they had proceeded a day's journey, a windstorm "arose" (עָמַד) upon them in the sea from their right and

---

[95] Jastrow, *A Dictionary* 243. The Aramaic plural can also be the same.

[96] BDB 1060. One of the four other occurrences of the verb is Prov 26:20, where quarreling "ceases." Cf. also Jastrow, *A Dictionary* 1640.

[97] The *Targum* employs נוּח (Sperber 3.436; Levine 41), and the Vulgate *cessabit* here.

[98] Cf. BDB 764,2.d, stop, cease doing a thing. In *Ant.* 9.213 Josephus states: "And so the storm was stilled." The Greek ἐστάλη here is the aorist passive of στέλλω, to check or repress (LSJ 1637–1638). It may very well derive from Josephus' original root עָמַד, to stand = to cease, passive "to be brought to a standstill."

[99] *Pirq. R. El.* 10 in Eshkol 30.

their left.[1] All the rest of the ships (v. 1. "the other ships") were crossing over and returning "in peace and in the silence / calm of the sea." But the ship in which Jonah embarked was in great distress and threatened to break up, as in Jonah 1:4.[2]

The Hebrew for "in peace [and] in the silence / calm of the sea" here is בשלום בשתיקת הים.[3] The noun שְׁתִיקָה, with its variant שְׁתִיקוּת here,[4] means "silence,"[5] signifying the sea's "calm." An intentional contrast is made between the quiet state of the sea on both sides of Jonah's ship and the sea there. He is the only one caught in a "great windstorm."

bb) After the captain of Jonah's ship tells him to call upon his god because he could do for them what he miraculously did for the Israelites at the Reed Sea (cf. Jonah 1:6), the prophet tells them (the sailors) to cast him into the sea. Then "the sea 'will become calm' for you," as in Jonah 1:12.[6] The verb וְיִשְׁתֹּק here is borrowed from the latter verse.

After the discussion between the sailors and Jonah in 1:7-14, including their desire that the sea "calm down" in vv 11-12, the *Jonah Midrash* relates in comment on v 15 that the sailors finally decided to cast the prophet into the sea.

They first cast him (into the water) up to his knees, "and the sea 'ceased' (עָמַד) from its raging." The sailors took him out, and the sea began to storm against them. Then they cast him in up to his belly button (or neck), "and the sea 'ceased' (עָמַד) from its raging." They took him out, and the sea began to storm against them until they cast him into the sea entirely. "And immediately the sea 'calmed down' (שָׁתַק) from its raging," as in Jonah 1:15.[7]

---

[1] On the latter phrase, cf. similar imagery in Jonah 4:11.

[2] Higger 8.115-116, Eshkol 30.

[3] Higger 8.115. *Yalquṭ Shem'oni* Jonah § 550 has "and"; *Midrash Jonah* only "in peace" (Jellinek 1.97).

[4] Cf. Eshkol 30.

[5] Jastrow, *A Dictionary* 1638.

[6] Eshkol 31. In Higger 8.116 the quotation of Jonah 1:12 is lacking. *Midrash Jonah* also has it (Jellinek 1.97). "And the sea will become calm for you" is lacking in *Yalquṭ Shem'oni* Jonah § 550.

[7] Cf. *Pirq. R. El.* 10 in Eshkol 31 with four attempts: up to the knees, the belly button, the neck, and then entirely; Higger 8.117 with שׁתק; *Midrash Jonah* in Jellinek 1.97; and *Yalquṭ Shem'oni* Jonah § 550.

Here the sea's "ceasing" (עמד) from its raging in Jonah 1:15 is emphasized by repetition three (or four) times, including once with the verb שׁתק, which also means "to be silent."

*   *   *

The above analysis of Jonah One, especially in Judaic tradition, makes it probable that the sentence "And the wind 'ceased,' and there was a great 'calm'" in Mark 4:39 is based on the שָׁתַק of Jonah 1:11–12, in the LXX also with κοπάζω, and on שְׁתִיקָה, used of the silence / tranquility / calm of the sea in connection with ships other than Jonah's when it was caught in a windstorm in the *Jonah Midrash*. However, the Palestinian Jewish Christian author of Mark 4:35–41 may have employed the synonym and rabbinic loanword "calm" (גליני), contrasting it to the raging "waves" (גלין), as indicated above.

The foregoing discussion of the Jonah background to Mark 4:39b leads one to ask whether there is also a similar background to Jesus' words in the first half of the verse. This is indeed the case.

14. *Rebuking the Wind, and Commanding the Sea to be Silent.*

Jesus rebuked the wind and gave a double command to the sea to be silent / be silenced in Mark 4:39a. The Palestinian Jewish Christian author of 4:35–41 was aware of the narrative of Jesus' exorcising an unclean "spirit" (in Hebrew also רוח, Aramaic רוחא)[8] from a man in Capernaum by "rebuking" it, and then commanding the unclean spirit: " 'Be silent' (φιμώθητι) and come out of him!" The bystanders are then amazed that the unclean spirits "obey" Jesus (Mark 1:21–27). These three expressions in quotation marks (to rebuke, be silent / be silenced, obey) he then transferred to his own narrative of Jesus' stilling the windstorm. At this point I shall comment on the first two.

A. Rebuking the Wind.

Mark 4:37 states that a furious storm of "wind" / windstorm (λαῖλαψ μεγάλη ἀνέμου) arose, causing the waves (of the Sea of Galilee) to beat upon the boat and to begin to swamp it. In v 39 Jesus rebukes this "wind," and the "wind" ceases. In the final verse of the pericope (41), the disciples ask who this is that even the "wind" and the sea obey him. The fourfold repetition of the "wind" in the narrative emphasizes its importance.

---

8 Jastrow, *A Dictionary* 1458.

The background of this windstorm is the "great wind" (רוּחַ-גְּדוֹלָה) the Lord hurls upon the sea in Jonah 1:4, also designated a great storm-wind or tempest (סַעַר-גָּדוֹל). The latter noun is repeated in v 12, and the same root is found as a verb in vv 11 and 13.[9]

When Jesus rebukes the "wind" (רוּחַ), as he rebuked the unclean "spirit" (πνεῦμα = רוּחַ) in Mark 1:25, the wind is thought of as hypostatized.[10] P. Schäfer cites several rabbinic sources where this is most probably the case.[11] That is, an angel is thought of as being in charge of the wind(s). This is understandable, for Amos 4:13 states that God Himself creates the wind.[12] His adjutants, the angels, then take over control of it for Him.

In the Hebrew Bible it is always God who "rebukes" (גָּעַר) the sea, as in Nah 1:4 and Ps 106:9.[13] When Jesus is described as rebuking the wind, which causes a storm or tempest in the sea and makes it rage, a divine attribute is transferred to him already during his lifetime, and not only after his Resurrection. Therefore his disciples ask in awe in Mark 4:41 who this is whom the wind obeys.

Three rabbinic passages dealing with rebuke help to better understand Jesus' rebuking the wind of the ferocious storm on the Sea of Galilee. In *b. Yoma* 39b a Tannaitic legend relates that for forty years before the Jerusalem Temple was destroyed in 70 CE, "the doors of the *Hekhal* would open by themselves, until R. Yoḥanan b. Zakkai 'rebuked' (גער) them, saying: 'Hekhal, Hekhal, why will you be the alarmer yourself? I know about you that you will be destroyed,'" as Zech 11:1 is then interpreted.[14] Here a first generation Tanna[15] is described as

---

[9] Cf. BDB 704 on the noun and the verb, as well as סְעָרָה, storm-wind, tempest, and references to רוּחַ סְעָרָה in Ps 107:25 and 148:8. The latter noun is also found in rabbinic Hebrew (Jastrow, *A Dictionary* 1010).

[10] Cf. in this respect Jonah 1:4, where the ship "thought" (חִשְּׁבָה) of being broken up, as if it were capable of "thinking" (BDB 362–363 on חשׁב).

[11] *Rivalität zwischen Engeln und Menschen. Untersuchungen zur rabbinischen Engelvorstellung* (SJ 8; Berlin and New York: de Gruyter, 1975) 57. See especially *Midrash ha-Gadol* Vayyigash on Gen 44:18 (Margulies 752), where an angel in charge of the wind(s) causes them to be silent (משׁתקן).

[12] Cf. in this respect *b. Ḥag.* 12b (Soncino 68).

[13] Cf. also Isa 17:13, as well as the "rebuke" (גְּעָרָה) of the Lord in 2 Sam 22:16 // Ps 18:16 (Eng. 15); Isa 50:2; and Ps 104:7. In *Aggadat Bereshit* 8 (Buber 21), the rebuke of Nah 1:4 is applied to Jonah 1:15. Rebuking the sea causes it to cease its raging.

[14] Cf. Soncino 186, which I slightly modify.

[15] Strack and Stemberger, *Introduction* 74–75.

"rebuking" the doors of the inner sanctuary of the Temple, which then cease their action. That is, his rebuke causes them to stop opening.

A baraitha in *b. B. Meṣ.* 59b also states that when R. Eliezer b. Hyrcanus, a second generation Tanna,[16] was excommunicated he urged: " 'If the *halakhah* agrees with me, let the walls of the schoolhouse prove it,' whereupon the walls inclined to fall. But R. Yehoshua 'rebuked' (גער) them, saying: 'When scholars are engaged in a *halakhic* dispute, what do you have to interfere?' Hence they did not fall in honor of R. Yehoshua, nor did they resume the upright, in honor of R. Eliezer. And they are still standing thus inclined."[17] Here in a haggadic narrative an early rabbi is described as "rebuking" walls, which then cease (to fall) at his command.

Finally, *t. Ḥag.* 2:12 relates regarding a dispute between a disciple of the House of Hillel and a disciple of the House of Shammai: "And he silenced him 'through a rebuke' (בגערה)."[18] Here a rebuke is also described as producing "silence" (שְׁתִיקָה), as there is a silence or calm after Jesus rebukes the wind (-storm) on the Sea of Galilee.[19]

The main impetus for Jesus' "rebuking" the "wind" in Mark 4:39, however, was his "rebuking" the unclean "spirit" of a man in 1:25. As I pointed out above, the Palestinian Jewish Christian who composed 4:35–41 knew this narrative and borrowed expressions from it.

---

[16] *Ibid.*, 77. His contemporary was Yehoshua b. Ḥananyah (77 – 78).

[17] Soncino 353, which I also slightly modify. For the combination of rebuking and causing to cease / stop, see also *b. Ḥag.* 12a (Soncino 65), where rebuke is also the fifth of the ten things by which the world was created.

[18] Zuckermandel / Liebermann 236. For a different translation, see Neusner, *The Tosefta* 2.317. Silencing by a rebuke (וְזִיפָּה, Jastrow, *A Dictionary* 891) is also found in *m. Meg.* 4:9 (Albeck 2.368; Danby 207; Neusner 323) in regard to Leviticus 18, read along with Jonah at the afternoon service on the Day of Atonement.

[19] Against M. Smith in *Jesus the Magician* (San Francisco: Harper & Row, 1978) 119, I doubt whether Jesus' rebuking the wind and calming the sea must have had magical parallels already in the first century CE. In J.-H. Niggemeyer, *Beschwörungsformeln aus dem "Buch der Geheimnisse" (Sefär ha-razim). Zur Topologie der magischen Rede* (Judaistische Texte und Studien 3; Hildesheim: Olms, 1975), the incantation formula of text 15 has "who rebuked the water" and "who rebuked the sea" (81, 153, n. 25-26, 198). These are biblical phrases. On גער, see also p. 50. Text 29 has "who calms the sea by His power" (82, 153, n. 30 with רגע, 212). The Book of Mysteries may in part go back to the talmudic period (p. 7), yet a first century dating is very improbable.

B. Commanding the Sea to be Silent.

Jesus not only rebuked the wind in Mark 4:39. He also commanded the Sea: "Be silent / be silenced! Be muzzled!" (σιώπα, πεφίμωσο).

Literally, "he commanded" is "he said" (εἶπεν). Yet λέγω, as here, can also mean "order, command."[20] The same is true for the Semitic אָמַר.[21]

Like the wind, the sea is also hypostatized here. In numerous rabbinic sources the angel in charge of the sea is called the "prince of the sea" (שַׂר הַיָּם).[22] At the Reed Sea, for example, God is described as "rebuking" him, as Jesus rebukes the windstorm on the Sea of Galilee.[23]

The latter Sea was also thought to have its own "prince." In *y. Sanh.* 7:13, 25d the early rabbis Eleazar, Yehoshua and Aqiba are portrayed in an haggadic account as wanting to bathe in the public baths of Tiberias on the Sea of Galilee. A heretic (*min*) performs magic upon them, which is countered by R. Yehoshua's magic, and all are held firm until they agree to release each other. Finally, R. Yehoshua challenges the heretic to walk through the Sea, as Moses did. When the heretic does so, Yehoshua gives instructions to the "prince of the sea" (שרה דימא), who then swallows the man.[24]

This passage shows that even after the Palestinian Jewish Christian narrative of Jesus' stilling the storm was composed, the Sea of Galilee was considered to have its own "prince." He could be given a command as in Mark 4:39, where Jesus commands the (hypostatized) Sea: "Be silent / be silenced! Be muzzled!"

The first command, "Be silent / be silenced!" is σιώπα, the present singular imperative of σιωπάω, meaning to keep silent, become quiet.[25] In the LXX it translates a number of Hebrew verbs, including the niphal of אָלַם, the importance of which I shall show in regard to "Be muzzled!"[26]

---

[20] BAGD 469, II.1.c.

[21] BDB 56,4., command.

[22] Cf. the sources cited by Schäfer, *Rivalität* 56.

[23] One instance of this is *Exod. Rab.* Beshallaḥ 24/1 on Exod 15:22, interpreting Ps 106:7 and 9, and Nah 1:4 (Soncino 3.296).

[24] Neusner 31.258–259; in the German translation of Wewers (209) it is labeled 7:19 (11), 25d.

[25] LSJ 1603, BAGD 752.

[26] Cf. the concordance of Hatch-Redpath 1267–1268. The singular imperative form σιώπα is found in LXX Judg 3:19, and the plural in Neh 8:11. The plural

As noted above, I suggest that because of the great emphasis on the verb שָׁתַק, to be quiet / silent, in Jonah 1:11–12 and in the *Jonah Midrash*, including the noun שְׁתִיקָה, silence, tranquility, this root stands behind σιώπα in Mark 4:39. The passage *t. Ḥag.* 2:12 cited above in section A. supports this assertion, for it states that a disciple "silenced him" (שְׁתִיקוֹ) through a "rebuke."[27] The Hebrew nithpael and the Aramaic ithpael forms mean: to become speechless, be struck dumb, become mute, still.[28] Thus σιώπα in Hebrew could be שְׁתוֹק or נִשְׁתַּתֵּק, the latter a good synonym of πεφίμωσο, "Be muzzled!"

The form πεφίμωσο is the second person singular passive imperative of φιμόω, to tie shut or muzzle, to silence.[29] A rare verb, it occurs only three times in the LXX, and in the passive in the NT elsewhere only in Mark 1:25 (// in Luke 4:35) and in Matt 22:12.[30] The latter Markan passage, as pointed out above, provided the basis for part of the imagery in Mark 4:39–41. The following table indicates the similarities.

aa) Jesus rebukes an unclean spirit	–	Mark	1:25
Jesus rebukes the wind / spirit	–		4:39
bb) Be muzzled / silenced!	–		1:25
Be muzzled / silenced!	–		4:39
cc) To be amazed	–		1:27
To be filled with awe	–		4:41
dd) The unclean spirits obey Jesus	–		1:27
Wind / spirit and sea obey Jesus	–		4:41

It is thus quite probable that the Palestinian Jewish Christian author of Mark 4:35–41 was also aware of the Semitic original behind "Be muzzled / be silenced!" (φιμώθητι) in what is now 1:25, and employed it at his own "exorcism" of the wind / spirit and sea in 4:39.

---

also occurs in *Test. Job.* 33:2 (*OTP* 1.855) and *4 Bar* 9:24 (*OTP* 2.424). In Josephus, *Bell.* 2.177, the Jewish historian relates that Pilate in Jerusalem "silenced" the crowd: ἐσιώπησεν.

[27] Cf. in this respect also Mark 10:48 (and the parallel in Matt 20:31), as well as 8:33. For Jesus' rebuking other unclean spirits, see 3:12 and 9:25.

[28] Jastrow, *A Dictionary* 1640. In his *Orte und Wege* (Gütersloh: Bertelsmann, 1924³) 198, G. Dalman proposes *ishtattaq* as the Aramaic behind Jesus' first command.

[29] LSJ 1943, BAGD 861–862. Cf. the cognate nouns φιμός, muzzle, silencing; φίμωσις, muzzling, silencing; and τὸ φιμωτικόν, a spell for silencing (LSJ *ibid.*).

[30] Josephus in *Bell.* 1.16 has the perfect passive πεφίμωνται, "they are muzzled/ mute / silent"; see also 1.438 for Herod's being "spellbound" (πεφίμωτο) by his infatuation for Mariamne.

I suggest that the Semitic verb behind πεφίμωσο was the niphal or ithpael imperative of אָלַם: to be bound, be dumb, silent.[31] In his Hebrew New Testament, Delitzsch for example has הֵאָלֵם at both Mark 1:25 and Luke 4:35.[32] Aquila and Symmachus also employ the cognate noun φιμός, muzzle, for "I will muzzle my mouth" in Ps 39:2 (Eng. 1). Verse 3 (Eng. 2) then states in parallelism: "I was dumb and silent..." (נֶאֱלַמְתִּי דוּמִיָּה). *Targum Psalms* on the latter reads: אִיתְאַלֵּימִית שְׁתִיקִית.[33] The latter are the same verbal roots I posit for the Semitic behind Mark 4:39 – שתק and אלם.

It is early Judaic comment on Exod 15:11, connected to the Jonah narrative in Jonah One, however, which also influenced in a major way the choice of πεφίμωσο in Mark 4:39. According to *b. Meg.* 31a the Book of Jonah was recited as the *haftarah* or reading from the prophets at the *minḥah* or afternoon service on the Day of Atonement.[34] The *Jonah Midrash* was most probably designed to emphasize the theme of repentance on this most sacred day, the liturgical highpoint of the entire year.[35] In the afternoon Sabbath service of Rosh Hashanah or New Year's just before the Day of Atonement, first Exod 15:1–10, then vv 11–18, were read.[36] Jonah One and Exod 15:11 thus appear to have been liturgical readings which were associated with festivals very close to each other chronologically. Indeed, the ten days between New Year's and the Day of Atonement were to be used to recall and repent of all one's sins.[37]

---

[31] BDB 47; Jastrow, *A Dictionary* 71.

[32] Pp. 62 and 108 respectively. The United Bible Societies' Hebrew New Testament has the root שתק both times (pp. 90 and 157).

[33] Merino, *Targum de Salmos* 105. Ps 39:10 (Eng. 9) also has the niphal of אלם. The verb in the well-known passage about the servant of the Lord in Isa 53:7, "like a sheep that before its shearers 'is dumb / silent'" (נאלמה), is rendered by שתקא in the *Targum* (Stenning, *The Targum of Isaiah* 180–181).

[34] Soncino 188.

[35] Cf. for example the remarks of G. Friedlander in regard to *Pirq. R. El.* 10 in his *Pirkê de Rabbi Eliezer* 66, n. 5; and 343, n. 10, on chapter 43 dealing with the power of repentance, probably employed on the Sabbath of Repentance, just before the Day of Atonement. The latter chapter contains part of the *Jonah Midrash* with Exod 15:11 on pp. 341–343.

[36] Cf. *b. Roš Haš.* 31a (Soncino 147) in the name of R. Yoḥanan, a second generation Palestinian Amora (Strack and Stemberger, *Introduction* 94–95).

[37] Cf. *b. Roš Haš.* 16a (Soncino 59), 17b (Soncino 68); *y. Roš Haš.* 1:3, 57a (Neusner / Goldman 42); the Sabbath between New Year's and the Day of Atonement as the "Sabbath of Repentance" ; and the art. "Sabbaths, Special," 3) in *EJ* (1971) 14.572–573.

In the *Mekilta* of R. Ishmael, an older second generation Tanna,[38] Shirata 8 on Exod 15:11, one interpretation of "Who is like You 'among the gods' (באלם), O Lord?", takes the defective אלם to mean "strong."[39] One example of the Lord's strength is His performing miracles and mighty deeds at the Reed Sea (Ps 106:22), including His "rebuking" it (v 9).

Then the anonymous *Mekilta* asks: "Who is like You 'in silence' (באלים), O Lord? Who is like You 'among the silent ones' (באילמים), O Lord? Who is like You who, seeing the humiliation of Your children, nevertheless 'keep calm' (שותק)?" as Isa 42:14 is interpreted.[40]

Here אלם is rendered to be tied up, mute, silenced / silent.[41] It is associated with שתק, just as I propose these as the Semitic background of the two Greek verbs in Mark 4:39.

Just before this in the *Mekilta* on the same verse, Pharaoh is cited as representative of the "gods" (אלים), to whom the Lord is superior. Indeed, as the *Mekilta* then notes, the Egyptian ruler even called himself a god, as Ezek 29:9 and 3 are interpreted.[42] J. Goldin correctly remarks here: "the passage has all the earmarks of polemic against the cult of emperor worship."[43] Pharaoh in *Mek.* Beshallaḥ 2 on Exod 14:5, for example, is portrayed as ruling from one end of the world to the other.[44] In *Exodus Rabbah* he is described as being crowned "cosmocrator,"[45] a title appropriated by the Roman emperors.[46]

---

[38] Strack and Stemberger, *Introduction* 77.

[39] Jastrow, *A Dictionary* 71, on אָלַם, 2) to grow, be strong, as well as the Aramaic equivalent. See also אַיְלִים as strong (p. 69).

[40] Cf. the Hebrew in Lauterbach 2.60.

[41] Jastrow, *A Dictionary* 71, on אֵלֶם, 2), and the Aramaic equivalent, 3), as well as אֱלַם or אִילֵם, mute.

[42] Lauterbach 2.59–61. Sennacherib, Nebuchadnezzar and the prince of Tyre are the other examples given.

[43] *The Song at the Sea* 193; see also 199.

[44] Lauterbach 1.196.

[45] Shemoth 5/14 on Exod 5:1 (Mirqin 5.97; Soncino 3.93); see also a parallel in *Tanḥ.* Va'era 5 (Eshkol 1.241).

[46] Cf. the discussion of other relevant rabbinic sources in my *"Caught in the Act," Walking on the Sea, and the Release of Barabbas Revisited* (USFSHJ 157; Atlanta: Scholars, 1998) 118–126, especially on the mad emperor Gaius Caligula.

I suggest that very early Judaic interpretation of Exod 15:11 [47] not only encouraged the selection of the two Semitic verbs for the "silencing" of the sea in Mark 4:39. It also allowed the Palestinian Jewish Christian author of Mark 4:35–41 to incorporate motifs from a very similar sea journey in a storm by the Roman emperor Julius Caesar, who after his death was deified. I shall comment on this in section II.11 below.

Confirmation of the close association of early Judaic traditions on Exod 15:11 and Jonah One is found in the legendary account of (the later Roman emperor) Titus' desecrating the Jerusalem Temple, claiming to be a god, and dying after a sea voyage back to Rome. The narrative is found in many variations, showing its great popularity.

In *b. Giṭ.* 56b Titus is described as polluting the Holy of Holies with a harlot and then slashing the Temple curtain with his sword. Abba Ḥanan, a third generation Tanna and student of R. Ishmael,[48] quotes here regarding Titus Ps 89:9 (Eng. 8), "Who is as mighty as You, O Lord?" "Who is mighty in self-restraint, that You heard the blaspheming and insults of that wicked man and 'keep silent' (שׁותק) ? In the school of R. Ishmael it was taught: 'Who is like You among the אלם?' (Exod 15:11). Who is like You among the mute ones?" Then Titus gathers all the vessels of the Sanctuary in the curtain and takes them along in the ship which was to carry him to Rome for his triumph. "A gale 'sprang up' (עמד) at sea which 'threatened to wreck / sink / drown him' (לטובעו; cf. a similar phrase in Jonah 1:4)." Titus reasons that God drowned Pharaoh in the sea, and also Sisera. If He is really mighty, He should fight with him on land. This God does by means of a very small creature, a gnat in his brain, which grows to such an extent that it kills him.[49]

In the version of this narrative found in *'Avot R. Nat.* B 7, the account also has God "keep silent" (שׁתק). It then states: "God gave a sign to the sea, and it ceased storming to fulfill what Scripture says: 'And the sea ceased from its raging' (Jonah 1:15)."[50] The latter tradition is also found

---

[47] In *Pirq. R. El.* 43 on the power of repentance, R. Neḥunya b. ha-Qanah, a first generation Tanna and according to *b. Šebu.* 26a (Soncino 138) the teacher of R. Ishmael (Strack and Stemberger, *Introduction* 74), also comments on Pharaoh and Exod 15:11 (Friedlander 341–342; Eshkol 167). As stated above, this chapter retains a section of the *Jonah Midrash*, which describes Pharaoh as escaping the Reed Sea and becoming the ruler of Nineveh, to which Jonah went (Friedlander 341–343).

[48] Strack and Stemberger, *Introduction* 83.

[49] Cf. Soncino 259 – 260, which I slightly modify.

[50] Schechter 21; Saldarini 70.

in *Lev. Rab.* Aḥare Moth 22/3 on Lev 17:3.[51] God's "giving a sign" here is רמז, to nod, gesticulate, hint, notion.[52] It recalls the Son of God, Jesus, who gives a sign by commanding the sea to be silent / silenced and muzzled in Mark 4:39. Here a divine attribute is applied to Jesus.

Qoh. Rab. 5:8 § 4 also relates the Titus anecdote. After his boasting at sea, God immediately " 'rebuked' the sea, and 'it became still from its raging.'"[53] The first expression in single quotation marks recalls Jesus' "rebuking" the windstorm on the Sea of Galilee and its becoming calm (Mark 4:39), and the latter is a quotation of Jonah 1:15.[54]

The above versions of the Titus narrative, most probably already from the end of the first century and the first half of the second century CE, and independent of Mark 4:35–41, show how Judaic comment on Exod 15:11, including the motifs of silence and might / power, was connected to a sea voyage and the ceasing of a storm on it, and to imagery borrowed from Jonah One. The same was also true of the Palestinian Jewish Christian author of Mark 4:35–41, who (in addition to 1:25) borrowed the motif of "being muzzled / silenced" from Exod 15:11 and "being silent / silenced" from the *Jonah Midrash*, which also cites the latter verse.

15. *Great Fear.*

a) After Jesus rebuked the wind and commanded the raging Sea of Galilee to be silent and muzzled, the wind ceased and there was a great calm. Then Jesus in Mark 4:40 said to the disciples: "Why are you 'afraid'? Have you still no faith?" Verse 41 continues literally: "And they feared with great fear...."

The first expression in single quotation marks from v 40 employs the plural of the adjective δειλός. It means "cowardly, timid."[55] It occurs in the Gospels only here and in the parallel Matt 8:26, where the Evangelist couples it with the adjective "of little faith."[56] Luke omits it at 8:25.

---

[51] Margulies 501; Soncino 4.279.

[52] Jastrow, *A Dictionary* 1481–1482.

[53] Cf. the Vilna edition of *Midrash Rabba*, Qoheleth, p. 29.

[54] For other versions of the Titus narrative, see Saldarini 67, n. 14.

[55] BAGD 173, LSJ 374.

[56] Its only other occurrence in the NT is in Rev 21:8, where it is also coupled with "unbelieving."

The Greek for the above phrase quoted from Mark 4:41 is καὶ ἐφοβήθησαν φόβον μέγαν. The verb φοβέομαι basically means to be afraid. This is how BAGD interpret Mark 4:41 – "they were very much afraid." Nevertheless, the translation of the NRSV is preferable here: "And they were filled with great awe...," for fear of God is also to have respect for Him, to revere Him.[57] Luke 8:25 retains at this point the aorist participle of φοβέομαι, yet adds θαυμάζω to it: "Having become afraid / filled with awe, 'they marveled.'"[58] Matt 8:27 omits φοβέομαι altogether and only has the disciples "marvel."

Logically, Jesus' questions "Why are you afraid? Have you still no faith?" in Mark 4:40 should come after the disciples half reproach him in v 38 with the question: "Don't you care that we are perishing?" This would be followed by Jesus' rebuking the wind and calming the Sea in v 39. The disciples' reaction of great reverence or awe in v 41 would then follow Jesus' action. This is why Matthew rewrote the narrative accordingly in 8:26, as did Luke in 8:24–25.[59]

The disciples' "fear," the rare φοβέομαι with the cognate accusative noun,[60] indicating Semitic influence, and the illogical order of the Markan narrative at this point, all derive from the Hebrew text of Jonah One and its Judaic interpretation in the *Jonah Midrash*.

b) Fear and reverential awe play major roles in Jonah One at four points.

aa) When a mighty windstorm arose on the sea and their ships threatened to break up, the sailors " 'were afraid' (וַיִּֽירְא֗וּ), and each cried to his god" (1:5). The *Targum* repeats the first in Aramaic and then paraphrases: "and each man prayed to 'his fear' (דְחַלְתֵיהּ), but they saw that they (the idols) were useless."[61] The noun דַּחֲלְתָּא here means both "fear" and "deity."[62] The same is true for the Hebrew יִרְאָה, "fear" and "idol."[63]

---

[57] Cf. BAGD 862,1.a., and 863,2., respectively. The cognate noun φόβος can mean either fear or reverence / respect (863).

[58] Cf. θαυμάζω in BAGD 352 as wonder, marvel, be astonished.

[59] Luke in 8:25 retains, however, the question of the disciples' faith at its Markan position.

[60] It is only found elsewhere in the NT at Luke 2:9. Cf. also Matt 17:6 and 27:54 with σφόδρα. See BDF § 153,1) (p. 85).

[61] Sperber 3.436; Levine 40, whose English on p. 49 I slightly modify.

[62] Jastrow, *A Dictionary* 292.

[63] *Ibid.*, 593.

In the *Jonah Midrash* at this point R. Ḥananya or Ḥanina, either a first or second generation Tanna,[64] says that there were men (sailors) from seventy tongues (all the peoples of the earth)[65] on the ship, and each had his idol in his hand, as in Jonah 1:5. They then fell down and said: "Let each man call upon the name of his god. The god who will answer and save us from this affliction shall be (the true) god." They did so, but it was to no avail.[66] Thus the captain approached Jonah.

Here the sailors' "fearing" in Jonah 1:5 is interpreted as each man's revering his own god / idol, all of which proved useless. Only Jonah's God has the power to still the storm and to save them all from perishing.

bb) When the sailors on his ship determined by lot that the ferocious windstorm was due to Jonah's presence on board, they asked him various questions (1:8). His reply was: "I am a Hebrew, and 'I fear / revere' (אֲנִי יָרֵא) the Lord God of heaven, who made the sea and the dry land" (v 9).

This is the basis for a phrase at the very end of the *Jonah Midrash*, where Jonah 1:16 is interpreted to mean that each of the (seventy) sailors then made a vow and kept (it): to bring his wife and his whole household "to the fear of" (לְיִרְאַת) the God of Jonah.[67] Here "fear" of God is also meant as reverence for Him.

cc) As a reaction to Jonah's statement in 1:9, the sailors in v 10 "feared with great fear" (וַיִּירְאוּ ... יִרְאָה גְדוֹלָה). This is true fear / dread / terror of perishing (vv 6 and 14). It led to the men's throwing Jonah into the sea in v 15.

This is also what Josephus means in his retelling of the Jonah narrative in *Ant.* 9.212. When the sailors noted that their vessel was about to sink, and that they were urged on to the deed by the prophet himself and by "fear" (τὸ δέος) of their own deliverance, they finally cast

---

[64] Apparently the rabbi went by both names, perhaps in different places.   Cf. Strack and Stemberger, *Introduction* 74 and 82.

[65] On the seventy languages and nations, see the sources listed under these headings in the index of Ginzberg, *The Legends of the Jews*, 7.429, as well as Luke 10:1.

[66] *Pirq. R. El.* 10 in Eshkol 31; Higger 8.116; Friedlander 67–68 with the notes; *Yalquṭ Shem'oni* Jonah § 550 (Wünsche 242); and *Midrash Jonah* (Jellinek 1.97; Wünsche 41).

[67] *Pirq. R. El.* 10 in Eshkol 33; see also Friedlander, *Pirkê de Rabbi Eliezer* 72, n. 12.   For Jonah as one of the three "early fathers" who served (God) out of fear and reverence, thus inheriting both this and the coming world, see *'Abot R. Nat.* B 10 (Schechter 26; Saldarini 88, with n. 13).

Jonah into the sea. One classical source notes that this Greek term, fear or alarm, is more lasting than φόβος.[68]

The LXX of Jonah 1:10 has ἐφοβήθησαν ... φόβον μέγαν.[69] This is the exact same wording as in Mark 4:41. Yet it is much more probable that the Semitic behind the Markan expression derives from Jonah 1:16, now to be analyzed.

dd) Chapter One of the Book of Jonah ends at (Heb.) v 16. When the sailors saw that the sea ceased from its raging, " 'they feared / revered with a great fear / reverence' the Lord, and offered an offering to the Lord, and vowed vows" (literal translation). The Hebrew for the first phrase is וַיִּירְאוּ ... יִרְאָה גְדוֹלָה, exactly as in v 10. I suggest that "And they feared / revered with a great fear / reverence" in Mark 4:41 is based on the equivalent Hebrew phrase in Jonah 1:16 for the following reasons.

First, it follows the ceasing of the raging of the sea in 1:15, just as Mark 4:41 follows Jesus' silencing the sea and the great calm in v 39.

Secondly, Jonah 1:16 is the culmination of the episode of the ferocious windstorm at sea in chapter one, which may originally have been a separate episode.[70] The first expression in Mark 4:41 is also the logical culmination of the entire account, the disciples' reaction of fear / reverence / awe in regard to Jesus' ability to rebuke the wind (רוּחַ) and calm the Sea of Galilee. It corresponds to the basic outline of another Gospel story the Palestinian Jewish Christian author of 4:35–41 followed at this point. After Jesus rebuked the unclean "spirit" (רוּחַ) and said to it "Be muzzled / silenced!," Mark 1:27 has all the bystanders be "amazed" and ask themselves how unclean spirits "obey" Jesus. The Palestinian Jewish Christian author or narrator retained this outline and these motifs in 4:41.

Thirdly, the *Jonah Midrash* corroborates the above. It moves from comment on Jonah 1:15 to the account of Jonah and the fish in chapter two, which ends with the fish's vomiting Jonah upon the dry land. Omitting any reference to chapters 3–4, the *Jonah Midrash* then states: When the sailors saw all the signs and miracles and great wonders which God did to Jonah, each threw his god into the sea, as in 2:9 (Eng.8). Then they returned to Joppa, went up to Jerusalem and circumcised the flesh

---

[68] LSJ 379. For the fear of sinking and the panic of the sailors, cf. also *De Jona* 11 (42, 44, p. 15).

[69] Elsewhere in the LXX it is found only in 1 Macc 10:8. Ps 52(53):5 in some Greek versions has a similar reading without "great." Jonah 1:16 has the dative, φόβῳ μεγάλῳ.

[70] Cf. for example A. Weiser, *Das Buch der zwölf Kleinen Propheten*, 220.

of their foreskins, as it is written: "And the men feared with a great fear the Lord, and they offered an offering to the Lord and vowed vows" (1:16). Is it not so, however, that an offering from the Gentiles is not acceptable? Rather, this is the blood of the covenant which is like the blood of a sacrifice. And they vowed and kept[71] (the vow) that each bring his wife and all his household "to the fear of" the God of Jonah. They made the vow and performed it. And of these it is said: "Concerning the proselytes, the proselytes of righteousness."[72]

The latter phrase, the very end of the *Jonah Midrash*, is a quotation from the thirteenth benediction of the "Eighteen Prayer" (Shemoneh 'Esreh), the benedictions of which E. Hirsch maintains "date from the earliest days of the Pharisaic Synagogue."[73] The thirteenth benediction begins: "May Thy mercies, O Lord our God, be stirred over the righteous and over the pious and over the elders of Thy people, the House of Israel, and over the remnant of their scribes, 'and over the righteous proselytes'...."[74]

It is significant that the *Jonah Midrash* as described above ends with a quotation of Jonah 1:16, and that the heathen sailors on board Jonah's ship all (seventy, representing all the nations) now "fear" or "revere" the God of Jonah, becoming proselytes of righteousness.[75] Since the *Jonah Midrash* was designed to further repentance just before and on the Day of Atonement, when the Book of Jonah was read at the afternoon service, the same may plausibly be attributed to the Palestinian Jewish Christian author of Mark 4:35–41 as one of his intentions.

---

[71] On this imagery, cf. Jonah 2:10 (Eng. 9).

[72] *Pirq. R. El.* 10 in Eshkol 33; cf. also variants in Higger 8.119, and in the notes of Friedlander, *Pirķê de Rabbi Eliezer* 72–73. *Midrash Jonah* and *Yalquṭ Shem'oni* then proceed to comment on the rest of the Book of Jonah.

[73] Art. "Shemoneh 'Esreh" in *JE* (1905) 11.277. It is also called the prayer spoken while "standing," thus Amidah. I. Heinemann notes concerning it in his art. "Amidah" in *EJ* (1971) 2.839: "It is almost certain that by the end of the Temple period the 18 benedictions of the weekday *Amidah* had become the general custom. However, their exact sequence and the content of the individual benedictions probably still varied."

[74] Hirsch, art. "Shemoneh 'Esreh" 11.271. Cf. the reference to the "proselytes of righteousness" in a discussion of the Eighteen Prayer in *b. Meg.* 17b (Soncino 107).

[75] Cf. already J. Smart on the Hebrew text of Jonah 1:16 in "The Book of Jonah" in *IB* (1956) 6.885: "The author undoubtedly means to suggest ... in closing the incident in this way, how heathens might be led to become worshipers of the one true God." See also *De Jona* 39 (157, p. 37) on the Ninevites' later "fear of God."

Jesus' disciples, like the sailors in Jonah's ship after the calming of the sea, "were filled with great awe" (NRSV) or "feared with great fear." This reaction on part of the (Jewish) disciples was reverential awe. While they already believed in God, they are now also described as revering Jesus as the Son of God, who calms the sea as God does. Yet the narrator, like the original narrator(s) of the *Jonah Midrash* as employed in the synagogue, also wanted to address the "God-fearers" (φοβούμενοι and σεβούμενοι), adherents of the synagogue who were formerly pagan. They too now have the opportunity to repent, to be converted to messianic Judaism, thus now believing in Jesus, the Lord of wind and sea, as the Son of God. One purpose of the narrative now found in Mark 4:35-41 may thus have been to convince formerly pagan "God-fearers" who now attended the Jewish synagogues in Palestine that Jesus is the Son of God. His power, attested in calming the Sea of Galilee, can only be divine.

16. *Divine Power and Might.*

a) In Mark 4:41 the disciples, filled with great awe, say to one another:[76] "Who then is this, that (both) the wind and the sea 'obey' him?" The Greek for "obey" here is ὑπακούω. The question is designed to be the culmination of the narrative, forcing the first hearers (and later readers) to ask the same question of themselves. If Jesus can rebuke the windstorm and calm the Sea, which thus both obey him, is he not the Son of God, for only God is described as doing so in the Hebrew Bible? The final sentence of the pericope thus attests to Jesus' divine power and might.

The Palestinian Jewish Christian author of what is now Mark 4:35-41 knew of the incident now recounted in 1:21-27. There, after Jesus rebuked the unclean spirit in a man, all were amazed and asked: "What is this? A new teaching with authority! He even commands the unclean spirits, and they 'obey' him" (v 27). Here the same Greek word for "obey" is employed as found above. The sentence, in its earlier Semitic form, was the narrator's model for his question in 4:41.

Although not specifically named, Jesus' (divine) power and might or strength are emphasized here. The emphasis on God's power and might is also found in *Midrash Jonah*.

b) Before analyzing *Midrash Jonah* in this respect, I would first like to call attention to a relevant liturgical tradition. The *Mishnah* at *Ber.* 9:2

---

[76] Cf. the phrase "saying to one another" in Mark 1:27, as well as Jonah 1:7, "they said to one another."

states that if one sees "windstorms" (רוּחוֹת), one should say: "Blessed (are You, O Lord our God), whose 'power and might' fill the world."[77] The Hebrew of the latter is כֹּחוֹ וּגְבוּרָתוֹ. Here windstorms demonstrate God's great strength. In *b. Ber.* 59a Abaye defines such a windstorm as a "hurricane" (זַעְפָּא).[78] In *y. Ber.* 9:2, 13c, R. Yehoshua b. Hananya, a second generation Tanna,[79] comments on these ferocious winds. Then the especially severe wind of Jonah 1:4 is noted as one of three winds which were boundless in force.[80]

The latter shows the early liturgical connection of God's power and might with a windstorm such as that in Jonah One, the background of the windstorm on the Sea of Galilee in Mark 4:35–41. Since wind and sea "obey" Jesus' commands, this also demonstrates that he as the Son of God has the power and might of God.

Midrash Jonah begins by stating in regard to Jonah 1:1–2 that God's mercy over all His creatures is great. When He sent Jonah to Nineveh to prophesy concerning it, He encountered him only in His attribute of mercy in order to proclaim "His power and His might" (כוחו וגבורתו) in the sea, as in v 3.[81] The same Hebrew phrase is employed in regard to God's causing a windstorm only to affect Jonah's ship in the sea, and not others (Jonah 1:4).[82] At the end of the Midrash, when God saw that the Ninevites had repented, He moved from the throne of judgment to the throne of mercy. Then Jonah fell on his face and asked God to forgive him for fleeing to the sea (1:3–4). He states: "I did not know the power of Your might, but now I know it," as it is written: "You are a gracious God and mercyful" (4:2).[83]

---

[77] Albeck 1.31; Neusner, *The Mishnah* 13, has "winds"; Danby in *The Mishnah* 9 has "storms." Storm winds are meant, as the gemara indicates.

[78] Soncino 368. On the noun, see Jastrow, *A Dictionary* 408: stormwind, hurricane.

[79] Strack and Stemberger, *Introduction* 77.

[80] Neusner 1.325–326. This mentions that the latter wind only sought to destroy Jonah (and not the other boats with him).

[81] The first printed edition of Prague, 1595; Jellinek 1.96 (Wünsche 2.39); and Horowitz, *Sammlung Kleiner Midraschim* 1.16.

[82] The first printed edition of Prague, 1595; Jellinek 1.97 (Wünsche 2.41); and Horowitz 1.17.

[83] Jellinek 1.102; Wünsche 2.50; Horowitz 1.21 assumes it under "etc." The De Rossi MS has at this point: "And now I know the power of Your deeds and Your mighty acts" (Eisenstein, *Ozar Midrashim* 1.221b). God's power is also emphasized in *De Jona* at 6 (21, p. 12), 20 (73, p. 21), 23 (83, p. 23), 25 (98, p.

This threefold emphasis on God's power and might in regard to the windstorm of Jonah One is part of the background of the power and might shown by Jesus when he stills the windstorm on the Sea of Galilee. Wind and sea obey him (Mark 4:41) because he as the Son of God takes on His attributes of power and might in regard to the sea.

The first Palestinian Jewish Christian hearers (and later readers) of what is now the Markan narrative may also have contrasted Jonah, who shows disobedience in fleeing from God in a ship towards Tarshish in the remote west,[84] to Jesus, who does not flee from God. Indeed, the wind and the sea obey him, for he is more than Jonah.

*   *   *

The above sixteen similarities in the basic plot outline, motifs and specific expressions between the narrative of Jesus' stilling the storm in Mark 4:35–41 and Jonah One, especially in Judaic tradition, can be questioned individually. Some similarities, such as the "other boats," found nowhere else, are much more compelling than others, such as "teacher." Cumulatively, however, they provide a convincing argument that the Palestinian Jewish Christian author of the Markan narrative not only employed some elements from the story of Jesus' rebuking an unclean spirit from a man in what is now found in 1:21–28. For his portrayal of Jesus' being more than Jonah by stilling a windstorm on the Sea of Galilee, he primarily employed materials known to him from the Hebrew text of Jonah One and its interpretation in Judaic tradition.

Before discussing questions such as the original language, extent, possible Markan editing, date and provenance of the narrative, as well as its genre and purpose(s), I would like to call attention to a similar narrative of Julius Caesar's unsuccessful attempt to cross the Adriatic Sea during a severe storm in 48 BCE. It deals with a deified emperor thought to be the lord of land and sea. The narrator of the Markan episode most probably saw it as a clear foil to his own account of Jesus' successful calming of the Sea of Galilee (and then completing his crossing of it).

---

25), 42 (163, p. 38) and 49 (199–200, p. 44). See also 45 (179–180, p. 41), which emphasizes that everything must "obey" God, including the waves of the sea.

[84] Cf. the emphasis on the motif of Jonah's disobedience in almost all the commentaries on Jonah One, for example in L. Allen, *The Books of Joel, Obadiah, Jonah and Micah* 202–205 ("A. Jonah's Disobedience"), as well as the motif of God's power and might (209–213).

II. Julius Caesar's Unsuccessful Attempt to Cross the Adriatic Sea During a Severe Storm.

Introduction

After Gaius Julius Caesar spoke the now famous words "Let the die be cast," he crossed the Rubicon River with his forces from Cisalpine Gaul into the rest of Italy and began the Civil War against Pompey in 49 BCE.[85] Although Pompey's military forces were superior to Caesar's, he abandoned Rome and took the consuls and senators south to Brundisium (modern Brundisi),[86] from which they crossed the Adriatic or Ionic Sea to Dyrrhachium (the modern Durrës in Albania). Since Caesar lacked ships, he could not pursue Pompey at this point. He thus returned to Rome and first consolidated his power there.

In 48 BCE, at the time of the winter solstice in early January, Caesar then crossed the Ionian Sea, took Oricum and Apollonia, and ordered his transport ships to return to Brundisium for the many soldiers who had not reached the city in time to cross over with him. He encamped on the River Apsus (modern Semeni)[87] north of Apollonia, with Pompey's camp directly opposite. Later, Antony crossed with the remaining Italian forces to join Caesar. On August 9th in 48 BCE Caesar thoroughly routed Pompey on the plain of Pharsalus some 280 km southeast of Apollonia.

---

[85] Cf. Suetonius, *The Lives of the Caesars*, "The Deified Julius" 1.31–32 (*Iacta alea est*), and Plutarch's *Lives*, "Caesar" 32 ('Ανερρίφθω κύβος). The latter notes that Caesar's friend Asinius Pollio was present, the importance of which will be shown below.

[86] This harbor on the southeast side of Italy was also employed by Palestinian Jews when they journeyed to Rome. Cf. for example the sea voyage of four early second century CE rabbis mentioned in *m. 'Erub.* 4:1 (Danby 126, with n. 1).

[87] Lucan in "The Civil War" 5.462–464 calls it the Hapsus, which "is made navigable by a lake (before its entrance into the Adriatic), which it drains imperceptibly with quiet flow" (LCL translation by Duff). For the position of the camps, see also Gaius Julius Caesar, *The Civil Wars* 3.13 and 19. Dio Cassius in his "Roman History" 47.1 also notes the Apsus River; he implies that Caesar earlier tried to sail to Italy via the Aoüs River to the south of Apollonia (45.2). Strabo, who wrote his "Geography" in 7 BCE, in 7.5.8 first mentions Dyrrhachium and the Apsus River, and then that Apollonia is located on the Aoüs River (i.e., ten stadia from it and sixty from the Adriatic Sea). See *The Geography of Strabo*, trans. H. Jones, I. xxv–xxvi for the dating, and xiv for Strabo's being born in 64 or 63 BCE. For my purposes it is immaterial which of the two rivers is meant, although I favor the Apsus because of the navigable lake at its mouth, just before the Sea. Appian in II.8.56 falsely speaks of the Alor River between Caesar and Pompey.

He then pursued him to Alexandria, Egypt, but arrived there only after Pompey had already been decapitated. Installing Cleopatra as ruler, Caesar then departed for Syria[88] and eventually returned to Rome.

Caesar's Egyptian campaign was viewed very positively by Palestinian Jews for a long period. Josephus for example, writing at the end of the first century CE, notes that Aristobulus fought in Syria for Caesar, but was poisoned by friends of Pompey. Aristobulus' son Alexander was also beheaded in Antioch by Scipio, Pompey's father-in-law. When Pompey perished, Antipater, the father of Herod the Great, sided with Caesar. With 3000 Jewish infantry Antipater fought so bravely for him against the Egyptians that Caesar conferred not only Roman citizenship on him, but also many honors. He also made him viceroy of all Judea.[89]

Caesar was also later remembered very positively for having reconfirmed the privileges of the Jews in Alexandria.[90]

All the above makes it probable that the Palestinian Jewish Christian author of Mark 4:35–41 was not only aware of the positive impression his fellow Jews had of the first Caesar. He could also assume their knowledge of a very famous incident involving Caesar's attempt to cross the Adriatic or Ionian Sea to Brundisium in a severe storm in early 48 BCE by first sailing or rowing down the Apsus River to its mouth in a lake, and from there entering the raging Sea. I suggest that, by means of contrast, this unsuccessful crossing was also part of the background for Jesus' calming the Sea of Galilee during a storm.

Gaius Julius Caesar himself does not mention this incident in his own commentary on the Civil War, probably because its lack of success would have distracted from his military reputation.[91] It is, however, related by four different authors:

a) Marcus Annaeus *Lucanus* was born in what is now Cordova, Spain, in 39 CE and died in 65 CE in Rome. In Book V. 425–720 of his

---

[88] Suetonius, "The Deified Julius" 35; Plutarch, "Caesar" 39–49.

[89] *Bell.* 1.183–200; *Ant.* 14.123–143.

[90] Cf. Josephus, *Ap.* 2.37 (see also 61); *Bell.* 2.488; *Ant.* 14.188 (see also 190).

[91] Cf. the A. Peskett translation of Caesar, Gaius Julius: *The Civil Wars*, 3.13–30. One would have expected the narrative between 25–26. Caesar's style with the present tense should be noted and compared to similar usage in Mark 4:35–41. See also J. Carter, *Julius Caesar. The Civil War, Book III* (Warminster: Aris and Phillips, 1993) 165, who speaks of the narrative as an "incredible tale." I find it hard to believe the account was not historical at least in its core because of its being related by four different authors in different versions, and because of its probable origin in Asinius Pollio (see below).

"The Civil War" the very young author describes in flowery, poetic Latin Caesar's attempt to cross the Adriatic Sea in a severe storm.[92]

b) Plutarch was born in Chaeroneia, Boeotia, in the middle of Greece about 50 CE, and died ca. 120 CE. In his "Lives" he coupled those of Alexander the Great and Caesar. In "Caesar" XXXVIII he recounts in Greek the Roman emperor's attempted sea crossing.[93]

c) The Alexandrian historian Appian may have been born ca. 95 CE and died ca. 165 CE. His "Roman History," The Civil Wars, Book II, 8–9, deals in Greek with Caesar's attempted crossing.[94]

d) Cassius Dio was born sometime between 155–164, and was known to have still been alive in 229 CE. In his "Roman History" 46.46 he also recalls in Greek Caesar's attempt to cross the Adriatic Sea in a ferocious storm.[95]

While special studies have been made of this particular incident,[96] it nevertheless remains unclear who provided the above four authors with their basic source material. A favorite theory is that it is the eyewitness Asinius Pollio, who is known to have fought with his friend Caesar both before and after the attempted crossing.[97] E. Schürer notes that he wrote "a history of the civil wars between Caesar and Pompey in seventeen books in the Latin language...." This history, now lost, was employed both by Plutarch and Appian, and Josephus in *Ant.* 14.138 states that Strabo of Cappadocia also cites Asinius Pollio in regard to Caesar's campaign in Egypt.[98]

---

[92] Cf. J. Duff, Lucan. *The Civil War*, Books I–X (Pharsalia) ix on the dates.

[93] Cf. B. Perrin, *Plutarch's Lives* I.xi–xii for the dates. The text of the anecdote is found in vol. VII as II.9.57–58.

[94] Cf. H. White, *Appian's Roman History* I.vii for the dates. The text of the incident is in vol. III.

[95] Cf. E. Cary, *Dio's Roman History* I.vii and x on the dates. The incident is found in vol. IV.

[96] Cf. the six works cited by B. Scardigli, *Die Römerbiographien Plutarchs* (Munich: Beck, 1979) 133.

[97] Cf. Plutarch, "Caesar" 32.7; 46.2; and 52.8. In his art. "Asinius Pollio" in *PW* 2.1589–1602, P. Groebe notes that he was born in 76 BCE and died in 5 CE. He was perhaps employed by Dio Cassius, but definitely by Appian and Plutarch (pp. 1589, 1592 and 1596, respectively).

[98] Cf. *The History of the Jewish People* 1.23. Unfortunately, only fragments of this history remain (p. 24). Strabo of Pontus, who lived 64–63 BCE to beyond 21 CE, also wrote a history which is no longer extant (1.64–65). It too may have mentioned Caesar's unsuccessful attempt to cross the Adriatic Sea. The poetic account by Lucan, the earliest available, unfortunately betrays no sources at this point.

The following motifs and expressions from Caesar's unsuccessful attempt to cross the Adriatic Sea in a severe storm early in 48 BCE are also of relevance to Jesus' stilling the storm in Mark 4:35-41.

1. Caesar's Crossing the Adriatic Sea, and Jesus' Crossing the Sea of Galilee.

Lacking sufficient troops to engage Pompey near Apollonia, Caesar sent numerous messengers to Antony in Brundisium to cross over the Adriatic Sea immediately, although it was the winter of 48 BCE, the period of severe storms. Receiving no reply, Caesar in desperation decided to cross over by himself, to quell any possible new support for Pompey, and above all to accompany his troops to the scene of the impending battle.

Lucan in 5.492 employs *ire per* for "going through" or "crossing" the sea, and in 573 *oras* for reaching the "shore" of Italy. After Caesar returns from his unsuccessful attempt, his soldiers in 690-692 also reproach him with the words: "You 'made for' Italy yourself, because you deemed it heartless to bid any 'cross' such a stormy sea."[99] In his "Caesar" 37.4, Plutarch speaks of Caesar's "crossing" (διαβάλλω)[100] the Ionian Gulf towards Macedonia, and in 38.1 of his plan then to "go over" (ἀνάγομαι)[101] to Brundisium. Appian notes in II. 8.56 that when Caesar's troops there "did not start, he decided to 'cross over' (διαπλεῦσαι) secretly to that army, because no one else could bring them so easily."[102] Finally, Dio Cassius in 46.46.4 remarks that in spite of all his efforts, Caesar "did not 'get across' (ἐπεραιώθη) ...."[103]

The various expressions employed above of Caesar's "crossing over" to the other (Italian) side of the Adriatic Sea made it easy for the Palestinian Jewish Christian narrator of Mark 4:35-41, acquainted with the narrative in a Semitic form, to associate this incident with his own on the Sea of Galilee. There Jesus also says to the disciples in v 35: "Let us 'go across' to the other side."

---

[99] Translation Duff. The Latin is *peto* (cf. W. Smith and J. Lockwood, *Chambers Murray latin-english Dictionary* 539, I., to direct one's course to, to make for) and *mitto* (Chambers Murray 439, C.d.: to let pass, to pass over in silence).

[100] Cf. LSJ 389, 2., pass over, cross.

[101] LSJ 102, B., put out to sea, set sail.

[102] Translation White. Cf. LSJ 407 on διαπλέω : sail across. Cf. also ἐπιπλευσεῖσθαι in 8.52 and διάπλουν also in 8.49, as well as περᾶν in 8.53.

[103] LSJ 1364 on περαιόω passive: pass over, cross. Cf. also 47.1, and Caesar's original crossing in 44.1 and 3.

2.   Caesar and Sailors in a Boat, and Jesus and the Disciples in a Boat.

When Lucan poetically describes Caesar's attempted crossing to Brundisium, he mentions only one other person, the skipper and owner of the boat, whose name was Amyclas ("The Civil War," 5.520, 539).   On board the vessel, Caesar explains in 5.655: "What trouble the gods take ... to work my ruins, assailing me on my little 'boat' with such a mighty storm!"[1]   The noun for "boat" here is *puppis*, which can mean either the stern of a ship, or a ship itself.[2]   It is used elsewhere in the Lucan account also, as well as *carina* (the keel of a ship, or a ship itself)[3] and *ratis*, which is either a raft or a bark, a boat, also implying a small vessel.[4] Plutarch in "Caesar" 38.1 notes that at Apollonia "Caesar conceived the dangerous plan of 'embarking in a twelve-oared boat' (πλοῖον ἐμβὰς τὸ μέγεθος δωδεκάσκαλμον)[5] ... and going over to Brundisium ...."   In 38.2 he labels it a ναῦς, ship.[6]   In addition to the twelve rowers or "sailors" (38.3-4), there was a master of the boat, pilot or helmsman (κυβερνήτης : 38.3, twice).[7]   With Caesar, there were thus fourteen persons on board in this account.   In his "Roman History" 8.56, Appian has Caesar send three servants the twelve stades to the river to obtain a "quick little boat" (κελήτιον ὀξύ).   This Greek noun is the diminutive of κέλης, a fast-sailing yacht (with one bank of oars).[8]   The Alexandrian historian mentions the rowers in 9.57, as well as the pilot in 8.56 and 9.57.   Elsewhere he also calls the vessel a ship, ναῦς (9.57).[9]   For him there were thus at least

---

[1] Translation Duff in the LCL edition.   Ammianus in XVI.10.3 labels the boat a "fisherman's skiff" (*lenunculo ... piscantis*).   See *Ammianus Marcellinus*, trans. J. Rolfe,   3 volumes.   In I. ix, Rolfe notes that Ammianus was born ca. 330 CE in Syrian Antioch, but was in Rome before 383 CE (xiii).

[2] Chambers Murray 599.

[3] Chambers Murray 98.

[4] Cf.   Chambers Murray 616.   The term *puppis* is found in 5.570, 575, 585, 590, 594, 647; *carina* in 514, 533; and *ratis* in 515, 560 and 587.

[5] LSJ 464 only cite this passage on the term.

[6] LSJ 1162.

[7] LSJ 1004: steersman, pilot.

[8] LSJ 937.

[9] In 8.54 he differentiates this from merchant-ships and war-ships, employing the general term τὰ πλοῖα for them together.   In 8.56 Pompey's triremes are mentioned.

seven persons (Caesar, his three servants, the pilot, and rowers) on board.   Finally, Dio Cassius in his "Roman History" 46.46.2 writes that Caesar embarked in a "small light boat" (ἀκάτιον), the diminutive of ἄκατος, light vessel, boat, ship.[10]   Like Lucan, he mentions only the pilot as also being on board (46.3), yet a crew may simply be assumed.

If the Palestinian Jewish Christian author of Mark 4:35-41 knew of a version of the Caesar incident in which a twelve-oared boat was mentioned, as in Plutarch, this too would have made him think of the twelve disciples together with Jesus in their boat, crossing the Sea of Galilee.   Even if less than twelve persons were implied, as in Appian's minimum of seven, the fact that in three versions of the incident Caesar is accompanied by others would have reminded him of Jesus' followers' accompanying him when crossing the Sea.

3. *Caesar's Attempt to Cross the Sea at Night, and Jesus' Crossing the Sea at Night.*

In "The Civil War" 5.500-501, Lucan states that Caesar "ventured in the 'dangerous darkness' (*incautas ... tenebras*) to defy the sea, thus doing of his own accord what others had feared to do when bidden."   In 504 he notes the "drowsy night" (*nox languida*), and that its third hour (9 p.m.) "had roused the second watch."[11]   At this time even the sentries were sleeping (511).   Then Caesar sought out a boat on the coast with which he could cross to Brundisium.   In his life of "Caesar" 38.2, Plutarch relates that it was "night" when Caesar went on board a twelve-oared boat in order to cross over.   During this night a strong wind was blowing from the sea.   Finally, Appian mentions in his "Roman History" II. 9.57 that after supper Caesar feigned being tired, drove in a carriage to the ship, and there was undisclosed and not at all recognized because of the night.[12]

The above evening / night setting for Caesar's attempted crossing of the Adriatic Sea was probably known to the Palestinian Jewish Christian author of Mark 4:35-41.   The phrase "when it had become late / evening" (ὀψίας γενομένης) in v 35 thus may *not* be a Markan redactional remark designed to adjust the narrative to the long day of teaching (4:1-34).   It may also be noted that the incident in the country of the Gerasenes, following the evening account of 5:1, is assumed to

---

[10] LSJ 48.

[11] Translation Duff in the LCL edition.

[12] Dio Cassius does not note the time of day.

take place during the day, when the events were visible.   The course of events here is thus due to the Evangelist himself.

The introduction to the originally independent narrative of Jesus' stilling the storm may thus have begun: "Once, when evening had come, Jesus said to his disciples: 'Let us cross over to the other side of the Sea.'"   This would betray influence from the Caesar narrative at this point, for the major background of the anecdote, Jonah One, especially in Judaic tradition, has the crossing of the sea take place during the day.

4.   *Caesar's Being Unrecognized in the Boat, and Jesus' Being "As He Was" in the Boat.*

Under the cover of darkness and incognito, so that his own and enemy soldiers would not note his absence, Caesar attempted to cross the Adriatic to Brundisium in a boat.   This motif is emphasized by all four writers who describe the incident.

In "The Civil War" 5.538–539 Lucan relates that Caesar spoke eloquently to the skipper Amyclas at the door of his humble cottage.   He acted this way, "for though disguised in humble garb, he knew not how to speak the language of a private man."[13]   In 5.581 Caesar tells the skipper at sea: "You do not recognize your passenger."   Plutarch in the life of "Caesar" 38.1 states that the emperor planned to cross to Brundisium "with the knowledge of none."   Therefore "at night he disguised himself in the garment of a slave, boarded, threw himself down 'as of no account' ($\dot{\omega}_S$ τινα τῶν παρημελημένων), and kept quiet."[14]   Later Caesar "discloses himself" to the pilot (38.3).   In his "Roman History" II. 8.56, Appian notes that Caesar thought it best to cross over to his troops in Italy "secretly"; thus he concealed his plan. In 9.57 Caesar then "put on the clothing of a private person" and drove off to the ship as if he were his own servant.   "He gave the rest of his orders through his (three) servants (in the boat) and remained concealed by the darkness of the night and unrecognized."[15]   At the height of the storm Caesar then revealed himself to the pilot.   Finally, Dio Cassius in his "Roman History" 46.46.2 states that Caesar desired to sail to Italy "by himself and alone" (αὐτὸς καὶ μόνος); thus he went on board a small light boat "like someone else" ($\dot{\omega}_S$ τις ἄλλος).   During the severe storm he then revealed himself to the captain (46.46.3).

---

[13] Translation Duff, which I slightly modify.

[14] Translation Perrin. Cf. LSJ 1317 on παραμελέω : disregard, pay no heed to.

[15] Translation White.

The Palestinian Jewish Christian author of Mark 4:35–41 describes the disciples at the Sea of Galilee in v 36 as "taking him (Jesus) along 'as he was' (ὡς ἦν) in the boat." The major background to this phrase, "as he was," is found in Judaic tradition on the sailors' taking Jonah along with them "by himself" (לוֹ). Yet the account of Caesar's attempting to cross the Adriatic Sea "by himself and alone," "like someone else" with ὡς, may also have encouraged him to describe Jesus in this somewhat awkward fashion.

5. Other Boats.

When Caesar covertly attempted to cross the Adriatic Sea to Brundisium, he traveled with only one boat, intentionally without accompaniment. Yet there were many other boats in the Sea, warships belonging to his opponent Pompey.

In "The Civil War" 5.420–421 Lucan describes Caesar's fear that Pompey's rowers could overtake his sailboats if there was a calm. The latter would expose his naval forces to great danger (5.447–448), for the enemy controlled the shores (5.488–489). In his life of "Caesar," Plutarch at 38.1 remarks that Caesar planned to cross to Brundisium although the Sea was surrounded by the enemy forces with such great armaments. Appian in "The Civil Wars" II. 8.49 notes that Pompey had earlier taken forty of Caesar's vessels in the Adriatic and now watched to prevent his crossing. In total, the son-in-law of Caesar had 600 warships.[16] Located in Dyrrachium, Pompey with his ships took back Oricum from Caesar and guarded the Sea extremely closely (8.56), searching it with his vessels (9.59).

The fact that there were many other (enemy) ships or boats in the Adriatic Sea when Caesar attempted to cross it may have also encouraged the Palestinian Jewish Christian author of Mark 4:35–41 to borrow the expression "other boats" from Judaic tradition on Jonah One and to insert it in v 36.

6. A Severe Windstorm.

When Gaius Julius Caesar attempted to cross the Adriatic Sea to Brundisium somewhat after the winter solstice, a severe windstorm prevented him from doing so. It is described extensively by the four narrators of the event.

In "The Civil War" 5.578 Lucan speaks of the "raging wind," in 583 of a hurricane, and in 588 of the "fury of the winds." In 595 it is a

---

[16] Cf. for example "The Civil War" 5.473–474, and n. 1 on this.

"raging whirlwind" which strikes Caesar's boat, breaking off important parts.   The entire section 597–653 portrays the storm with its terribly high waves, beating upon and threatening the boat.   In his life of "Caesar" 38.4, Plutarch notes that the sailors in Caesar's boat tried in vain to make progress during the storm. Appian remarks in "The Civil Wars" II. 9.57 that a windstorm forced the pilot, who could make no progress, to despair. Caesar thereupon urged him to brave the tempest. Nevertheless, the violent wind and waves "tossed the ship high on towards the bank."[17]   In his "Roman History" 46.46.3, Dio Cassius describes the wind (ἄνεμος) as violently driving the boat's passengers forward, with the waves throwing them into terrible confusion.

The ferocious windstorm described above in regard to Caesar certainly aided the Palestinian Jewish Christian narrator of Mark 4:35–41 in applying the motif of a severe windstorm from Jonah One, especially in Judaic tradition, to his account of Jesus' stilling a "great storm of wind," with waves beating against the boat, in v 37.   In part, he wanted to show that Jesus, the Son of God, is more than a "deified" Roman emperor (see below).

7. *The Boat's Swamping.*

In his life of "Caesar" 38.4, Plutarch relates that Caesar finally abandoned his attempt to cross the Adriatic Sea during a very severe windstorm only after the boat "took on much water" (δεξάμενος πολλὴν θάλατταν).

This motif, not explicitly mentioned by the other three writers who describe the incident, if known to the Palestinian Jewish Christian narrator of Mark 4:35–41, may also have encouraged him to apply the motif of Jonah's ship as swamping to Jesus' boat during the severe windstorm on the Sea of Galilee.   V 37 also describes it as already filling up with water from the waves.

8. *A Calm.*

In "The Civil War" 5.701–702, Lucan notes after the ferocious windstorm in which Caesar tried to cross the Adriatic Sea to Brundisium: "the weary sea, permitted by the winds, 'calmed' (*conposuit*) its swollen billows."[18]   Plutarch in "Caesar" 38.2 remarks that when a twelve-oared

---

[17] Translation White.

[18] Translation Duff. Cf. Chambers Murray 131, C.d. on *compono*: to lay, settle, allay, "calm."   See also 5.704.   Before Caesar left Brundisium for Macedonia, there was also a dead calm (5.434, 442, 447, 449, 453–454 with various nouns).

Heaven, he ventured in the dangerous darkness to defy the sea...."[25] When the skipper of the boat implored Caesar to turn about, he "was 'confident' (*fisus*) that all dangers would make way for him" (5.577).[26] As already noted above, in 581–583 Caesar describes himself to the pilot as "a man whom the gods never desert, whom 'Fortune' (*fortuna*) treats scurvily when she comes merely in answer to his 'prayer' (*vota*). Burst through the heart of the storm, relying on my protection."[27] He encourages the man to "believe" (*crede*) that he will reach Italy (5.589). When the windstorm refuses to let up and threatens to drown him, Caesar finally "believes" (*credit*) that the danger equals his "destiny" (*fata* – 5.653–654). Plutarch in his life of "Caesar" 38.4 notes that when the emperor returned from his dangerous attempt to cross the Adriatic Sea, his forces "found much fault with him and were very impatient with him because he did not 'believe' (πέπεισται) that he was able to conquer alone, but was troubled, and risked his life for the sake of the absent as though 'distrusting' (ἀπιστῶν) those who were present."[28] In his "The Civil Wars" II. 9.58, Appian describes Caesar's daring and dangerous attempt to cross the stormy Adriatic Sea as his " 'believing' (ἐπεποίθει) in 'fortune' (τύχη) rather than in reason." Dio Cassius in his "Roman History" 46.46.3 remarks that the captain of Caesar's boat did not "dare" to sail any further in the severe storm. Caesar therefore revealed himself to him and encouraged him: "Be brave, you are carrying Caesar." The Roman emperor had great "spirit" and "hope," having "faith" (πίστιν) in his "safety / deliverance" (σωτηρίας) in spite of the negative circumstances.

All the above sources express Caesar's great self-confidence, his "belief" in his personal fortune or destiny, including the mastering of a ferocious windstorm in the Adriatic Sea. His great faith in himself, and in the gods as favoring him, contrasted greatly to that of the pilot and rowers of his boat. They so greatly feared (section 9. above) the severe storm that they wanted to turn about.

I suggest that Caesar's great faith or confidence in himself during the storm at sea also encouraged the Palestinian Jewish Christian author of Mark 4:35–41 to describe Jesus in a similar way. During a severe windstorm on the Sea of Galilee Jesus went to the stern of the boat and

---

[25] Translation Duff.

[26] Cf. *fido, fidere* in Chambers Murray 272: to trust, confide, put confidence in. The cognate noun is *fides*, trust, faith.

[27] Translation Duff. For other instances of Caesar's prayers, cf. 5.450 and 491.

[28] Translation Perrin.

slept on a headrest (v 38).   This showed his great faith or confidence in God, the creator and Lord of the sea.   Then, after being awakened and both rebuking the wind and silencing the Sea, Jesus not only asked the disciples in the boat why they were afraid.   He also posed the question: "Have you no 'faith' (πίστις)?" (v 40).   Either the pre-Markan collector of these miracle stories, or more probably Mark himself, then later added "yet" ("Don't you have faith 'yet'?" – οὐ became οὔπω) in light of the numerous other opportunities earlier in the Gospel for the disciples to gain faith in Jesus.

The motif of "faith" as such is lacking in Jonah One and in Judaic tradition on this chapter, the major background for Mark 4:35-41.   The question in regard to the disciples' faith in v 40 may thus be the major contribution the narrative of Caesar's attempted crossing of the Adriatic in a windstorm made to the anecdote as now found in the Gospel.

11. *Divine Power and Might.*

As noted above in section 10., Caesar was extremely confident that his fortune or destiny would enable him to cross the Adriatic Sea even during a ferocious windstorm of the stormy winter season.   His lack of success in this endeavor contrasts him to Jesus, the Son of God, who calmed the Sea of Galilee also while crossing it during a ferocious windstorm.   This contrast was most probably intended by the Palestinian Jewish Christian author of Mark 4:35-41.   He not only could assume knowledge of the Jonah narrative and Judaic tradition on it in his hearers.   He also could assume that they were acquainted with the famous incident of Caesar's unsuccessful attempt to cross the Adriatic Sea.

I shall first make several relevant observations in regard to the latter, and then describe Julius Caesar as labeled "god" or divine already during his lifetime, and in a major way after his death in 44 BCE.

In "The Civil War" 5.581-582, Lucan has Caesar tell the pilot of his boat at the height of the windstorm at sea: "you know not whom you carry.   He is a man whom the gods (*numina*) never desert...."   In 585-586 Caesar maintains that the storm will not affect their boat, "for Caesar treads the deck, and her freight shall insure her against the waves."   In 685-686 his soldiers afterwards tell him: "When the existence and 'safety' (*salus*) of so many nations depend on your single life, and so large a part of the world has chosen you as its head, it is cruel of you to court death."   In 694 they call him "master of the world," and in 698-699 "the ruler of the world" and "the master of mankind."[29]   In his life of

---

[29] All translations by Duff.

"Caesar" 37.2, Plutarch notes that Caesar was made "dictator" by the senate in Rome, and in 8 he is labeled "Imperator" (αὐτοκράτωρ). Later in 42.2 his office of "Pontifex Maximus" (τῆς ... ἀρχιερωσύνης – "of the highpriesthood") is mentioned. Finally, Dio Cassius in his "Roman History" 46.46.3, as noted above in section 8, states that when the boat's captain did not dare to continue sailing forward in the severe storm, Caesar revealed himself to him, "as if by this act he could stop the storm."

Thus, although Caesar prayed to the gods, he had such faith or confidence in his own destiny or fortune that he attempted the impossible: crossing a sea during a ferocious winter windstorm. Very reluctantly, he had to resign himself to returning to shore. Although he was already dictator, imperator or emperor, and high priest, and was considered by his men to be the master of the entire world, he definitely was not the lord of the sea.[30] Jesus' rebuking the storm wind and silencing the Sea of Galilee, enabling him and his disciples to cross over it, point to him in contrast as the Son of God. As such he also has the divine power and might to still a severe windstorm, something the most powerful man in the world, the Roman emperor, cannot do.

In his recent fine study of the Roman imperial cult from the time of Julius Caesar to Trajan, H.-J. Klauck calls attention to an Ephesus inscription from 48 BCE which labels Caesar during his lifetime "him who has appeared as god, and general savior of human life." Another inscription from Demetrias from the same period also calls him "god." Klauck believes Caesar's victory over Pompey at Pharsalus is probably in the background here. At the latest in 29 BCE, however, when a temple was dedicated to Caesar in Rome, with his statue, cult personnel and regular sacrifices, the deceased emperor was definitely called *divus Julius*.[31]

Palestinian Jews in the first century CE were keenly aware of the Roman practice of considering an emperor divine upon his death.

---

[30] Contrast Josephus, *Bell.* 3.402, where the future Jewish historian prophesies to Vespasian at his capture that he will become emperor, "for you, Caesar, are master not of me only, but of land 'and sea' and the whole human race." Translation Thackeray. See also Pompey, whom "even the winds and the tempest obey," in *Cicero. The Speeches*, "Pro Lege Manilia," etc., 16.48, trans. H. Grose.

[31] Cf. Appian's "The Civil Wars" II.20.148, where already at Caesar's death, his adopted son Octavian "decreed divine honours to his father." Translation White. For this and the above references, with the exception of Josephus, see H.-J. Klauck, *Die religiöse Umwelt des Urchristentums. II. Herrscher- und Kaiserkult, Philosophie, Gnosis* (Kohlhammer Studienbücher Theologie 9,2; Stuttgart: Kohlhammer, 1996) 45–48.

When Gaius Caligula (37–41 CE), for example, maintained that he was divine during his lifetime and demanded worship as such, also from the Jews, including the erection of his statue in the Holy of Holies in the Jerusalem Temple, a tremendous crisis evolved.   As I have indicated elsewhere, Caligula's walking or riding over a large number of ships bound together in the Bay of Naples, to show that he was not only lord of the land but also of the sea, led to a Palestinian Jewish Christian's creating the narrative of Jesus' walking on the Sea of Galilee in what is now found in Mark 6:45–52.[32]   Part of the background of Jesus' stilling the storm (and successfully crossing the Sea) in 4:35–41 is found in turn in the *unsuccessful* attempt of an earlier Roman emperor, Julius Caesar, to cross the Adriatic Sea during a ferocious windstorm.   Although labeled "divine" and "cosmocrator,"[33] he was definitely not the lord of the sea. Its lord is rather Jesus, the true Son of God.   Like his heavenly Father, he alone can still the sea, for he participates in His might and power.

*   *   *

It is thus not only the Hebrew narrative found in Jonah One, and in Judaic interpretation of it, which informed the Palestinian Jewish Christian author of Mark 4:35–41.   The well-known attempt by Julius Caesar to cross the Adriatic Sea during a ferocious winter windstorm in 48 BCE most probably also influenced the narrative.   "When it became late / evening" in v 35, and "Have you no faith?" in an earlier form of v 40 (later "not 'yet'"), could very well have their background in the Caesar incident.   It took place at night and emphasized Caesar's faith or self-confidence in contrast to that of others with him in the boat.   Other motifs from the Caesar anecdote also encouraged the Palestinian Jewish Christian author to apply similar motifs from the Jonah story to his own narrative.

What is most important, however, is the foil character or function which the Caesar incident provides for Mark 4:35–41. Jesus shows he is not only more than the prophet Jonah. He is more than the most powerful man in the world, the Roman emperor, labeled and considered

---

[32] Cf. my *"Caught in the Act"* 53–133, especially pp. 117–126 on Gaius Caligula.

[33] Contrast *y. Ber.* 9:1, 13b (Neusner / Zahavy 1.315 – 316; German in Horowitz 222), an interpretation of Ps 146:6, God "who made heaven and earth, the sea, and all that is in them." A human "cosmocrator" (the Roman emperor is meant) can only rule over the land, but not also over the sea. God alone does both.   One example of His ruling over the sea is His rescuing Jonah from the belly of the whale.

by many to be divine. Through Jesus' calming the storm on the Sea of Galilee, he demonstrates that he, and he alone, is the true Son of God.

III. The Extent of the Original Narrative, and the Pre-Markan or Markan Editing.

On the basis of the above analysis of the Jonah and Julius Caesar narratives, which form a major part of the background to Mark 4:35-41, it is possible to posit the extent of the original narrative and any pre-Markan or Markan editing.

"On that day" in v 35 was added by the Evangelist when he inserted the incident of Jesus' stilling the storm after Jesus' extensive parable teaching from a boat off the shore of the Sea of Galilee (4:1-34). In contrast to the opinion of most commentators, I would maintain that "when it had become late / evening" in v 35 is probably part of the original setting. It was influenced by the account of Caesar's attempt to cross the Adriatic Sea under the cover of darkness in order to remain undetected by the forces of Pompey, which were not only on land but also at sea.

The original introduction probably began something like this: "Once when Jesus was at the Sea (of Galilee), when it had become late / evening, he said to the disciples: 'Let us cross over to the other side.'"

The words "and having dismissed the crowd" in v 36 are also Markan redaction, referring the incident back to the crowd of 4:1.[34]

In addition, as noted above in section I. C. 10, the aorist passive participle διεγερθείς in v 39 was probably originally ἐγερθείς, as translated by a Hellenistic Jewish Christian from the Semitic original. To vary the style (ἐγείρουσιν just before in v 38), either the pre-Markan collector of the miracle stories[35] or Mark himself changed ἐγερθείς to διεγερθείς. Unfortunately, the redactor did not notice that a change in meaning occurred thereby: "and having risen" became "and having awakened," now strange because the disciples have already spoken to Jesus.

Otherwise, there are no other signs of pre-Markan or Markan editing of the pericope. Except for the minor changes noted above, and some lesser attested textual variants, the original has been remarkably well preserved.

---

[34] Cf. the editorial dismissing of the crowd also in 6:45, another miracle on the Sea of Galilee which occurred when it had become late / evening (v 47).

[35] Cf. also the following nature miracles in 6:30-44; 6:45-52; and 8:1-10.

IV. The Original Language, Provenance and Date of the Narrative.

1. *The Original Language.*

Throughout section I. above I presented various arguments for a Semitic background to the narrative of Mark 4:35–41, the original extent of which I described in section III. This assertion is primarily due to the main background of the account as being found in the Hebrew text of Jonah One, especially as interpreted in Judaic tradition. The story line of the anecdote also follows that of Jonah One quite closely.   All of the Judaic traditions reflected in Jesus' stilling the storm, with the exception of *Targum Jonathan* and some later Talmudic passages, are also found in Hebrew.   The following examples point to a Semitic background to Mark 4:35–41.   Here I cite the Hebrew form, yet the Aramaic is usually quite similar.

1) The עֶרֶב, "evening," of v 35 is a word play with what directly follows it: נַעֲבֹר or נַעְבְּרָה, "Let us go across." If "to the other side" is הָעֵבֶר, as in Delitzsch's Hebrew New Testament,[36] the word play is intensified.

2) I also proposed the Hebrew לוֹ as found in Judaic tradition on Jonah's embarking in the ship "by himself" or "alone" as the background of the somewhat puzzling "as he was" (ὡς ἦν) in v 36.   Jesus was "alone" in the boat.

3) The phrase "other boats were with him" in v 36 is the strongest argument for a Semitic background to the narrative. "Other boats" (אֳנִיּוֹת אֲחֵרוֹת) is found in regard to Jonah's crossing the sea only in the Hebrew *Jonah Midrash*. It also attests to the Palestinian Jewish Christian's artistic skill, for a possible word play is created in association with Jesus' being in the "stern" (אֲחֹרֵי) of the boat in v 38.

4) I also suggested that "Teacher / Rabbi" (διδάσκαλε) in v 38 may be derived from the רַב of Jonah 1:6.

5) The Semitic behind "'Don't you care' that we are perishing?" in Mark 4:38 derives from מַה לְּךָ in Jonah 1:6, especially as interpreted in Judaic tradition. "Perish" derives from אבד in the same verse.

6) As related above, the participle διεγερθείς of Mark 4:39 was originally the Semitic equivalent of ἐγερθείς, which makes much better sense in the development of the narrative.   A word play then took place between "they wakened" him in v 38 (הֵעִירוּ) and "he stirred himself" (נִתְעוֹרֵר or הִתְעוֹרֵר) in v 39.

---

36 P. 68.

7) In v 39 the command σιώπα may derive from שְׁתֹק, and the noun γαλήνη from שְׁתִיקָה or שְׁתִיקוּת, as in the *Jonah Midrash*. If the latter, however, was the Hebrew loan word גַּלְנִי, it may have been a word play with "waves," גַּלִּין, in v 37.

8) Recognizing the Hebrew background of the phrase in v 41, "And they feared with great fear" (וַיִּירְאוּ ... יִרְאָה גְדוֹלָה), as deriving from Jonah 1:10 and 16, the Hellenistic Jewish Christian translator of the narrative also borrowed the equivalent Greek phrase from the LXX, well-known to him (Jonah 1:16 with the dative, and 1:10 with the accusative).

9) Finally, the phrase "and they said to one another" in regard to the sailor disciples in Mark 4:41 is probably based on the similar phrase employed by the sailors in Jonah 1:7, וַיֹּאמְרוּ אִישׁ אֶל-רֵעֵהוּ.

The above nine suggestions make it very probable that the original narrative of 4:35–41 was composed in a Semitic language. In light of the use of Hebrew at Qumran, in some of the Bar Kokhba letters from ca. 132–135 CE, and elsewhere,[37] and because almost all the Judaic traditions reflected in the Markan narrative are now found in Hebrew, I tend to believe the original was also first narrated in that language. There would have been many Palestinian Jewish Christians, however, who understood Aramaic more easily. It is thus probable that the narrative was also translated into Aramaic and circulated in that language very soon after it was composed. My main point, however, is simply that the original was Semitic and not Greek.

This thesis is not less attractive due to the fact that the narrative of Julius Caesar's attempt to cross the Adriatic Sea appears to have also influenced its formulation at several points. That anecdote, originally in Latin and Greek, was almost certainly known in Palestine via the many Greek-speaking communities there[38] and because of Palestinian Jewish aid to Caesar in Egypt, which the emperor amply rewarded. In many cities of Palestine both Greek and Aramaic (and or Hebrew) were spoken, for the population was often mixed. The Palestinian Jewish Christian author of Mark 4:35–41 probably knew of the Caesar narrative already from his own native Jewish community, or at the latest from such a mixed community.

A Hellenistic Jewish Christian from one of the many mixed communities in Palestine (or possibly Syria) may also have translated the narrative of Jesus' stilling the storm on the Sea of Galilee into Greek.

---

[37] Cf. the general discussion in Schürer, *The History* 2.20–28, especially 27 with notes 115–116; and 1.552 for the dating of the uprising.

[38] Schürer in *The History* 2.85–183 analyzes thirty-three of them.

There is no compelling reason to think of a distant diaspora setting for this process of translation, although it cannot be fully excluded.

2.   The Provenance of the Original Narrative.

Hebrew or possibly Aramaic as the original language in which the narrative of Mark 4:35-41 was formulated points to Palestine as its provenance, while the neighboring area in Syria cannot be completely excluded.   Because of the incident's setting on the Sea of Galilee, it is tempting to speculate that the author may even have been a Galilean Jewish Christian, well acquainted with severe windstorms on his native "Sea."   More, however, cannot be stated.

3.   The Date of the Original Narrative.

There is no way precisely to date the narrative now found in Mark 4:35-41. The Gospel of Mark is usually thought to have been composed shortly before or after the fall of Jerusalem to the Romans in 70 CE.[39] Written in Greek, it includes many narratives such as Jesus' stilling the storm which were originally composed in Hebrew or Aramaic.   Since it took some time for these to be translated into Greek and to become available to Mark, perhaps already in a collection such as the (nature) miracles, a date in the fifties for the original narrative may be the best informed guess, although an earlier dating in the forties is also possible.

V. The Historicity, Purposes and Genre of the Narrative.

1.   The Historicity.

Up until the advent of the historical-critical method of biblical criticism, the authenticity of Jesus' stilling the storm in Mark 4:35-41 was simply not questioned.   Even in modern times, the vivid language and many details, some of them ostensibly extraneous such as Jesus' sleeping in the stern on a headrest / pillow, have convinced many commentators of the narrative's historicity.[40]   Numerous scholars appealed to the

---

[39] Cf. J. Marcus, "The Jewish War and the Sitz im Leben of Mark" in *JBL* 111 (1992) 460; D. Lührmann, *Das Markus-Evangelium* 6; and J. Gnilka, *Das Evangelium nach Markus (Mk 1 – 8,28)* 34.

[40] Cf. A. Edersheim, *The Life and Times* 603: these "carry their own evidence"; on p. 604 he maintains the narrative is "an historical occurrence...."   See also V. Taylor, *The Gospel According to Mark* 272.

personal reminiscence of a disciple, especially Peter, for v 35,[41] v 36,[42] v 38a,[43] v 38b,[44] v 40,[45] or for the whole narrative.[46]

Yet vivid details do not necessarily point to authenticity. As J. Schniewind notes in regard to Jesus' stilling the storm: "auch die Legende kann anschaulich erzählen."[47] J. Goldin also correctly remarks that "imaginative dramatization and overdramatization" are two of the "familiar devices of haggadic Midrash...."[48] As pointed out in section I., most of the motifs and expressions found in Mark 4:35–41 derive from the Hebrew text of Jonah One, especially in Judaic tradition as represented by the *Jonah Midrash*. One example from it are the "other boats" which accompanied Jonah's ship as he was crossing the sea. They are found nowhere else and led to much puzzlement when the Palestinian Jewish Christian narrator of Jesus' stilling the storm also incorporated them into Mark 4:36.

The very vivid and detailed account of Jesus' stilling the storm, including "other boats," is not historically true. Yet it has its own *religious truths*, which I shall now describe.[49]

---

[41] G. Wohlenberg, *Das Evangelium des Markus* 144.

[42] Cf. F. Hauck, *Das Evangelium des Markus (Synoptiker I)* 62 (see also p. 61); J. Wellhausen, *Das Evangelium Marci* 39 ("real tradition"); and F. Grant, "The Gospel According to St. Mark" in *IB* 7.709–710.

[43] V. Taylor, *The Gospel According to Mark* 275.

[44] Cf. F. Grant, "The Gospel According to St. Mark" 710; and J. Bowman, *The Gospel of Mark. The New Christian Jewish Passover Haggadah* (SPB 8; Leiden: Brill, 1965) 141.

[45] P. Carrington, *According to Mark* 117.

[46] Cf. M.-J. Lagrange, *Évangile selon Saint Marc* 125, and W. Lane, *The Gospel According to Mark* (NICNT 2; Grand Rapids, Michigan: Eerdmans, 1974) 174. E. Gould in *The Gospel According to St. Mark* 86 also views the narrative as probably historical, as does R. Glöckner, *Neutestamentliche Wundergeschichten und das Lob der Wundertaten Gottes in den Psalmen* (Mainz: Grünewald, 1983) 67–69, who also lists several others who think similarly.

[47] *Das Evangelium nach Markus* (NTD 1; Göttingen: Vandenhoeck & Ruprecht, 1960⁹) 52.

[48] *The Song at the Sea* 27.

[49] Cf. the statement by M. Herr in the art. "Aggadah" in *EJ* (1971) 2.355: "the *aggadah* does contain truth which is greater than that of historical and philological reality, and more important than that of the natural sciences."

2. The Purposes of the Narrative.

The original narrative of Jesus' stilling the storm on the Sea of Galilee did not have a single purpose or meaning, but rather expressed several religious truths.   They are now described in sections A–E.   After this I shall analyze Mark's own understanding of the narrative (F).

A. Jesus as the Son of God is also Lord of the Sea.

When Jonah attempted to flee from God's presence by boarding a ship to Tarshish on the far western side of the Mediterranean Sea, and only this ship became involved in a ferocious windstorm (Jonah One), the prophet learned that God not only rules over heaven and earth, but also over the sea.[50]

Since Judaic traditions on Jonah One provide the major background to Mark 4:35–41, it is understandable that the same motif is mirrored in the narrative of Jesus' calming the Sea.   Here, however, Jesus does not pray in the boat to his heavenly Father for Him to show that He is Lord of all the elements.   Instead, he himself exercises the divine prerogative of commanding wind and waves to cease.   This portrays him as the Son of God, for only God possesses this power.[51]

Up to now it has usually been thought that such divine characteristics were attributed to Jesus only after the Resurrection, especially in eschatological contexts.   Here this is already done during his Galilean ministry.   The title "Son of God" is intentionally avoided in the account, however, for during Jesus' earthly ministry only God at his baptism (Mark 1:11) and transfiguration (9:7), and the unclean spirits / demons (3:11 and 5:7), acknowledge him as such.[52]   Nevertheless, Jesus shows that he is already the Son of God during his lifetime by appropriating a divine function, stilling the sea.   This demonstrates both his very intimate relationship to the Father, as well as his divine power.

(For Jesus as a contrast to the Roman emperor, thought to be lord of the sea, compare section C. below.)

---

[50] Cf. L. Ginzberg's statement regarding chapter one of Jonah in *The Legends* 4.247.

[51] For the motif of God's power and might as strongly emphasized in the midrash on Jonah One, see I. C. 16 above.

[52] The centurion's statement beneath the Cross in 15:39 is only after Jesus' death. The title "the Son of the Blessed" is part of a question posed by the high priest in 14:61.   D. Lührmann in *Das Markusevangelium* 97 also emphasizes the legitimization of Jesus as God's Son in the stilling of the storm.

B. Jesus Is "More / Greater Than."

1) The Jonah Midrash.

The motif of Jesus' being "more than" or superior to others is reflected in his ability to calm the wind and waves of the Sea of Galilee. In addition to the "Q" tradition described in section 2) and the material on the Messiah analyzed in section 3) below, this motif may also in part derive from Judaic interpretation of Jonah One.

In *Midrash Jonah* on 1:6, the captain of the ship approaches the prophet and informs him that they are standing between life and death, yet he is sleeping. After he asks Jonah from which people he is and the latter answers, "I am a Hebrew" (v 9), the head of the sailors states: "Have we not heard that the god / God of the Hebrews is 'greater than' (גדול הוא מ׳) all the gods?   Rise, call upon your god / God! (v 6) Perhaps the god / God will act as he / He did in regard to all the miracles at the Reed Sea."[53]

This is probably based on (the pagan) Jethro's "'hearing of' all that God had done for Moses and for Israel His people, how the Lord had brought Israel out of Egypt," in Exod 18:1. In v 11 Jethro states: "Now I know that the Lord is 'greater than' all gods...."[54]

In *Midrash Jonah* God is described as being "greater than" all the other gods because of the miracles He performed for the Israelites at the Reed Sea. In the Markan narrative of Jesus' calming the ferocious windstorm on the Sea of Galilee, based for the most part on Judaic traditions on Jonah One, Jesus is also presented as being "greater than" the winds and raging sea because, as the Son of God, he is also the Lord of the sea.

2) Gospel Traditions.

In the "Q" tradition now found in Matt 12:41 and Luke 11:32, Jesus is represented as saying regarding the men of Nineveh: they "will arise at the (Final) Judgment with this generation and condemn it; for they

---

[53] Cf. the first printed edition of Prague 1595, as well as Jellinek, *Bet ha-Midrasch* 1.97 (German in Wünsche, *Aus Israels Lehrhallen* 2.41). Parallel traditions simply have: "is great."   In *De Jona* 25 (93, p. 24), the King of the present generation (God) is described as "superseding" with new miracles the old ones.   In 94 the Hebrews' passing through the (Reed / Red) Sea is then mentioned. The whole incident is connected to believing.

[54] Cf. also the pagan Rahab's statements in Josh 2:10–11.

repented at the preaching of Jonah, and behold, 'something greater than' (πλεῖον) Jonah is here."

This alludes to Jonah's preaching in Jonah 3:4, which resulted in the men of Nineveh as "believing" in God (v 5), fasting, putting on sackcloth, sitting in ashes and repenting (vv 5–10).

Whether Jesus' being "more than" Jonah derives from him or was formulated by the first Palestinian Jewish Christians after his Resurrection,[55] this saying was almost certainly available to the Christian community out of which Mark 4:35–41 arose. The Palestinian Jewish Christian narrator knew of it and created his incident partially in order to illustrate it. He wanted to show Jesus' superiority to the prophet, especially as described in Jonah One and in Judaic traditions on it.

Jonah fled from God's commission to him to preach repentance to the city of Nineveh (Jonah 1:1–3), while early Christian tradition had Jesus accept divine recognition at his baptism and then begin to preach repentance (Mark 1:11 and 15). Jonah went down into the inside of the ship he was on, lay down and fell into deep sleep because of his mental anguish (Judaic tradition on Jonah 1:5). Jesus, in contrast, was asleep on a headrest in the stern of the boat while a great windstorm raged. This showed his confidence or faith in God. Also, the Mediterranean Sea only quieted down when the sailors on Jonah's ship threw him into it. The Sea of Galilee, in contrast, already calmed down when Jesus, remaining in the boat, rebuked the wind and commanded the Sea to be still.

The Palestinian Jewish Christian narrator knew that those hearing his account would most probably make the above comparisons between Jonah and Jesus and conclude: Here is indeed "more than" Jonah.

Yet why was Jonah considered so important since he was one of the twelve minor prophets and ostensibly not of such stature as the major figures Isaiah, Jeremiah, Ezekiel, or even Moses, also considered a prophet in Judaic tradition? The answer lies not only in the very significant early Palestinian Jewish Christian comparison of Jesus' being three days and three nights in his grave before he was resurrected, and Jonah's being three days and three nights in the belly of a large fish before it vomited him out upon dry land. It is probably also due to the close association in Judaic tradition of Jonah with the major miracle workers Elijah and Elisha.

---

[55] The latter is most probably true for the "sign of Jonah" in Luke 11:29–30, which Matthew spells out in 12:39–40 in light of the three days and three nights of Jonah 2:1 (Eng. 1:17).

When Jesus raised Jairus' daughter from the dead in Mark 5:21–43, for Palestinian Jewish Christians this recalled Elijah's raising the son of the widow of Zarephath from the dead in 1 Kgs 17:7–24.[56]   As noted above in section I. 1., Judaic tradition maintained this boy became the later prophet Jonah.   When Jesus fed the 5000 with five loaves of bread and two fish in Mark 6:30–44,[57] the incident showed that he was "greater than" Elisha, who only fed 100 men with twenty loaves of barley and fresh ears of grain in 2 Kgs 4:42–44.   When Jesus walked upon the Sea of Galilee in Mark 6:45–52, he was "more than" both Elijah and Elisha, who only caused the waters of the Jordan River to part so that they could walk through its dry bed in 2 Kgs 2:8.[58]

In Judaic tradition Jonah was a major disciple of the miracle worker Elisha.   The latter led Israel for more than sixty years,[59] and otherwise had thousands of disciples.[60]   Yet Elisha employed only Jonah, for example, for the important task of anointing Jehu king over Israel.[61]

---

[56] Jesus refers to Elijah and the widow of Zarephath elsewhere in Luke 4:26. Cf. also Elisha's raising the son of the Shunnamite woman from the dead in 2 Kgs 4:18–37.

[57] Cf. the variant with 4000 in Mark 8:1–10;   it has seven loaves of bread and a few small fish.

[58] Elisha performs this miracle alone in v 14.   Moses' passing through the Reed Sea on dry ground at the exodus is very similar.   Cf. also the worker of miracles Pinḥas b. Yair, a fourth generation Tanna (Strack and Stemberger, *Introduction* 87), who is said to have caused the River Ginnai to divide three times so that individuals could pass through it.   Concerning this R. Joseph (bar Ḥiyya), a third generation Babylonian Amora (Strack and Stemberger, *Introduction* 102), stated: "How great is this man! 'Greater than' Moses and sixty myriads of Israel!"   See *b. Ḥull.* 7a (Soncino 29).   As H.-J. Klauck states in *Allegorie und Allegorese in synoptischen Gleichnistexten* (NTAbh, Neue Folge 13;   Münster: Aschendorff, 1978) 346, n. 38, OT (and Judaic) sources make *theios anēr* ideas irrelevant here. R. Pesch in *Das Markusevangelium. I. Teil* 280–281 also cites others who believe the OT "men of God" were of much more importance than Hellenistic figures in regard to the Gospel miracles.

[59] Cf. *Seder 'Olam* 19 (Milikowsky 334, English 502).

[60] Cf. *b. Keth.* 106a (Soncino 680) with at least 2,200, and *Tg. Ps.-J.* Deut 34:3 (Rieder 2.308, English in Clarke, 104, and Etheridge 682) with 200,000.

[61] Cf. *Seder 'Olam* 18 (Milikowsky 328, English 500).   He is assumed to be "one of the sons of the prophets" called by Elisha in 2 Kgs 9:1, 4, 6.   In *Gen. Rab.* Bereshit 21/5 on Gen 3:22 (Theodor and Albeck 201;   Soncino 1.175), Jonah is identified as one of the sons of the prophets whose axe head fell into the Jordan River.   His master Elisha miraculously made the iron float up so that Jonah could retrieve it (2 Kgs 6:1–7).   For other Judaic references to Jonah and the two miracle workers Elijah and Elisha, see Ginzberg, *The Legends* 4.197 and 246, with the relevant notes in 6.318 and 348.

The close association of Jonah with the major miracle workers Elijah and Elisha in Judaic tradition certainly aided the Palestinian Jewish Christian narrator of Mark 4:35–41 in modeling his account of Jesus' miraculous stilling of the storm on chapter one of the prophetic book of Jonah, especially as found in Judaic tradition. Jesus is "more than" this famous prophet.

3) The Messiah in Judaic Tradition.

Rabbinic traditions on David, probably representing the son of David = Messiah, and on the King Messiah, also point to the Messiah as "greater than" other Judaic heroes. *Exod. Rab.* Beshallaḥ 25/8 on Exod 16:4 ("bread from heaven"), for example, has God in the time-to-come ask someone at the messianic banquet to say grace. After the angels Michael and Gabriel, the three patriarchs, Moses, Aaron and the elders defer, David is given the honor, for a king should bless a King.[62]   In *b. Pesaḥ.* 119b grace is said by David after this "great banquet," and the order is Abraham, Isaac, Jacob, Moses, Joshua and David.[63]

Another Judaic tradition on the "great mountain" of Zech 4:7 interprets it as the King Messiah. He is greater than the patriarchs, more exalted than Moses, and higher than the angels of service.[64]   Finally, *Midr. Pss.* 18/29 on Ps 18:38 relates that in the time-to-come God will seat the King Messiah at His right hand (the place of honor), as Ps 110:1 is interpreted.   When He seats Abraham at His left, the latter's face turns pale.[65]

Although the above rabbinic traditions are now found in late sources, they certainly reflect earlier Judaic thought in regard to the Messiah: he will be "greater than" the angels, the patriarchs, Moses,

---

[62] Mirqin 5.282; Soncino 3.310.

[63] Soncino 616.

[64]   *Tanḥ.* B. Toledoth 20 in Buber, *Midrasch Tanchuma* 139; German in Bietenhard, *Midrasch Tanḥuma B* 1.149. See also *Tanḥuma* Toledoth 14 (Eshkol 1.118); *Targ. Jon.* Zech 4:7 (Sperber 3.482); and *Yalquṭ Shem'oni* on the verse. In *Pesiq. R.* 37/1 the patriarchs acknowledge that the Messiah is greater than they because he has suffered for their children (Friedmann 162b; Braude 2.685, and n. 2 on the latter motif). See also *Yalquṭ Shem'oni* on Isa 52:13 as quoted in S. Levey, *The Messiah: An Aramaic Interpretation* (Cincinnati: Hebrew Union College – Jewish Institute of Religion, 1974) 67.

[65] Buber, *Midrasch Tehillim* 157, and Braude, *The Midrash on Psalms* 1.261.

Aaron and the elders.[66]   When Jesus, whom Christians held to be the Messiah, was described as being "greater than" Jonah, and this "Q" saying was illustrated in a concrete way by the narrative found in Mark 4:35–41 based on Jonah One, especially in Judaic tradition, this thus fit into the larger context of Jesus' being "greater than" all the venerated figures of early Judaism.

C. Jesus is Greater than the Roman Emperor.

Closely related to section B. above, yet important enough for special treatment, is an implied contrast between Jesus' calming a ferocious windstorm while crossing the Sea of Galilee in a boat, and Julius Caesar's well-known attempt to cross the Adriatic Sea in a boat in 48 BCE.   As related above in section II., the Roman emperor utterly fails to subdue the fierce elements and must return to the shore.   He may be called "cosmocrator," and his troops may rule over the land, but he is definitely not lord of the sea.   As the Son of God, who is the creator of heaven, earth and sea, Jesus, however, can rebuke the wind and command the sea to be peaceful.   He, and not the ostensibly most powerful person in the world, is thus truly Lord.

D. Jesus Strengthens Present-day Disciples' Weakened Faith.

The early Palestinian Jewish Christian community to which the narrator of Mark 4:35–41 addressed his narrative was experiencing turbulences in regard to its faith in Jesus as the Lord of their lives. When he asks "Why are you afraid?" in v 40, he speaks to the contemporary conditions of the Christian community.   It was affected by adverse circumstances, indicated in the narrative by waves thrashing against the boat, which resulted in its filling up with water.   The danger of sinking was imminent.   In addition, the disciples are represented as asking Jesus if he doesn't care about them, for they are about to perish (v 38).

While there are no clear indications in the episode in regard to the specific reasons for the Christian community's fears, the following may be surmised.   There was some scattered Jewish persecution of Christians, especially in Judea.[67]   Some of those who had first believed

---

[66] Cf. my treatment of this theme also in regard to Ahasuerus and John 2:1–11 in *Water into Wine and the Beheading of John the Baptist* (BJS 150; Atlanta: Scholars Press, 1988) 33–34.

[67] Cf. 1 Thess 2:14–16; Rom 15:31; Mark 13:9, 11–13; Acts 4:3; 5:18; 7:58; 8:1; 12:2; and Josephus, *Ant.* 20.200 on the stoning of Jesus' brother James.

were now also falling away.[68]   False prophets tended to lead others astray.[69]   And some members of the earliest Christian communities, as time passed, lost hope in the imminent return or parousia of Jesus, and began to doubt.[70]

Such "storms of life" suggested to the narrator of Mark 4:35–41 that his incident of Jesus' stilling the storm would offer consolation, encouragement and inner strength to those Christians who were being persecuted, or whose faith had begun to waver, who had begun to have serious doubts.   Jesus' sleeping on a headrest in the stern of a storm-tossed boat shows his own confidence in almighty God.   Jesus' present-day followers should now also share his faith in the heavenly Father and in his own ability to calm the rough seas in their lives.[71]

E. The Call to Decision in Regard to the Person of Jesus.

Like the question after the exorcism in Mark 1:27, the question in 4:41, "Who then is this, that even wind and sea obey him?" forces the hearer (and later the reader of the Gospel of Mark) to make a decision in regard to the identity of Jesus.   Is not he who can still a ferocious windstorm the true Son of God?   If so, they should "reverence him with great reverence."   This question gains much weight by being placed at the very end of the narrative.[72]

---

[68] Cf. for example Mark 4:17.

[69] Cf. Mark 13:5–6, 21–22; and Matt 7:15.

[70] Cf. Mark 4:26–29 and 30–32; 9:1 and 13:30; 11:22–23; and 13:32–37.

[71] On the immense secondary literature in regard to the theme of faith in the Gospel of Mark, and this pericope in particular, see for example E. Best, *Disciples and Discipleship.*   Studies in the Gospel According to Mark (Edinburgh: Clark, 1986) 193–194, and "The Church as Ship" on pp. 230–234; T. Vogt, *Angst und Identität im Markusevangelium.* Ein textpsychologischer und sozialgeschichtlicher Beitrag (NTOA 26; Freiburg, Switzerland: Universitätsverlag; Göttingen: Vandenhoeck & Ruprecht, 1993) 70 – 100; C. Marshall, *Faith as a Theme in Mark's Narrative* (SNTSMS 64; Cambridge: Cambridge University Press, 1989) 213–220; and T. Söding, *Glaube bei Markus* (SBB 12; Stuttgart: Katholisches Bibelwerk, 1987²) 441–446.

[72] Cf. P. Müller, *"Wer ist dieser?"* Jesus im Markusevangelium (Biblisch-theologische Studien 27; Neukirchen-Vluyn: Neukirchener, 1995) 33: "Die ganze Erzählung läuft auf die Frage 'Wer ist dieser?' hinaus.   Geschichten mit einer Frage am Schluß sind offen und wollen weiter erzählt werden."   I disagree, however, that v 41 was originally an acclamation, later turned into a question by Mark (p. 39).   It belonged rather to the narrative art of the Palestinian Jewish Christian who composed the original incident. He modeled it on the question in Mark 1:27, part of a story already known to him.

To this extent Mark 4:35-41 may also be thought of as "missionizing." It not only strengthens the weakened faith of those who already were believers in Jesus as the Son of God. It also seeks to persuade those on the edge of a Christian congregation that as God is Lord of the sea, so too is Jesus, who is thus His Son. Such possible converts to the Christian message (first Jews, then proselytes, God-fearers and Gentiles) are strongly encouraged to answer the question of v 41 positively: "This narrative has helped persuade me that Jesus is the true Son of God, and I thus now want to join the community of his followers." The latter is valid for all stages of the incident's development: the original Palestinian Jewish Christian community to which the anecdote was first addressed; the Hellenistic Jewish Christian community which first translated it into Greek; and the Gospel of Mark, where the narrative is now found. The basic message remains the same.

* * *

The narrative of Jesus' stilling the storm thus basically conveys four religious truths: Jesus is the Son of God and as such also Lord of the sea; he is more than the prophet Jonah, closely associated with the miracle-workers Elijah and Elisha; in contrast to the "divine" Roman emperor, he is the true Lord of the sea; and Jesus can strengthen the weakened faith of contemporary disciples. In addition, a major purpose of the narrative is to call the hearer, later the reader, to a decision in regard to the person of Jesus.

F. *Mark's Understanding of the Narrative.*

Finally, it is appropriate to briefly describe the meaning of Jesus' stilling the storm as now found in the Markan context.

Mark found the narrative already in Greek. There are no indications that he himself knew either Hebrew or Aramaic. After relating a number of Jesus' healings and exorcisms, the Evangelist employs it as his leadoff nature miracle. This primary position, before for example Jesus' feeding the 5000 and walking on the Sea of Galilee, by itself emphasizes its great importance for the earliest Evangelist.

As noted above, Mark added a reference to the crowd in 4:36 in order to relate the incident to the foregoing events of the same day. Jesus is not only a teacher / preacher, who tells parables (4:1-34). He is also a man of deeds, one who performs miracles. By commanding the wind and sea to obey him, Jesus demonstrates that he is stronger than the prince of demons, Beelzebul / Satan (3:27).

In addition, the first Evangelist most probably added "yet" (-πω to οὐ = οὔπω) in v 40. This changed the meaning of Jesus' original question to the disciples from "Have you no faith?" to "Don't you believe (even) yet?"   Mark thinks here of all the healings and exorcisms the disciples had already witnessed Jesus perform as of 1:21. With others they asked "What is this?" in 1:27.   Now the closest followers of Jesus should not ask "Who is this...?" (4:41), but should already bear witness to their faith in Jesus (v 40).   For Mark, however, they cannot proclaim him as the Son of God, in contrast to the evil spirits (1:24; 3:11; 5:7) and God (1:11), for Peter has not yet labeled Jesus the Christ (8:30).   Because of Mark's own theological emphasis on the "messianic secret," he underlines the disciples' lack of understanding in 4:40.[73]

Within Mark's Gospel the various points of comparison and contrast between Jesus and Jonah, easily perceived by the earliest Palestinian Jewish Christians in regard to 4:35-41, were now lost or at least much less apparent to the first Gentile Christian readers.   There are no indications that Mark expected them to have an extensive knowledge of Judaic traditions, including those on the prophet Jonah.   Only if they somehow also had access to the "Q" saying about Jesus' being more than Jonah, could they as Gentiles also have appreciated the Jonah background to Jesus' stilling the storm.

These, then, are the peculiarly Markan emphases in the narrative of Jesus' stilling the storm, and a description of how his first Gentile Christian readers would probably have perceived it (in addition to the meanings described above in sections A – E, excluding the Jonah material).

3. The Genre.

There is no question that Jesus' stilling the storm is a "miracle," and more exactly a "nature miracle."[74]   A closer characterization of it, however, becomes more difficult.   It has also been called a "rebuke of demons," to which the motif of aid to the disciples was added.[75]   Its proximity to the form of the "exorcism" of Mark 1:23-27 has also been

---

[73] On this, cf. M. Hooker, *The Gospel According to Mark* 140. Yet the disciples' inability to understand and to have faith is not "the" point of the narrative. The incident has several other meanings, as related above.

[74] Cf. H. Holtzmann, *Die Synoptiker* 74; H. Anderson, *The Gospel of Mark* (NCB; London: Oliphants, 1976) 142; W. Schmithals, *Das Evangelium nach Markus. Kapitel 1 – 9,1*, 255; and M. Hooker, *The Gospel According to St Mark* 138.

[75] E. Lohmeyer, *Das Evangelium des Markus* 92 and 106.

noted,[76] a pericope which the narrator knew and borrowed from in its pre-Gospel form, as I have proposed at several points above.   Other commentators emphasize the narrative of 4:35-41 as an "epiphany,"[77] more particularly a "rescue epiphany."[78]   M. Dibelius called it a "tale" ("Novelle").   He maintained that the tales reveal "self-convincing power," yet were not formed for public worship or preaching, nor do they provide didactic motifs.   Instead, they deal with Jesus as a thaumaturge, and were addressed to churches "which believed in and continually experienced miracles."[79]   D. Lührmann has justly chided Dibelius in this respect.   The purpose of the stilling of the storm is indeed proclamation.[80]   It was not composed and further related simply for the sheer joy of story-telling, shown in its colorful details.   Rather, it was narrated within the context of worship.

R. Pesch aptly notes that the pericope is intended to be an "Überbietungserzählung mit epiphanischem Einschlag."[81]   Pesch thinks here primarily of Jesus' being presented as "more than," or superior to, Jonah.   Above, I have pointed out that he is also presented as being superior to Julius Caesar, the deified Roman emperor who could not cross the Adriatic Sea in a severe windstorm.   Jesus is thus also more than even the Roman emperor, thought to be "cosmocrator," including his being lord of the sea.   In addition, the Messiah in Judaic sources is considered to be "more than" the great folk heroes of Judaism.

Pesch's term "narrative of superiority" is thus very appropriate for the genre, especially within the original Palestinian Jewish Christian

---

[76] M.-É. Boismard, *L'Évangile de Marc – sa préhistoire* (Ebib, N.S. 26; Paris: Gabalda, 1994) 102. Cf. also T. Dwyer, *The Motif of Wonder in the Gospel of Mark* (JSNT Supp. Ser. 128; Sheffield: Academic Press, 1996) 109. R. Gundry denies Jesus' exorcising a "particular storm-demon" here, but speaks of his "quelling the powers of chaos (the sea) in general" (*Mark* 241).

[77] K. Kertelge, *Die Wunder Jesu im Markusevangelium*. Eine redaktionsgeschicht-liche Untersuchung (SANT 23; Munich: Kösel, 1970) 98; it was later changed by Mark to fit the situation of the church in the apocalyptic distress of the final time (106). See also Klauck, *Allegorie und Allegorese* 346.

[78] D.-A. Koch, *Die Bedeutung der Wundererzählungen für die Christologie des Markusevangeliums* (BZNW 42; Berlin: de Gruyter, 1975) 93; it was expanded by means of the motif of aid to the disciples (106).

[79] *From Tradition to Gospel* 71, 80–81, 103, quotations from pp. 96 and 79. Dibelius also asserts that "the miracle is told as an epiphany of the divine on earth, and this epiphany in the miracle is for its own sake" (94).

[80] *Das Markusevangelium* 94.

[81] *Das Markusevangelium, I. Teil* 269. He also calls it a rescue miracle (268).

context.   Yet already at this primary stage the narrator intended Jesus to be considered as revealing his divine power as the Son of God.   Jesus does not pray to God that the heavenly Father calm the turbulent Sea of Galilee.   Instead, as His Son he does this himself.   Thus while the actual terminology of "epiphany" is not employed, Jesus indeed "reveals" himself as what he truly is: the Son of God.   To this extent Pesch's further description of the narrative as "with an epiphanic touch" is also appropriate.

The genre of the narrative cannot be separated from its various purposes, as I have described these above in sections A – E.   To the extent that the original anecdote also sought to attract other Jews to the Palestinian Jewish Christian community by maintaining that Jesus is "greater than" Jonah, associated with the greatest miracle workers of Judaism, Elijah and Elisha, it was "missionary propaganda" in the best sense of the term.   By showing that Jesus is the true Son of God, however, it also sought to win the formerly pagan "God-fearers" and proselytes for the Christian message.   This was especially true after the narrative was translated into Greek in Hellenistic Jewish Christian communities, and was later appropriated by primarily Gentile Christianity.   In the latter two, Jesus as a miracle worker would have been in competition with pagan thaumaturges.

Finally, the narrative of Jesus' stilling the storm also seeks to strengthen the weakened faith of contemporary disciples who are experiencing persecutions and other distress.   They can indeed rely on Jesus, who will accompany them during all the storms of life they encounter.   They will not be alone in their affliction.   To this extent the pericope may also be appropriately called a "narrative of consolation."

In conclusion, Jesus' stilling the storm in Mark 4:35–41 has numerous purposes.   Therefore describing its genre may not be oversimplified, but must also be conceived as many-faceted.   The most appropriate designation could thus be: "a nature miracle of rescue and consolation, showing Jesus' superiority and revealing him as the Son of God."

*   *   *

The original Palestinian Jewish Christian narrative of Jesus' stilling a ferocious windstorm on the Sea of Galilee is full of fascinating details and is painted in vivid colors.   It captivated the earliest Christian communities so much that it was soon translated from Semitic into Greek and later taken up by Mark into our earliest Gospel.   When he did so, he (gratefully) only slightly altered the original anecdote.   Matthew and Luke then appropriated the Markan narrative, beginning a long chain of interpretation from the early church fathers up to contemporary exegetes. Modern-day Christians should be appreciative not only of the original composer's narrative artistry, but also of the important meanings or religious truths the present form of the story conveys for Jesus' contemporary disciples, themselves caught in the various storms of life.

Chapter Two

Jesus' Calling the First Four Disciples in Mark 1:16-20 and Judaic Traditions on Elijah's Calling Elisha as his Disciple in 1 Kgs 19:19-21

Introduction

The narrative of Jesus' calling the fishermen Simon, Andrew, James and John at the Sea of Galilee to be his first disciples is found in Mark 1:16-20 (cf. also Matt 4:18-22 and Luke 5:1-11).[1] It includes his famous words: "Follow me, and I will make you fishers of people" (v 17).

The very compressed form of the present account "leaves much to the imagination."[2] Indeed, W. Schmithals maintains that here "Jesus is like a tourist."[3] He simply walks along the Sea of Galilee, tells four fishermen to follow him (as his disciples), and they immediately do so, leaving everything behind them. For this reason R. Gundry speaks at this point of "the miracle of sudden persuasion."[4]

---

[1] Cf. also the similar calling of Levi at the Sea of Galilee in 2:13–14.

[2] D. Juel, *Mark* (Minneapolis: Augsburg, 1990) 40.

[3] *Das Evangelium nach Markus, Kapitel 1–9,1* 109.

[4] *Mark* 67. See the secondary literature on the pericope he cites on pp. 66-68 and 70-73, as well as *The Gospel of Mark. A Cumulative Bibliography 1950-1990*, ed. F. Neirynck et al. 568-569.

Yet there is good reason to believe that the four future disciples had already known Jesus for at least some time before they decided to become his followers. It must therefore be asked whether the Palestinian Jewish Christian author of the narrative based his description of this call upon Judaic traditions regarding another famous call to discipleship in the Hebrew Bible. If it also contained the element of "sudden persuasion," this would help to explain the present compressed form of Mark 1:16–20.

I suggest that this is indeed the case. No calling of a disciple in the Hebrew Bible was more well-known in early Palestinian Judaism than that of Elijah's calling Elisha in 1 Kgs 19:19–21. While recent studies have shown the influence of Elijah traditions upon the Gospels,[5] and a number of scholars have dealt with the relevance of the Septuagintal (3 Kingdoms) form of 1 Kgs 19:19–21,[6] no one up to now has attempted to demonstrate in a major way the influence of Hebrew and Aramaic Judaic traditions on the latter Scriptural passage in regard to Mark 1:16–20.[7] In the excursus below on "Fishing in the Sea of Galilee with Nets, and 'Fishers of People' in Mark 1:17 par.," I also employ primarily Palestinian Judaic sources in Hebrew and Aramaic to point out the metaphorical use of "fishing" expressions, and the positive meaning of Jesus' saying on "fishers of people." This image up to now has been thought by commentators to be especially associated with negative judgment, particularly in the OT.

---

[5] Cf. M. Öhler, *Elia im Neuen Testament*. Untersuchungen zur Bedeutung des alttestamentlichen Propheten im frühen Christentum (BZNW 88; Berlin: de Gruyter, 1997), as well as the secondary literature he cites. He deals tersely with Mark 1:16–20 on p. 158, yet shows no knowledge of Judaic tradition on 1 Kings 19. The author of this Vienna dissertation openly acknowledges his lack of expertise in Judaic studies on p. IX. See also his art. "The Expectation of Elijah and the Presence of the Kingdom of God" in *JBL* 118 (1999) 461-476.

[6] Cf. L. Goppelt, *Typos*. 89; A. Schulz, *Nachfolgen und Nachahmen*. Studien über das Verhältnis der neutestamentlichen Jüngerschaft zur urchristlichen Vorbildethik (SANT 6; Munich: Kösel, 1962) 100-103 (see also 18-19); and especially the important study by R. Pesch, "Berufung und Sendung, Nachfolge und Mission. Eine Studie zu Mk 1,16–20" in *ZKT* 91 (1969) 1-31 (see especially 9, n. 49, and 11, n. 55).

[7] This is also true for the very brief analysis of the pericope by M. Hengel, *Nachfolge und Charisma*. Eine exegetisch-religionsgeschichtliche Studie zu Mt 8, 21f. und Jesu Ruf in die Nachfolge (BZNW 34; Berlin: Töpelmann, 1968) 85-87, and 18-20 on Elijah's calling Elisha. Hengel refers to R. Meyer, *Der Prophet aus Galiläa* (Leipzig: Lunkenbein, 1940), who also sees the background of Mark 1:16–20 and 2:14 in 1 Kgs 19:19–21 (pp. 32-35, also dependent on predecessors – n. 140).

Section I. points out eight similarities between Judaic traditions on Elijah's calling Elisha while the latter was plowing, and Jesus' calling his first four disciples while they were engaged in their trade of fishing in Mark 1:16–20. Section II. is concerned with the original language of the pericope, section III. with the purposes of the original narrative, section IV. with the question of historicity, and section V. with possible Markan editing and the dating of the account.

Because a major Judaic source I employ in my analysis is an account now found in *Eliyyahu Rabbah* 5, available only in a very periphrastic English translation, I offer my own rendering of it at this point.[8]

After discussing how Elijah merited reviving one dead person,[9] the midrash poses the question:

> For what reason did Elisha merit reviving two dead persons?[10] Because he did the will of Him who spoke and the world came into being. And from where does one know that it is so? From the time when the holy spirit said to Elijah,[11] "Go, return on your way to the wilderness of Damascus," etc. (1 Kgs 19:16). "Also you shall anoint Jehu the son of Nimshi as king over Israel; and Elisha ...you shall anoint as prophet in your place," etc. (vv 16-18). "So he set out from there, and found Elisha son of Shaphat of Abel-meholah,[12] who was plowing" (v 19).[13] [Elisha] was skilled in his trade [as a plowman]. A sign of this was that "there were twelve yoke of oxen ahead of him" (*ibid.*). "And Elijah passed by and cast his mantle over him" (*ibid.*). [Elisha] immediately left all that belonged to him and ran after him, as it is said: "And he left the

---

[8] Cf. the Hebrew in M. Friedmann, *Seder Eliahu Rabba and Seder Eliahu Zuta* 22-23, and the English in *Tanna debe Eliyyahu. The Lore of the School of Elijah*, trans. W. Braude and I. Kapstein, 91-92. This is the major Judaic source on Elijah's making Elisha his disciple. See Ginzberg, *The Legends* 4.239 and 6.343, n. 2. The talmudic passages he cites are relevant to the next chapter on Jesus' discussion with Cleopas and his companion on the road to Emmaus in Luke 24.

[9] Cf. 1 Kgs 17:17–24 on the son of the widow in Zarephath.

[10] Cf. his request for a "double share" of Elijah's spirit just before the latter's ascension (2 Kgs 2:9), fulfilled in his reviving the son of a woman from Shunem in 2 Kgs 4:8–37, as well as a dead man thrown into the prophet's grave in 1 Kgs 13:21. On this, see also Sir 48:12.

[11] "The Lord" tells this to Elijah when he is at Mount Horeb (Sinai): 1 Kgs 19:8.

[12] The place-name is inserted here from v 16.

[13] The quotation in the text ends already after "Abel-meholah"; it is followed by "etc."

oxen," etc. (v 20). [Elisha] immediately renounced ownership of all that belonged to him. And he sowed the entire field with salt, [its barrenness then preventing him from returning to it]. Scripture [further] indicates this [resolve] by stating: "And [Elisha] returned from following him, took the yoke of oxen, slaughtered them," etc. (v 21). It is not written "And he [Elijah] taught him [Elisha]," but "And he [Elisha] served him [Elijah]" (*ibid.*). This is the basis for the saying: "Attendance [of a pupil / disciple upon his master] is greater than study."

The above midrash then continues with the section regarding Elijah and Elisha's walking on the road, discussing the Torah, of vital importance to the Emmaus narrative, to be analyzed in the next chapter. Thus the call of Elisha to discipleship, connected here with the incident of Elijah's ascension, stands back to back with the Judaic tradition which forms the major background to the Emmaus narrative in Luke 24, just before Jesus' ascension. The following study indicates how important Elijah's call of Elisha as his disciple in Judaic tradition was for Jesus' call of his first four disciples, and for the conditions of that discipleship. Eight similarities can be noted.

I.   Elijah's Calling of Elisha, and Jesus' Calling of the First Four Disciples.

1.   *Becoming a Disciple.*

A.

a)   *Going After / Following.*

1 Kgs 19:20 has Elisha tell Elijah that after kissing / taking leave of his parents: "I will go after / follow you." The next verse (21) relates that after Elisha slaughtered his yoke of oxen, boiled their flesh and feasted the (local) people with it, he rose and "went after / followed" Elijah and served him.

Both instances here of "to go after / follow" someone are הלך אחרי in the Hebrew. In early Judaism this had become a technical term for "becoming / being someone's 'disciple' (תַּלְמִיד)," the latter expression also being applied to Elisha.[14] One example from shortly before the destruction of Jerusalem is found in '*Avot R. Nat.* A 4, which states: "One time Rabban Yoḥanan b. Zakkai was departing from Jerusalem, and R. Yehoshua 'went after him' (הָיָה הוֹלֵךְ אַחֲרָיו)...."[15] R. Yehoshua (b. Ḥananyah) was an older second generation Tanna, a pupil of Yoḥanan b. Zakkai, a first generation Tanna.[16] The pupil or disciple "went after" his teacher wherever the latter went in order to gain not only theoretical, but also practical knowledge.

In his paraphrase of the calling of Elisha by Elijah, the Jewish historian Josephus, a native of Jerusalem whose native tongue was Aramaic, only decades after the fall of the city to the Romans in 70 CE[17] noted in *Ant.* 8.354 that at his calling, Elisha "followed" (ἀκολουθέω for "to run after" in 1 Kgs 19:20) Elijah. This Greek term was a translation of the Hebrew for "going after" someone already in the Septuagint.[18] Josephus notes in the same paragraph that Elisha "followed" (ἕπτομαι) Elijah and was both his "disciple and attendant" as long as his master lived.   The Greek of "disciple" here is μαθητής (cf. also 9.28), a paraphrase of הָלַךְ אַחֲרֵי in 1 Kgs 19:21. On the basis of this and the (later) rabbinic examples cited above in n. 14, there can be no doubt that first century Palestinian Judaism considered Elisha, who "went after / followed" Elijah when the latter called him, to be Elijah's (main) "disciple" (μαθητής / תַּלְמִיד).

---

[14] On תַּלְמִיד, cf. Jastrow 1673. Cf. the many examples cited by P. Billerbeck in Str-B 1.187-188 and 528-529. In early Judaic sources a pupil is represented as selecting his own teacher, and not the reverse. That is, the teacher did not "call" someone to become his disciple, as Jesus did. Nevertheless, the term "to go / follow after" someone meant to become and to be someone's disciple. Elisha is labeled Elijah's "disciple" (תלמיד) in *Mek. R. Ish.* Pisha 1 on Exod 12:1 (Lauterbach 1.14), *b. Sanh.* 105b (Soncino 720), *Eliyyahu Rabbah* 17 (Friedmann 87; Braude and Kapstein 232), and *Midr. Ma'aseh Torah* (Jellinek, *Bet ha-Midrasch* 2.95; German in A. Wünsche, *Aus Israels Lehrhallen* 4.287). Elijah's "disciples" are also mentioned in *y. Ta'an.* 2:8, 65d (Neusner 18.196) and *Targ. Pal.* Deut 34:3 (Rieder 2.308; Clarke, 104). In *t. Soṭah* 12:5 (Zuckermandel 318; Neusner 3.200) Elijah's relationship to Elisha is referred to as the former being "his master" (רבו). In *Targ. Jon.* 2 Kgs 2:12 Elisha does not address Elijah as "My father," as in the Hebrew, but also as "My master" (רבי; Sperber 2.274; Harrington and Saldarini 267).

[15] Schechter 21; Goldin 34; Neusner 41.

[16] Strack and Stemberger, *Introduction* 77-78 and 74-75 respectively.

[17] Cf. *Vita* 7 for Jerusalem, *Bell.* 1.3 for Jerusalem and his native tongue, and *Ant.* 20.267 for the conclusion of the *Antiquities* in 93/94 CE.

[18] Cf. 3 Kgdms 19:20, Isa 45:14, and Hos 2:5 (Heb. 7).

This terminology influenced the narrative of Jesus' calling his first disciples, as will be indicated in section B. below.

b) *Serving.*

1 Kgs 19:21 states that after Elisha feasted the people with the oxen he had slaughtered and boiled, thus thoroughly breaking with his past, "he set out and followed Elijah and 'became his servant.'" The latter is literally: "and he served him," with שָׁרַת, the piel in the MT meaning "to minister, serve."[19] Countless rabbinic passages show that a disciple's personal attendance upon his teacher in daily life enabled him to recognize how the latter interpreted and put Scriptural and post-biblical injunctions into practice.[20]

Elisha's "serving" Elijah as his disciple is also emphasized in two Judaic traditions on 1 Kgs 19:19–21.

In *Ant.* 8.354 Josephus states that after Elisha took leave of his parents, he followed Elijah. "And as long as Elijah lived he was both his disciple and 'servant' (διάκονος)." Here the Jewish historian transforms the Hebrew verb in 1 Kgs 19:21, "and he served him," into the Greek noun "servant."

The second instance is *Eliyyahu Rabbah* 5. It comments on "and he served him" as follows: "'And he [Elijah] taught him' (וילמדהו) is not written here, but 'and he [Elisha] served him' (וישרתהו). This [incident between Elisha and Elijah] is the derivation of the saying: 'Serving is greater than teaching.'"[21]

R. Simeon b. Yoḥai, a third generation Tanna,[22] in *b. Ber.* 7b comments in regard to the latter: "The service of the Torah is greater than the study thereof. For it is said: 'Here is Elisha the son of Shaphat, who poured water on the hands of Elijah' (2 Kgs 3:11). It is not said, 'who learned,' but 'who poured water.' This teaches that the service of the Torah is greater than the study thereof."[23]

---

[19] BDB 1058, especially 1.c., with reference to here and to Joshua's serving Moses. See also Jastrow 1635. In 1 Kgs 18:43 and 19:3, Elisha is considered to be Elijah's "boy / servant" (נַעַר; BDB 655, 2.a).

[20] See again the passages cited in Str-B 1.527–529.

[21] Cf. Friedmann 23, and Braude and Kapstein's paraphrase on p. 92. See their n. 34: "The disciple is thus constantly with the master who instructs by example as well as by word."

[22] Strack and Stemberger, *Introduction* 84.

[23] Soncino 83; cf. n. 3. Reference from Friedmann 23, n. 25. See also *Targ. Jon.* 2 Kgs 3:11 on Elisha's "serving" Elijah (Sperber 2.276; Harrington and Saldarini

The above Tannaitic explanation of a disciple's learning best by "serving" his teacher derives from the example of Elisha's "serving" Elijah in a concrete way in 2 Kgs 3:11. *Eliyyahu Rabbah* 5 also derives it from Elisha's "serving" Elijah, however, by quoting 1 Kgs 19:21. No doubt both Scriptural passages were employed as proof texts.

The description of Elisha's becoming a servant of / serving Elijah when the latter called him also influenced the Gospel narratives of Jesus' calling his disciples, as will be seen in B. b) below.

B.

a) *Going After / Following.*

In the Gospel of Mark, long before Jesus is represented as appointing twelve of his followers "to be with him, and to be sent out to proclaim the message, and to have authority to cast out demons" (= to heal sicknesses: 3:13–19, quotation vv 14–15), the Evangelist employs the expression "the disciples" (οἱ μαθηταί) in 2:15, 16, 18, 23 and 3:7. The latter are already thought of by him as a fixed group, labeled "his" (Jesus') disciples in four of these instances and "your" (Jesus') disciples in one instance. Yet originally, before the selection of only twelve of them, all those who "went after / followed" Jesus would technically have been his "disciples." This included the first four whom he called in Mark 1:16–20, also described otherwise (Josephus) in terms of Elisha's becoming a "disciple" of Elijah at his calling.[24]

When Jesus called his first disciples at the Sea of Galilee, he said to Simon and Andrew: " 'Follow me' and I will make you fish for people" (NRSV; RSV – "fishers of men": Mark 1:17 // Matt 4:19). The Greek of

---

268). For Elisha's pouring water over Elijah's hands at Mount Carmel as one of his "disciples" (תלמידים), see *Eliyyahu Rabbah* 17 (Friedmann 87; Braude and Kapstein 232). For Elisha's "serving" Elijah as his (main) disciple, see also *Mek. R. Ish.* Pisḥa 1 on Exod 12:1 (Lauterbach 1.14).

[24] Interestingly, the late *Midrash Ma'aseh Torah* states that Elijah had four disciples: Micah, Jona, Obadiah and Elisha (Jellinek, *Bet ha-Midrasch* 2.95; German in Wünsche, *Aus Israels Lehrhallen* 4.287). If this part goes back to an older source (cf. Strack and Stemberger, *Introduction* 372), may the motif have influenced Jesus' first calling "four" disciples, and only then the other eight? Elsewhere in Judaic sources, however, Jona is considered a disciple of Elisha. For Obadiah as a disciple of Elijah, see already the *Lives of the Prophets* 9:2 (Charlesworth 2.392), perhaps from the time of Jesus (D. Hare in 2.381).

the first phrase is δεῦτε ὀπίσω μου, literally "Come after me."[25] This is a Semitism, reflecting the Hebrew הֵלֵךְ אַחֲרֵי or its Aramaic equivalent. As described above, it was a technical term for becoming and being a disciple / pupil. The usual Greek translation of this is ἀκολουθέω, employed of Elisha as a "disciple" of Elijah in Josephus (*Ant.* 8.254) and in the LXX references cited above. The Semitic expression most probably lies behind ἠκολούθησαν αὐτῷ in Mark 1:18, as well as ἀπῆλθον ὀπίσω αὐτοῦ in v 20.[26]

It is significant that Jesus' call of his first disciples at the Sea of Galilee is the only instance in the four Gospels which reflects the Semitic phrase "to go behind / after." I propose that it derives from OT and Judaic tradition on Elijah's calling Elisha, who then "went after" him as a disciple.

b) *Serving.*

The Gospel of Mark simply assumes that after Jesus called his first disciples in 1:16–20, they not only "went after / followed" him, but also "served" Jesus. This is shown for example in a concrete way in 6:35–44 and 8:1–10, as well as in 14:12–16. The model for the disciples' doing so, however, was Elisha's "serving" Elijah after his calling in 1 Kgs 19:21, specifically labeled so by Josephus and emphasized as such in *Eliyyahu Rabbah* 5.

2. *The Number Twelve.*

A.

When Elijah called Elisha to be his disciple, he found the latter plowing.[27] 1 Kgs 19:19 states that "There were twelve yoke of oxen

---

[25] Cf. BAGD 176,2 on δεῦτε with τινός. The same Greek phrase in 4 Kgdms 6:19, although spoken by Elisha, has nothing to do with discipleship. Against Pesch, "Berufung" 15.

[26] The same is true for the call of Levi in 2:14. On these, cf. the Hebrew New Testament of Delitzsch (pp. 62 and 64).

[27] Cf. in this respect Eliezer b. Hyrcanus' "plowing" with a cow which became injured, whereupon he went off to become a pupil of Rabban Yoḥanan b. Zakkai in Jerusalem. I analyze the rabbinic sources on this incident in "Luke 15:11–32 and R. Eliezer b. Hyrcanus' Rise to Fame" in *JBL* 104 (1985) 443-469. See especially *Gen. Rab.* Lech Lecha 42/1 on Gen 14:1 (Theodor and Albeck 1.398; Soncino 1.340).

ahead of him, and he was with the twelfth." The LXX modifies this somewhat ambiguous passage to mean that Elijah was ἐν τοῖς δώδεκα, "among the twelve [pairs]." *Targum Jonathan* at this point states that Elisha "was driving twelve yoke of oxen yoked before him; and he was on one of the twelve."[28] Here the animals of Elisha are not the twelfth pair, but are indefinite, as in the LXX. In his retelling of this narrative, Josephus in *Ant.* 8.353 states that Elijah came up with Elisha "as he was plowing, and certain others were with him, [all together] driving (pl.) twelve yoke of oxen." Here the Jewish historian certainly reflects early Judaic interpretation of 1 Kgs 19:19 to mean that Elisha was not alone with the twelve yoke of oxen. Indeed, it could even be implied that one plowman was behind each yoke, for a total of twelve plowmen.

I suggest that the twofold mention of the number "twelve" at Elijah's call of Elisha[29] to be his disciple in 1 Kgs 19:19 helped to stimulate the Palestinian Jewish Christian author of Jesus' calling his first disciples at the Sea of Galilee to employ imagery at this point from the MT and Judaic tradition on the call of Elisha.

B.

When Jesus calls his first four disciples at the Sea of Galilee (Mark 1:16–20 par.), there is admittedly no mention of the final number "twelve." It occurs for the first time in the Gospel (twice) in 3:13–19 par., where all twelve are explicitly named. Jesus' calling twelve disciples, however, certainly goes back to the period of his own ministry.[30]

The original author of Mark 1:16–20 par. definitely knew of the twelve disciples of Jesus, even if they later lost much of their original importance. The number "twelve" thus may also have helped him apply imagery from Elijah's calling of Elisha in 1 Kgs 19:19–21, with its twofold mention of "twelve," to Jesus' calling of the first four of his twelve disciples in Mark 1:16–20.

---

[28] Sperber 2.262; Harrington and Saldarini 254. The preposition ּ can mean "on," as in Judg 8:21 (" 'on' the necks of their camels"), but here more probably "with" one of the twelve (BDB 89: III.1.a, citing MT 1 Kgs 19:19).

[29] Cf. S. De Vries, *1 Kings* (WBC 12; Waco, Texas: Word Books, 1985) 238: "the number twelve is certainly symbolic of the tribes...." He suggests that all the village ox-teams were working together in a common field. See also n. 39 below.

[30] Cf. the persuasive arguments of J. Meier in "The Circle of the Twelve: Did It Exist During Jesus' Public Ministry?" in *JBL* 116 (1997) 635-672.

3. The Call of Workers Engaged in Their Trades (Plowing, Fishing).

A.

When Elijah set out to call Elisha, 1 Kgs 19:19 simply states that he found him plowing: "There were twelve yoke of oxen ahead of him, and he was with the twelfth." In *Ant.* 8.353 Josephus inserts early Judaic tradition at this point by adding: Elijah "came upon Elisha plowing, and certain others with him, [all together] driving (pl.)[31] twelve yoke of oxen."

The biblical verse 1 Kgs 19:19 was also employed in Judaic tradition to describe the selection by lot of the high priest Phannias / Pinḥas b. Samuel of Ḥabbata in 67/68 CE. In *t. Yoma* 1:6 it is stated that, after the lot fell on him, the revenuers and supervisors of the Jerusalem Temple found him as he was "plowing," as it is said regarding Elisha...."[32] In *Bell.* 4.156, Josephus relates at this point that Phannias was dragged "out of the 'country'" (χώρα),[33] probably meaning the same.

While Phannias was not called to be the disciple of a prophet, the early application of 1 Kgs 19:19 to describe his being called from "plowing" to a most significant office, the high priesthood, shows that the verse was not just limited to the call of a disciple. It could be employed for another important kind of calling, the determination by lot of a high priest.

The same motif of being "called" from plowing to a high office was already employed of Saul, the first king of Israel. 1 Sam 11:5 states that he "was coming from the field [plowing] behind the oxen." Shortly thereafter he is made king (v 15).

It should also be noted that the "call" or decision of Eliezer b. Hyrcanus to study with and become a disciple of Yoḥanan b. Zakkai in Jerusalem is related to have occurred while he was "plowing." Eliezer's cow fell down and was maimed, which caused him to resolve to study with the famous rabbi.[34]

---

[31] *Targum Jonathan* also has "driving" here, as stated above.

[32] Zuckermandel / Liebermann 180; Neusner 2.186. A parallel is found in *Sifra* 'Emor 2, § 213, on Lev 21:10 (Neusner 3.173).

[33] Cf. LSJ 2015, II. Josephus also mentions Phannias in *Ant.* 20.227. For variants of his name, see Schürer, *The history* 1.496-497 and 2.232.

[34] Cf. the sources cited in n. 27.

Elisha's calling to be Elijah's disciple is emphasized as occurring while the former was at work in *Midr. Tannaim* Deut 5:14. It states: "Beloved is work, for the Holy Spirit only rested upon Elisha ben Shaphat from the midst of work, as it is written: "And [Elijah] went and found Elisha ben Shaphat, and he was plowing" (1 Kgs 19:19).[35]

Finally, *Eliyyahu Rabbah* 5 also emphasizes Elisha's calling while being at work. It comments on 1 Kgs 19:19, where Elijah finds Elisha "plowing," as follows: "[Elisha] was skilled in his trade [as a plowman]. [A sign of this was that] 'there were twelve yoke of oxen ahead of him' (v 19)."[36] The Hebrew of "skilled in his trade" is קל במלאכתו.[37] The first printed edition of *Eliyyahu Rabbah* (Venice, 1598) reads here instead: "in the work of 'twelve.' And he was skilled in his work, for he remained at the end, as it is written, 'and he was with the twelfth.' Truly he was designated / prepared for greater things than this."[38]

Here Elisha at his calling by Elijah is not described as a simple farmer, but as a skilled worker, who is plowing at the moment of his call. In one MS tradition, his plowing abilities also point to his being prepared to take on greater tasks.[39] The same motif of being called at work is true for Jesus' first disciples.

B.

Acts 4:13 has the members of the Sanhedrin in Jerusalem describe Peter and John as "uneducated and ordinary men." While this probably referred to their lack of formal training with the leading teachers of the day, it in part later led to the romantic notion of Peter and the three other Galilean fishermen of Mark 1:16–20 as simple, unskilled workers. Their social standing may not have been the highest, yet fishermen at this time

---

[35] Cf. *Midrasch Tannaim zum Deuteronomium*, ed. D. Hoffmann, 22.

[36] Friedmann 23; Braude and Kapstein 92.

[37] The meaning of קל as "skilled" is discussed by Saul Liebermann in the references cited in Braude and Kapstein 92, n. 31. See also Jastrow 1371, with "easy to achieve."

[38] Friedmann 23, n. 22. See his p. 2 on the Venice edition, as well as Braude and Kapstein 5, 11 and 546. The hif. pass. part. מוּכָן can mean: prepared, designated, ready (Jastrow 621). I thank N. Oswald of Berlin for discussing this passage with me.

[39] Cf. the related statement by C. Keil, *Die Bücher der Könige* (Leipzig: Dörffling and Franke, 1876²) 217: "Wie er mit seinen 12 Paar Rindern seinen irdischen Acker gepflügt hatte, so sollte er nun den geistigen Acker der 12 Stämme Israels pflügen (Luc. 9,62)."

were indeed members of a special trade with its own expertise. Since fish was a major staple in the diet, their services were not only needed but also greatly appreciated.

I suggest that just as Elijah called his disciple Elisha while he was working, so the Palestinian Jewish Christian author of Mark 1:16–20 described Jesus as calling his first four disciples at the Sea of Galilee while they too were working. They could instead have been shopping in the marketplace, walking on the road, praying in the synagogue, resting on the Sabbath, or doing something else. Yet the author of the Gospel narrative has them working (fishing) precisely because Judaic tradition emphasized Elijah's calling his disciple Elisha while he was working (plowing).

4. Finding and Passing By.

A.

a) *Finding.*

The same verse as in 3.A. above, 1 Kgs 19:19, states that after Elijah departed from Mount Horeb, he "found" Elisha plowing. The Hebrew for "and he found" is וימצא, for which *Targum Jonathan* has ואשכח[40] and the LXX εὑρίσκει. In *Ant.* 8.353, Josephus states that Elijah "came upon" (the verb καταλαμβάνω)[41] Elisha plowing with some other persons.

b) *Passing By.*

After noting that Elisha was with the twelfth pair of oxen before him, 1 Kgs 19:19 continues by stating: "Elijah 'passed by' him and threw his mantle over him," thus making Elisha his disciple. The Hebrew here is עבר with אל. It can mean that Elijah first "passed on" or "went on"[42] (beyond Elisha – and the other eleven pairs of oxen) and only then cast his mantle upon Elisha, making him his disciple. *Targum Jonathan* employs the same verb, with ל: "And Elijah passed unto him...."[43] The LXX employs the verb ἐπέρχομαι with ἐπί at this point, "to come

---

[40] Sperber 2.262. On the verb שכב, cf. Jastrow 1572.

[41] LSJ 897, II: catch, overtake, come up with.

[42] On these meanings of עבר, cf. BDB 718, 5.a.

[43] Sperber 2.262; Harrington and Saldarini 254.

upon."[44] Josephus in *Ant.* 8.353 has the very similar προσέρχομαι, to come or go to,[45] which R. Marcus translates as "and, going up to him...."[46]

I suggest that the above two verbs from the Elijah / Elisha calling narrative, "finding" and "passing by," were appropriated, in partly modified form, by the Palestinian Jewish Christian who originally formulated the account of Jesus' calling his first disciples in Mark 1:16-20. This took place, however, in reverse order, as will now be shown.

B.

b)   *Passing By.*

Mark 1:16 states that "As Jesus 'passed along' the Sea of Galilee, he saw Simon and his brother Andrew casting a net into the sea – for they were fishermen." Then Jesus called them to be his disciples (v 17). The Greek for "pass along" in v 16 is παράγω, which can also mean "pass by,"[47] as does the Hebrew and Aramaic עבר.

The Palestinian Jewish Christian author of the calling narrative now found in Mark 1:16–20 here borrowed the verb "to pass by" (עבר) from his model in 1 Kgs 19:19 and applied it to the new circumstance of the Sea of Galilee. He knew that Jesus had made Capernaum on its north shore the center of his public ministry (Mark 1:21; 2:1; 3:19). He therefore had Jesus "pass by / along" the Sea of Galilee until he saw those he wanted to call to be his disciples.

a)   *Finding.*

Mark 1:16 notes that "as Jesus passed along the Sea of Galilee, he 'saw' Simon and his brother Andrew...," whom he then made his disciples in v 18. The same is true for Jesus' "seeing" James the son of Zebedee and his brother John in v 19, whom Jesus also calls to be his disciples in v 20.[48]

---

[44] LSJ 618, I. It also means to approach.

[45] LSJ 1511.

[46] Cf. the LCL edition of Josephus.

[47] BAGD 613.2.a. The same verb is employed of Jesus' "passing by" (the sea) when he sees Levi and calls him in 2:14.

[48] Cf. also Jesus' "seeing" and calling Levi the son of Alphaeus when he walked along the Sea of Galilee in Mark 2:14.

I suggest that the Palestinian Jewish Christian author of Mark 1:16–20 knew of Elijah's "finding" Elisha among twelve yoke of oxen in 1 Kgs 19:19, and his then making Elisha his disciple. Instead of describing Jesus at the Sea of Galilee as passing by and similarly "finding" four disciples, which could make the impression they were lost or simply accidentally found, he substituted the verb "to see" (רָאָה; here ὁράω).[49] He may also have chosen the term "to see" in order to emphasize that it was Jesus' choice to call precisely these four and not others he encountered (cf. 3:13 – Jesus "called to him those whom he wanted"). When Jesus "sighted" (= found) suitable candidates, he certainly "looked (them) over" very carefully before calling them to become members of the Twelve.[50]

5. *Casting.*

A.

1 Kgs 19:19 states that "Elijah passed by him [Elisha] 'and cast' his mantle over him." The Hebrew verb behind "and cast" here is וַיַּשְׁלֵךְ, the hiphil of שָׁלַךְ, meaning "to throw, fling, cast."[51] The LXX employs ἀπορρίπτέω at this point, which Josephus follows in *Ant.* 8.353. The Greek verb is also used of "casting" a net.[52] As a result of this encounter, Elisha "went after" (= followed) Elijah and "served" him (as a disciple) in v 21.

I suggest that the Palestinian Jewish Christian who first formulated Mark 1:16 borrowed the term "cast" from his model of Elijah's making Elisha his disciple in 1 Kgs 19:19.

B.

Mark 1:16 describes Jesus as passing along the Sea of Galilee when he sees Simon and his brother Andrew " 'casting nets' in the Sea, for they

---

[49] On the Semitic form of the original narrative, see section II. below.

[50] Historically, Jesus very probably knew his future disciples for some time before he "called" them. Mark 1:16–20 (as well as 2:13–14) is a compressed haggadic account later created by a Palestinian Jewish Christian. On this, see section IV. below.

[51] BDB 1020.

[52] Cf. LSJ 216, with their reference to Hesiod.

were fishermen." The Greek for "casting nets" is the acc. pl. present participle of ἀμφιβάλλω.[53] The parallel in Matt 4:18 makes the phrase more precise by rephrasing it to "casting 'net[s],' " employing the verb βάλλω together with the noun ἀμφίβληστρον, a term restricted to a "casting" net.[54] Since the Greek noun means "anything thrown round," it is also used for example of "the garment thrown like a net over" Agamemnon, and of other similar pieces of clothing.[55] This shows how the same term could also have been associated with the "garment cast over" Elisha by Elijah in 1 Kgs 19:19 when a Hellenistic Jewish Christian, aware of the background of the account, translated the original Semitic narrative of Mark 1:16–20 into Greek before it reached Mark (see section II. below).

I suggest that the Semitic original of Simon and Andrew's "casting nets" (ἀμφιβάλλω) in the Sea of Galilee was the Hebrew מַשְׁלִיכִים מְצוֹדָה.[56] This employs the hiphil of שׁלך, as in 1 Kgs 19:19. The following passages support this suggestion.

Isa 19:8 states that "all who 'cast hooks' (מַשְׁלִיכֵי חַכָּה) in the Nile will lament."[57] A parable in *Midr. Prov.* 1:19 also relates that someone took a hook " 'and cast it' (והשליכה) into the sea."[58]

The best rabbinic parallel to Mark 1:16, however, is found in *Eliyyahu Zuṭa* 14. It states that once Elijah was "passing along" (עובר)[59] from one place to another and met a man who maintained that God had not granted him understanding and knowledge. Thus he excused himself from any moral responsibility on the Day of Judgment. When Elijah

---

[53] BAGD 47; LSJ 89, I.4.b.

[54] BAGD 47; LSJ 90, 1. This is in contrast to a seine or dragnet (see below).

[55] Cf. the sources cited in LSJ 90, 1.b.

[56] In his Hebrew New Testament Delitzsch employs this phrase at Matt 4:18 (p. 5), but not at Mark 1:16 (p. 62). Cf. also his rendering of John 21:6 (p. 210), taken up in part by the United Bible Societies' Hebrew New Testament (298; see also 8 on Matt 4:18). The plural "nets" (מְצוֹדוֹת) is also possible. *Targum Jonathan* on Elijah's "casting" his mantle over Elisha has the Aramaic verb רמא (Jastrow 1482, to throw, cast; Sperber 2.262). It does not appear to be used for "casting" nets, thus my preference for the Hebrew form. See also n. 64 below.

[57] BDB 1020 on שׁלך states regarding this phrase: "i.e. fishermen." Cf. the other terminology in this Isaiah verse of "fishing" and "spreading nets."

[58] Buber 47; Visotzky 26. This leads to a large fish's being "caught." See also Matt 17:27 for Peter's "casting a hook" into the Sea of Galilee at Capernaum (v 24).

[59] Cf. Jesus' "passing along" the Sea of Galilee in Mark 1:16, analyzed in section 4.B above.

asked him his occupation and he replied "fisherman" (צָיָיד), the prophet
asked him further: "My son, who told you to bring linen cord, weave it
into nets (מְצוּדוֹת), 'cast them' (וְתַשְׁלִיכֵן) into the sea (לְיָם), and bring
fish up from the sea?" When the man had to concede that Heaven had
granted him understanding and knowledge to do so, Elijah continued:
"My son, if understanding and knowledge were given you 'to cast nets'
(לְהַשְׁלִיךְ מְצוּדוֹת) and bring up fish from the sea...."[60]

Here "casting nets in(to) the sea" (הַשְׁלִיךְ מְצוּדוֹת לְיָם) is mentioned
twice, exactly the same verbal form[61] behind the Semitic original of Mark
1:16's ἀμφιβάλλοντας ἐν τῇ θαλάσσῃ and the βάλλοντας ἀμφίβληστρον
εἰς τὴν θάλασσαν of Matt 4:18. Both Gospel accounts continue: "for they
were fishermen" (ἦσαν γὰρ ἁλιεῖς). The Hebrew of the latter noun is
צַיָּ(י)דִים, the plural of צַיָּיד,[62] as found in the *Eliyyahu Zuta* narrative
above. A wordplay is intentional here. Simon and Andrew were casting
"nets" (מְצוּדָה / מְצוּדוֹת) into the Sea, for they were "fishermen"
(צַיָּידִים). Both terms derive from the common root צוּד, which when
employed of fish means "to catch" them.[63]

In light of the above, although the disciples themselves cast their
nets, and not Jesus his net upon them, it seems probable on the basis of
the catchword "casting" that Elijah's "casting" his mantle over Elijah,
making him his disciple, was the basis for a Palestinian Jewish
Christian's having Jesus make Simon and Andrew into his disciples
when they were "casting" their nets in(to) the Sea of Galilee. For both
expressions, the hiphil of the verb שָׁלַךְ was employed.[64]

---

[60] Friedmann 195-196; I have slightly modified the translation of Braude and
Kapstein 458. It should be noted that Isa 19:9 is quoted at the end of this
narrative, adjacent to v 8, quoted above. Imagery from both verses informs the
account. A parallel tradition in *Tanḥ*. Deut. Vayelek 2 (Eshkol 993) employs
slightly different terminology.

[61] S. Krauss in *Talmudische Archäologie* 2.144 notes that פָּרַשׂ, "spreading," is
employed of a net, while "throwing" would actually be more appropriate. He
apparently was not aware of the hiphil of שָׁלַךְ used in this sense.

[62] Jastrow 1276.

[63] Jastrow 1265-1266.

[64] Cf. also the more common rabbinic Hebrew term for "casting / spreading" a
net, פָּרַס / פֶּרֶס, also used of a father's casting / spreading a garment or cloak
over his son in *Mek. R. Ish.* Beshallaḥ 5 on Exod 14:19 (Lauterbach 1.225).

EXCURSUS

Fishing in the Sea of Galilee with Nets,

and

"Fishers of People" in Mark 1:17 par.

A. *Fishing Towns on the Sea of Galilee.*

After he departed from Nazareth, his home in SW Galilee (Mark 1:9, 24; 6:1; 10:47; 14:67; 16:6), according to the Evangelist Mark Jesus let himself be baptized by John the Baptist in the Jordan River (1:9). When John was later arrested, Jesus returned to Galilee (1:14) and began his own public ministry at the Sea of Galilee, where he first called Simon, Andrew, James and John (1:16–20). This took place on the north shore, for after making disciples of these men, he continued on to Capernaum (1:21), the home of the fishermen Simon and Andrew (1:29). It was this town which Jesus then made the center of his ministry (2:1; 9:33).

Capernaum.

According to Judaic interpretation of Deut 33:23, Joshua the son of Nun (here as "fish") stipulated that only the tribe of Naphtali was allowed to fish in the Sea of Galilee. Yet as long as navigation was not impeded, others were also permitted to fish there with hooks, nets and traps.[65] The northern section of the Sea was especially noted for its large quantities of fish,[66] in part due to the nutrients from the Jordan River

---

[65] Cf. *t. B. Qam.* 8:18 (Zuckermandel / Liebermann 363; Neusner 4.49); *b. B. Qam.* 81b and a (Soncino 461 and 459); *y. B. Bat.* 5:1, 15a (Neusner 30.97); and *Sifre* Wezot ha-Berakah 355 on Deut 33:23 (Finkelstein 419; Hammer 373).

[66] On fishing in this freshwater lake, cf. the sources cited in S. Krauss, *Talmudische Archäologie* 2.145-146 and the relevant notes; Str-B 1.185-186; W. Wuellner, art. "Fishermen (NT)" in *IDBSup* 338-339; *idem, The Meaning of "Fishers of Men"* (Philadelphia: Westminster, 1967); M. Nun, *The Sea of Galilee and its Fishermen in the New Testament; idem,* "Cast Your Net Upon the Waters. Fish and Fishermen in Jesus' Time" in *BARev* 19/6 (1993) 46-56, 70; and the art. "Fishing, Nets," in *Jesus & His World. An Archaeological and Cultural Dictionary,* ed. J. Rousseau and R. Arav (Minneapolis: Fortress, 1995) 93-97. An older study by F. Dunkel, "Die Fischerei am See Genezareth und das Neue Testament" in *Bib* 5 (1924) 375-390, deals with five different kinds of nets (pp. 376-380) and fishing techniques employed at the beginning of this century, with their Arabic

which entered the Lake at this point. This helps to explain why Peter and Andrew were fishermen at home in Capernaum, located only some 2 miles (3 kilometers) west of the Jordan on the Via Maris.[67]

Bethsaida.

The Gospel of John, however, maintains that Peter and Andrew were from Bethsaida, as was Philip (1:44; cf. 12:21). While Capernaum is much more probable for Peter and Andrew, the Palestinian Jewish Christian tradition behind the Gospel of John at this point may have located them in Bethsaida precisely because they were fishermen. The place-name "Bethsaida" is Aramaic   (בֵּית צַיְידָא), meaning literally "place of the fisherman"[68] or "fishville." It derives from the same noun employed of Peter and Andrew as "fishermen" (Hebrew צַיָּדִים) in Mark 1:16. Bethsaida was located on the Jordan River just before it entered the Sea of Galilee, and it had its own harbor on the old river bed.[69] Unfortunately, Jesus' ministry was basically unfruitful here, as in Capernaum (Matt 11:21 and 23; Luke 10:13 and 15).

Magdala.

One of Jesus' most faithful followers was Mary Magdalene (Mark 15:40, 47; 16:1; and Luke 8:2), from Magdala on the WNW side of the Sea of Galilee. The Aramaic name of this town was Migdal Nunayya (מִגְדַּל נוּנַיָּא), "Tower of Fish."[70]

---

designations, the best fishing grounds (381-382), and the different kinds of fish (383-386). No Hebrew or Aramaic terms, or Judaic sources, are cited. In *Bethsaida, Home of the Apostles* (Collegeville, Minnesota: The Liturgical Press, 1998) 47-56, F. Strickert surveys fishing in a general way; the lead and ring weights, as well as hooks, found in Bethsaida (50-55) are solid archaeological evidence for the importance of fishing there.

[67] Cf. the art. "Capernaum" in *Jesus & His World* 39-47.

[68] Jastrow 1276 on צַיָּד, צַיְידָא.

[69] Cf. the art. "Bethsaida" in *Jesus & His World* 19-24, as well as B. Strickert, *Bethsaida. Home of the Apostles*, maps on pp. 34 and 38.

[70] Jastrow 888 on נוּן, נוּנָא. Cf. the art. "Magdala," etc. in *Jesus & His World* 189-190, and its other designation Taricheae as "salted fish."

Tiberias.

Finally, according to *b. Pesaḥ.* 46a the standard for a *mil* was the short walk from Magdala to Tiberias, some 3 miles (5 kilometers) south.[71] Jesus the son of Sapphias was the chief magistrate of Tiberias at the time of the outbreak of the Jewish-Roman War in 66 CE according to Josephus, who also notes that he was of the party of the "sailors" (ναυτῶν) and the poor.[72] If these "boatmen" on the Sea of Galilee were also fishermen, as seems probable,[73] this corroborates the later mention in the Palestinian Talmud of the "dragnet fishermen of Tiberias" (חרמי טיבריה).[74]

* * *

The above close connections between Capernaum, Bethsaida, Magdala, Tiberias and fishing show how appropriate it was for Jesus in Mark 1:16 to pass along the (northern shore of the) Sea of Galilee, encounter two fishermen, and make them into fishers of people.

In Mark 2:13-14 Jesus is also described as "passing along" the Sea of Galilee (at Capernaum), seeing Levi the son of Alphaeus sitting at the "tax booth," and successfully calling him to be his disciple with the words "Follow me." A. Schlatter was of the opinion that the tax collectors of Capernaum primarily taxed the fish which had been caught in the Sea of Galilee.[75] If the latter is true, the call of the disciple Levi at Capernaum was also connected with fishing, as in Mark 1:16-20.

---

[71] Soncino 219. N. 6 remarks that this was 2000 cubits, or an eighteen minutes' walk.

[72] Cf. *Vita* 66 and *Bell.* 2.599.

[73] Cf. S. Wachsmann's remarks on the remains of an almost nine meter long boat from the first century BCE to the end of the first century CE found in 1986 in the Sea of Galilee between Magdala and Kibbutz Ginosar: "The craft was primarily used for fishing; however, it no doubt also served to transport passengers and supplies...," in *The Excavations of an Ancient Boat in the Sea of Galilee (Lake Kinneret)* 132, and 129-130 on the dating. In the off-season, or their spare time, the fishermen would have transported cargo with their boats in order to improve their income. See also W. Wuellner, art. "Fishermen (NT)" in *IDBSup* 338: "The use of ships [boats] for fishing led to the equating of fishermen with sailors...."

[74] Cf. *y. Mo'ed Qaṭ.* 2:5, 81b (Neusner 20.169, who translates here "fish trappers"), and *y. Pesaḥ.* 4:1, 30d (Bokser / Schiffman 13.153: "net-fishers"). I differentiate below between the various kinds of nets.

[75] Cf. his *Der Evangelist Matthäus* (Stuttgart: Calwer, 1929) 302 on the parallel in Matt 9:9. He compares an Ephesian inscription, for which see the art. τελώνης by O. Michel in *TDNT* 8.98, n. 113, which incorrectly speaks of "dues for fishing

B. Nets.

It was a great exception that "fish" (pl. of the Hebrew דָּג;[76] Aramaic
נוּן, נוּנָא[77]) were caught on a "hook" (חַכָּה),[78] or in a basket-like "trap"
(אַקוֹן).[79] The usual method employed the net, of which there were
various forms. The biblical term רֶשֶׁת[80] almost never appears in later
Hebrew.[81] The מִכְמֶרֶת or מִכְמֹרֶת was a trap or small fishing net,[82] like
the hook also primarily employed by an individual, non-professional
fisherman. The term קֶלַע designated a casting net. It derived from the
same root, "to cast, sling."[83]   Although the equivalent of the
ἀμφίβληστρον of Matt 4:18 and presupposed in Mark 1:16, it too was
very seldom employed in rabbinic Hebrew.[84] The large "dragnet" or
"seine" was חֵרֶם,[85] and a חָרָם could be one who fished (together with
others) by means of such a large net.[86] It was thrown or let out from a

---

rights" in Schlatter.   The latter is unfortunately repeated in W. Wuellner, *The
Meaning of "Fishers of Men"* 23 (and 43), who speaks of fishermen as "leasing
rights from *telōnai.*"   I am aware of no sources which attest precisely such leases
in Palestine.

[76] BDB 185; Jastrow 279. The feminine דגה is employed almost always in the
collective sense.

[77] Jastrow 888. The term כַּוְרָא (Jastrow 617) occurs relatively seldom and
appears to be primarily Babylonian usage.

[78] Cf. BDB 335 and the discussion of Isa 19:8 above; Jastrow 461; and Matt 17:27.

[79] Cf. Jastrow 112 and the references in the Mishnah which he cites. See also
other "baskets" (נְחִיל – Jastrow 894; כְּפִיפָה – Jastrow 659, and *t. Makš.* 3:12
[Zuckermandel and Liebermann 676; Neusner 6.311]).

[80] BDB 440.

[81] Jastrow at 1502 can only cite *m. Kel.* 23:5 (Albeck 6.98). Cf., however, 1QH 2.29
(10.29) in Martínez and Tigchelaar, *The Dead Sea Scrolls Study Edition* 1.162–163.

[82] BDB 485, only in Hab 1:15 and Isa 19:8; Jastrow 783. In *y. Mo'ed Qaṭ.* 2:5, 81b
(Neusner 20.169) and *y. Pesaḥ.* 4:1, 30d (Bokser / Schiffman 13.153), the hook
and small net are allowed for individuals on the Sea of Tiberias. On this term,
see also 1QH 3.26 (11.26) and 5.8 (13.8) in Martínez and Tigchelaar 1.166–167 and
170–171.

[83] Cf. the verb in BDB 887; the noun is used in biblical Hebrew only of a sling,
associated with stones, but not fish. See also Jastrow 1380, 1.

[84] Cf. the general term in *m. 'Ed.* 3:5 (Albeck 4.294; Danby 427 and Neusner 647
as "a sling"), and in connection with fishing in *t. B. Qam.* 8:17 (Zuckermandel /
Liebermann 363; Neusner 4.49 as "a sling").

[85] BDB 357; Jastrow 504, 1).

[86] Jastrow 504, referring to such professional fishermen from Tiberias.

boat somewhat offshore, then pulled or dragged in. It probably was the type of net employed by James, John, their father Zebedee and the hired men (thus at least five persons) in Mark 1:19-20, which also mentions the brothers' mending the nets (δίκτυα). Jesus definitely meant it when in a parable he compared the kingdom of heaven to a net (σαγήνη)[87] that was thrown into the sea and caught fish of every kind. After it was full, the fishermen "drew it ashore" (Matt 13:47-50).

The general and the most frequent term for a fishing net in rabbinic Hebrew, however, was מְצוּדָה, Aramaic מְצוּדְתָא.[88] The casting net, the rare term קֶלַע, may be meant by the type of fishing done by Simon and Andrew in Mark 1:16. Yet "for they were 'fishermen'" (ἀλιεῖς = Hebrew צַיָּידִים) directly afterwards in the same verse makes it extremely probable that the author intended a wordplay here with מְצוּדָה (pl. מְצוּדוֹת), the general and most frequent term for a fishing net, from the same Semitic root (Hebrew or Aramaic). Numerous examples from passages cited in the following section corroborate this.

C. Fishers of People.

Mark 1:17 has Jesus say to Simon and Andrew: Follow me, and I will make you into / cause you to become "fishers of people" (ἀλιεῖς ἀνθρώπων). That is, in the positive sense of the term they will "catch" people and win them over to follow Jesus and his teachings regarding the inbreaking of the kingdom of God. Up to now Simon and Andrew as fishermen had cast their nets into the Sea of Galilee and "caught" only fish. Now they should "catch" people.

A number of Hebrew and Aramaic terms are employed in the Bible and in rabbinic works for "catching" fish. The Hebrew דּוּג, דִּיג is found only in Jer 16:16 and not in rabbinic sources.[89] The verb אָחַז[90] occurs in Eccl 9:12 in a simile for fish "taken" in a cruel net (מְצוּדָה). It should be noted in this respect that in *Ecclesiastes Rabbah* on this verse the verb אָחַז is omitted and צוּד is substituted for it, the latter occurring six times.[91] In *Pirq. R. El.* 51 fish in the eschatological time are described as ascending

---

[87] BAGD 739; it only occurs here in the NT. Cf. also LSJ 1580.

[88] Jastrow 823. A glance at the concordances of the Tannaitic works corroborates this. For Qumran, see 1QH 3.26 (11.26) and CD-A 4.15 (Martínez and Tigchelaar 1.166-167 and 556-557).

[89] BDB 185.

[90] BDB 28.

[91] Vilna 49; Soncino 8.247-248.

the (Kidron) Brook as far as Jerusalem and being "caught" there, with אֶחֹז.[92]

Another term for "catching" fish is לקח, employed of "taking"[93] fish by means of nets (מְצוֹדוֹת) in *Tanḥ.* Deut. Vayelek 2.[94] It too is only seldom used in this meaning in rabbinic sources.

The verb תפס - תפש, literally "to lay hold of, seize,"[95] is employed of "catching" fish in *Gen. Rab.* Vayechi 97/3 on Gen 48:16;[96] *Deut. Rab.* Ki Thabo 7/6 on Deut 28:12;[97] and in *Midr. Prov.* 1:19.[98]

With these relatively few exceptions, the verb for "catching" fish in rabbinic sources is always צוד, as a glance at the various relevant concordances indicates. Examples from the Mishnah are *Šabb.* 1:6;[99] *Beṣ.* 3:1-2;[100] and *'Uq.* 3:8,[101] from the Tosefta *Beṣ.* 3:1;[102] *B. Qam.* 8:17 (and 18 on the Sea of Tiberias);[103] *'Abod. Zar.* 4:11;[104] and *Makš.* 3:12;[105] and

---

[92] Eshkol 208: Friedlander 418. Ezek 47:10 with its "fishermen" is then cited.

[93] BDB 543-544; Jastrow 717.

[94] Eshkol 993. As pointed out above, this is a parallel tradition to *Eliyyahu Zuṭa* 14.

[95] BDB 1074-1075; Jastrow 1687-1688.

[96] Theodor and Albeck 1246; Soncino 2.940.

[97] Mirqin 11.115; Soncino 7.138.

[98] Buber 47; Visotzky 26. Cf. also Ezek 12:13 (=17:20) of being "caught" in a net (מְצוּדָה), perhaps for fishing. On the latter at Qumran, see also CD-A 4.15 (Martínez and Tigchelaar 1.556-557).

[99] Albeck 2.19; Danby 101; Neusner 180.

[100] Albeck 2.294; Danby 184-185; Neusner 295.

[101] Albeck 6.502; Danby 789; Neusner 1136.

[102] Zuckermandel / Liebermann 205 (lacking fish); Neusner 2.239-240.

[103] Zuckermandel / Liebermann 363; Neusner 4.49.

[104] Zuckermandel / Liebermann 467; Neusner 4.327.

[105] Zuckermandel / Liebermann 675-676; Neusner 6.311.

from the Babylonian Talmud *Šabb.* 26a, 75a and 106b;[1] *Yoma* 84b;[2] *Mo'ed Qaṭ.* 11a and 13b;[3] *Qidd.* 72a;[4] *B. Qam.* 81b;[5] and *Ḥull.* 75a.[6]

Yet "catching" can also be used of human beings, as already found in the Hebrew Bible. Jer 16:16, for example, employs דיג of fishermen sent by the Lord as "catching" others. In Hebrew parallelism, "hunters" (צַיָּדִים) are then mentioned. "Hunting down" or "capturing" (צוד, piel) human lives (souls - נְפָשׁוֹת) is found in Ezek 13:18. Mic 7:2 states that men "hunt" (צוד) each other with nets. Eccl 9:12 notes that mortals (בְּנֵי הָאָדָם) snared at a time of evil are like fish caught / taken (אחז) in an evil net (מְצוֹדָה). Ezek 12:13 (=17:20) has the Lord say regarding the prince in Jerusalem, probably Zedekiah: "I will spread My net over him, and he shall be 'caught' (תפשׂ) in My snare (מְצוּדָה)." Finally, Ezek 32:3 has the Lord state in regard to Pharaoh: "I will throw My net (רשׁת) over you; and they will haul you up in My dragnet (חרם)."

The above biblical examples show how "catching" fish, by means of a net, was already transferred to human beings in the biblical period, even if almost exclusively in a negative sense.

Post-biblical, metaphorical rabbinic sources broaden the above impression and present new possibilities for a better understanding of the phrase "fishers of people" in Mark 1:17. I shall now analyze thirteen passages, beginning with other metaphorical usages of fish, nets, being caught and catching, and conclude with the two passages most relevant to the phrase "fishers of people." In the following examples it should be recalled that the term צוד basically means "to catch," and it is used of catching not only fish, but also wild animals and birds.[7] Thus a צַיָּד is either a fisherman or a hunter, depending on the context. "Hunting" an object or a person thus also means "catching" it, him or her.

1) In *b. B. Bat.* 161b it is related that "Rab drew a fish" (as his signature), and other rabbis drew other things.[8] Rab (Abba Arikha) was a first

---

[1] Soncino 113, 357 and 513, the first two dealing with a purple-fish.

[2] Soncino 416.

[3] Soncino 60 and 77.

[4] Soncino 368 in regard to a fishpond.

[5] Soncino 461, on the Sea of Tiberias.

[6] Soncino 412.

[7] Cf. for example *m. Šabb.* 1:6 (Albeck 2.19), with nets (מְצוּדוֹת).

[8] Soncino 705.

generation Babylonian Amora.[9] Reminiscent of Christians' drawing a fish with Greek letters as a sign of their allegiance to Jesus Christ, Rab's deed shows how a fish could be used to signify a person.

2) In *b. Pesah.* 23a[10] and *Ber.* 9b[11] it is stated: "They made it like a net without fish."[12] Here a net and fish are used in order to make a comparison with another object.

3) In *b. Yebam.* 63b a passage from Ben Sirach is quoted in Hebrew: "Turn your eyes away from (your neighbor's) charming wife so that you won't be caught in her net (מצודה)."[13] Here a human being is warned, metaphorically, of being caught in the net or charms of a married woman.

4) In *b. Pesah.* 3b it is related that R. Yehuda b. Bathyra, a second generation Tanna who first lived in Palestine and later in Nisibis in Babylonia,[14] was instrumental in causing a Gentile to be apprehended. The latter had defiled the Jerusalem Temple's inner Sanctuary by entering it. The Temple officials thus wrote Yehuda the following: "Peace be with you, R. Yehuda b. Bathyra, for you are in Nisibis, yet 'your net is spread' (ומצודתך פרוסה) in Jerusalem!"[15] This early rabbi is figuratively described here as a fisherman or hunter who employed his net to catch a delinquent human.

5) In *b. Ber.* 61b R. Aqiba, a second generation Tanna,[16] employs a parable of a fox and fish in a river. When asked by the fox what they were fleeing from, the fish answered: "From the nets which humans (בני אדם) cast over us."[17] Here Jews who openly practice their piety are metaphorically meant by the fish who flee together from one place to another in order to avoid the oppressive Roman

---

[9] Strack and Stemberger, *Introduction* 93.

[10] Soncino 614.

[11] Soncino 48.

[12] In both passages there are variant readings.

[13] Soncino 426, which I modify. The niphal of the verb לכד (Jastrow 710) is employed here for being caught or seized. Cf. the present form of Sir 9:8, which differs in the second half.

[14] Strack and Stemberger, *Introduction* 83.

[15] Cf. Soncino 10, which I modify, and n. 7.

[16] Strack and Stemberger, *Introduction* 79.

[17] Soncino 386, which I modify.

government. The Romans "cast their nets" over these Jews who remain in their element, the Torah.

6) To R. Aqiba is also attributed the saying in *m.'Avot* 3:16: "All is handed over as a pledge, and 'a net is cast over all the living' (ומצודה פרוסה על כל החיים)."[18] Here God is represented metaphorically as a fisherman, who casts His net over everyone, catching them so that they cannot escape. The unit continues with reference to the final Judgment and the (messianic) banquet.[19] This saying of R. Aqiba recalls Jesus' parable of the dragnet thrown into the sea, catching fish of every kind. As the good fish are now separated from the bad ones, so the final Judgment will be (Matt 13:47–50).

7) *Gen. Rab.* Vayechi 97/3 on Gen 48:16 interprets the verb וידגו as a reference to fish, דג. It therefore states that "As fish are only caught by their throat [mouth], so your children are only caught by their throat." This refers to some Israelites' saying "Sibboleth" and not "Shibboleth" in Judg 12:6.[20] That is, their mouths caused them to be caught. Here a simile is made between the catching of fish and the catching of humans.

8) Commenting on Nimrod as a great "catcher / hunter" (גִּבּוֹר – צָיִד) in Gen 10:9, *Gen. Rab.* Noach 37/2 in the name of R. Hanna bar Isaac[21] emphasizes the term "like" Nimrod. "Just as one [Nimrod] 'caught people by their mouth' (צד את הבריות בפיהם), so the other [Esau, standing for the evil Roman government] caught people through their mouth."[22] Examples of such "snaring" behavior are then given. Here in a simile, two different figures are described as "catching people" negatively, by deception.

9) Esau also plays a major role in *Gen. Rab.* Toledoth 67/2 on Gen 27:33, "Who was it then 'that hunted game' (הוא הצד ציד) and brought it to me...?" Isaac here questions Esau. After the former had blessed Jacob, the comment is made: "He [Jacob] caught the catcher / hunter [Esau]": הוא צד הצייד. Here the deceiver is himself deceived. Then

---

[18] Albeck 4.367; English by Neusner 681. On Aqiba, see 3:13. Cf. also *'Avot R. Nat.* A 39 (Schechter 123; Goldin 161) and B 44 (Schechter 123; Saldarini 275). The latter has R. Eliezer b. R. Yose the Galilean as the author.

[19] Cf. the notes in the Soncino edition, pp. 39–40, which also call attention to Ezek 32:3, where the Lord God will throw His net over people, and they will be hauled up in His dragnet.

[20] Theodor and Albeck 1246; Soncino 2.940, with n. 4.

[21] Str-B 5/6.139 has R. Hanina b. Isaac as Palestinian, ca. 325 CE.

[22] Theodor and Albeck 345; Soncino 1.296, which I modify.

R. Leazar b. R. Simeon, probably a fourth generation Tanna,[23] states in Aramaic regarding Esau what may have been proverbial: "O catcher / hunter, how you are caught!" (צַיָּידָא הֵיךְ צָדוּךְ).[24] Here a human known as a catcher / hunter is himself caught or deceived, and imagery is employed which can mean a catcher / fisherman if used in the context of fishing.

10) In *b. Ḥull.* 63b R. Zera, perhaps a first generation Babylonian Amora,[25] asks: "Does 'master' (רב) mean 'a master of wisdom' (רבו חכם) or 'a master of catching' (רבו צייד)?"[26] Here a scholar adept at "catching" others at their argumentation in the often very complicated legal debates of the rabbinical schoolhouses is probably meant. The connotation could be positive, but is more likely negative here because of the contrast to a master of (true) wisdom.

11) In *Gen. Rab.* Bereshith 7/4 on Gen 1:21 two similar statements are made. "With this Ben Laqish 'spread his net over' (R.) Kahana," and "With this (R.) Kahana 'spread his net over' Ben Laqish." Both phrases in single quotation marks are פרס מצדתיה על.[27] R. Simeon ben Laqish (Resh Laqish) and Rab Kahana were second generation Palestinian Amoraim associated with Tiberias on the Sea of Galilee.[28] This may help to explain the metaphor from the realm of fishing of "spreading / casting one's net" over another scholar. It probably means that the one who successfully cast the net won a point in a legal debate. This would explain how each rabbi mentioned above could cast a net over the other.

The same imagery is also found in *y. Kil.* 1:6, 27a, where the fifth generation Palestinian Amora R. Yose b. R. Bun[29] states: "Here Kahana 'has cast his net over' (פרס מצודתיה על) Resh Laqish and

---

[23] Cf. Strack and Stemberger, *Introduction* 87, on R. Eleazar b. Simon (b. Yoḥai).

[24] Theodor and Albeck 753; I restate the English of Soncino 2.607, with notes 1–2. Cf. also *Lev. Rab.* Behar 34/12 on someone from the Roman government who "caught them" (וצדון), the nephews of R. Simeon b. Yoḥai, and put them in prison (Margulies 797, apparatus; Soncino 4.438).

[25] Strack and Stemberger, *Introduction* 93; other rabbis of this name are found on pp. 99 and 106.

[26] Soncino 346, which I modify. After this R. Yoḥanan (bar Nappaḥa), a second generation Palestinian Amora (Strack and Stemberger, *Introduction* 94–95), employs the same phrases.

[27] Theodor and Albeck 53; Soncino 1.52.

[28] Strack and Stemberger, *Introduction* 95.

[29] Strack and Stemberger, *Introduction* 106.

'caught him' (וצדייה)."[30]   This is a more complete form of the imagery noted above. There is no pejorative connotation intended, for example deception. The metaphorical expression basically means winning a particular point in a legal debate.

12) In *b. 'Erub.* 54b R. Eleazar b. Azariah, a second generation Tanna,[31] is quoted as asking what Prov 12:27 means: "The slothful man shall not hunt his prey." Interpreting the Hebrew צידו, "his prey," as צייד, "hunter," and רמיה, "slothful," as רמאי, "cunning," "deceptive," Eleazar states: "The cunning hunter will not live long."[32] I. Slotki interprets this to be "one who possesses no knowledge and pretends to be a scholar."[33] Here a very early Tanna also employs צייד, "hunter / catcher," in a metaphorical sense, albeit negative.

The above is directly followed by the third generation Babylonian Amora R. Shesheth's[34] interpretation of Prov 12:27 in a positive sense. For him it means: "The cunning hunter will roast" (what he has caught).[35] That is, the צייד (disciple or student of a teacher) who learns well will retain his catch. This positive interpretation is strengthened by the comparison R. Dimi, a fourth generation Palestinian Amora,[36] made in this regard when he journeyed from Palestine to Babylonia: "This may be likened to a hunter / catcher (צייד) who hunts (צד) birds. If he breaks the wings of each bird as he shoots it down, his catch is secure, otherwise it is not."[37]

Here a disciple or student who learns well, piece by piece, is described metaphorically, in a positive sense, as a clever "hunter / catcher" (צייד).

---

[30] Neusner / Mandelbaum 4.33.

[31] Strack and Stemberger, *Introduction* 78.

[32] Soncino 380, with I. Slotki's n. 12.

[33] *Ibid.* Cf. also Goldschmidt 2.180, n. 51.

[34] Strack and Stemberger, *Introduction* 101.

[35] Cf. Soncino 380, n. 15. On another positive case of "cunning," cf. Jastrow 1482 on רמי, רמה: to be cunning in charitable deeds.

[36] Strack and Stemberger, *Introduction* 104.

[37] Soncino 381, which I slightly modify. A parallel tradition is found in *b. 'Aboda Zara* 19a (Soncino 99–100), with slight variants. Cf. the similar statement by R. Huna on p. 99. I owe this reference to S. Lachs, *A Rabbinic Commentary* 59, n. 10. His other references derive from Jastrow's *Dictionary* and are frequently quoted wrong. I have not been able to trace the planned article he mentions in n. 11.

13) The Judaic passage, however, which is closest to Jesus' calling Peter and Andrew to be "fishers / catchers of men" is found in *b. B. Qam.* 41b–42a. The second generation Palestinian Amora Rab Kahana, cited above in 11), compares R. Eliezer (b. Hyrcanus), a second generation Tanna,[38] "to a fisherman who had been catching fish in the sea" (לצייד ששולה דגים מן הים).[39] Catching large ones, he kept them, and (catching) small ones, he kept them (also). R. Ṭabyomi, a fourth century CE Palestinian,[40] then follows in *b. B. Qam.* 42a by comparing R. Eliezer "to a fisherman who had been catching fish in the sea" (same Hebrew as above). Catching little ones, he kept them. (Later) catching large ones, he threw away the little ones and kept the large ones.[41]

As remarked above, Rab Kahana was associated with the Sea of Tiberias, which probably influenced his choice of fishing imagery here. In describing R. Eliezer, he compared (משל ל) the rabbi to a fisherman (צייד) who not only retained larger matters, but also smaller ones. This agrees with the description by Yoḥanan b. Zakkai of his pupil Eliezer as a plastered cistern which doesn't lose a drop (*m. 'Abot* 2:8).[42]

R. Ṭabyomi enlarged on the above Kahana tradition by stating that R. Eliezer was capable of changing his opinion for the better in a legal dispute (replacing smaller by larger fish).

Both Rab Kahana and R. Ṭabyomi here label another person a "fisherman" (צייד) in the positive sense of the term, just as Jesus calls Peter and Andrew to be "fishers" of people, also meant positively. They as disciples are to win over or "catch" others and make them acquainted with Jesus' teachings. They are called to invite them to become a part of the eschatological community which experiences the inbreaking of God's kingdom, especially in and through Jesus. There is thus no negative connotation to the term "catcher (fisher – צייד) of people" in Mark 1:17.[43]

---

[38] Strack and Stemberger, *Introduction* 77.

[39] The verb שלי, שלה literally means to draw out or pull (Jastrow 1582).

[40] Cf. Str-B 5/6.242, who equates him with Ṭabuth.

[41] Cf. Soncino 237, with notes 2–3. On keeping the good, but throwing out the bad fish caught in a dragnet, see also Matt 13:48.

[42] Albeck 4.359–360; Danby 448; Neusner 676.

[43] The "catching" and "net" imagery from Qumran (1QH 2.29; 3.26; and CD 4.15–18) is negative, like almost all the rabbinic examples. One possible exception may be 1QH 5.8 (13.8), translated by Martínez and Tigchelaar (*The Dead Sea Scrolls Study Edition* 1.170–171) as: "You [God] made my [the

While Kahana and Ṭabyomi are Amoraim, they reflect the positive metaphorical usage of the term "fisherman" already employed earlier by another person closely associated with the Sea of Tiberias / Galilee, Jesus of Nazareth. Although the present form of Mark 1:16–20 is very compressed and in a dramatic scene represents what most probably evolved over a longer period of time between Jesus and the four fishermen he called to be his first disciples (see section IV. below), there is no reason to deny the sentence "Follow me, and I will make you become / turn you into fishers of people" to Jesus himself.[44]

6. The Immediateness of the Disciple's Following.

A.

1 Kgs 19:20 simply states that after Elijah threw his mantle over Elisha, "he left the oxen, ran after Elijah," and asked permission to bid farewell to his parents before following him. Only after doing all the things mentioned in v 21 does Elisha actually follow Elijah. Judaic tradition on this passage adds the motif of "immediateness," probably in part influenced by Elijah's not going, but "running" after Elijah at this point.

Certainly reflecting first-century CE Judaic opinion, Josephus in *Ant.* 8.354 states regarding 1 Kgs 19:20 : "Then Elisha 'immediately' (εὐθέως) began to prophesy and, having abandoned his oxen, followed Elijah." While the Jewish historian then mentions Elisha's request to say farewell to his parents, the events of v 21 are omitted. Elisha then follows the prophet.

---

community leader's] lodging with many fishermen (דייגים), those who spread the net upon the surface of the water, those who go hunting (וצידים) the sons of injustice." Even if the Qumranites are characterized as "fishermen" here, their tracking down / hunting evil-doers is essentially a negative task. My search for other relevant passages in Charlesworth *et al.*, *Graphic Concordance to the Dead Sea Scrolls*, produced no other results. For the passages noted above, see already O. Betz, "Donnersöhne, Menschenfischer und der Davidische Messias" in *RevQ* 3 (1961) 54.

[44] For possible Hebrew, Aramaic and Syriac reconstructions of the sentence, cf. Hengel, *Nachfolge und Charisma* 85. An alternative for "people," though less probable, could also be נְפָשׁוֹת, as in Ezek 13:18.

Scripture nowhere indicates that Elisha began to prophesy when Elijah threw his mantle over him. This is a haggadic addition, as is the motif of "immediateness."

Eliyyahu Rabbah 5 also emphasizes the latter motif. After citing 1 Kgs 19:19 it states: "Immediately (מיד) [Elisha] left[45] all that belonged to him, and he ran after [Elijah], as it is written: 'and he left[46] the oxen,' etc." (v 20).

The narrative then continues: "'Immediately' (מיד) [Elisha] renounced ownership of all that belonged to him, and he sowed the entire field with salt, as is written ... (v 21)."[47]

Here, precisely in connection with Elisha's following Elijah after the latter called him to be his disciple, the motif of "immediateness" is emphasized twice. I suggest that its occurrence in Judaic tradition on 1 Kgs 19:20-21 influenced the narrative of Jesus' calling his first disciples.

B.

After Jesus told Simon and Andrew, who were fishing, to follow him and that he would make them into fishers of people (Mark 1:16-17), v 18 continues: "And 'immediately' (εὐθύς), having left the[ir] nets, they followed him."[48]

Here too the motif of the disciples' leaving everything "immediately" is emphasized. The Palestinian Jewish Christian author of Mark 1:16-20 borrowed it from Judaic tradition on 1 Kgs 19: 20.

7. *Leaving One's Possessions.*

A.

---

[45] The hiphil of נוה (Jastrow 885) is employed here.

[46] The verb עזב (BDB 736-737) occurs here: leave, abandon, forsake.

[47] Friedmann 23. Cf. the paraphrastic translation of Braude and Kapstein 92. "Thereat" for the second מיד is misleading.

[48] Jesus' "immediately" calling James and John in v 20, however, probably derives from the Evangelist Mark. See Pesch, "Berufung" 7. In 4:22, Matthew applies it to James and John's leaving their boat and following Jesus. When Levi is called by Jesus in Mark 2:14, he also gets up from his tax booth and follows Jesus. Although the term "immediately" is lacking, it is implied here.

1 Kgs 19:20 states that after Elijah called Elisha to be his disciple by throwing his mantle over him, Elisha "left (עזב) the oxen, ran after Elijah," etc. Here Elisha is represented as owning the oxen with which he had been plowing up to then, for in v 21 he slaughters them, boils their flesh and makes a feast for the people.[49]

The motif of Elisha's "leaving" his possessions at his calling is emphasized in Judaic tradition on 1 Kgs 19:20, as found in *Eliyyahu Rabbah* 5. After quoting v 19, the narrative continues: "[Elisha] immediately 'left all that belonged to him' (הניח את כל אשר לו) and ran after [Elijah], as it is stated: 'And 'he left' the oxen,' etc. (v 20). [Elisha] immediately 'renounced ownership of all that belonged to him' (הפקיר את כל אשר לו). He sowed the entire field with salt, [its barrenness then preventing him from returning to it]. Scripture [further indicates this resolve when it] states: 'And [Elisha] returned from following him, took the yoke of oxen, slaughtered them,' etc. (v 21)."[50]

Elisha's "leaving all that belonged to him / all his possessions" is emphasized here by repetition. The second statement to this effect employs the hiphil of the verb פקר, meaning "to renounce ownership of."[51] It is the correct reading here, as indicated in *Yalquṭ Shem'oni* Kings 224 *ad loc*.[52] The misreading of ר as ד, which happened frequently, led to the form הפקיד, meaning: "He 'deposited' all that belonged to him [with others, until he would later return]."[53] Yet this reading makes no sense in light of Elisha's following behavior.

"To indicate the irrevocability of his resolve to join Elijah,"[54] Elisha then sowed with salt the entire field he had been plowing. Judg 9:45

---

[49] If Elisha is meant to own all twelve pairs of oxen, he is represented as a wealthy person who would lose a great deal if he left all his possessions and followed Elijah. For this view, cf. J. Montgomery and H. Lehman, *The Books of Kings* (ICC 11–12; Edinburgh: Clark, 1960) 315, who also call attention to the five yoke of oxen in Luke 14:19. See also C. Keil, *Die Bücher der Könige* 216 ("einen recht vermögenden Mann"); R. Kittel, *Die Bücher der Könige* (HAT 1.5; Göttingen: Vandenhoeck & Ruprecht, 1900) 154 ("vermögender Grundbesitzer"); and M. Rehm, *Das erste Buch der Könige* (Würzburg: Echter Verlag, 1979) 191.

[50] Friedmann 23; Braude and Kapstein translate paraphrastically on p. 92.

[51] Cf. Jastrow 1212 for this meaning in both Hebrew and Aramaic. The verb is not found in biblical Hebrew.

[52] Cf. Jastrow's remark on p. 1212, as well as Braude and Kapstein 92, n. 32, who apparently believe Friedmann misread the Vatican MS 31 from 1073 CE (his "R" on p. 545). The latter, however, is improbable in light of his n. 24.

[53] Cf. Jastrow 1207, hiphil of פקד: to give in charge, deposit.

[54] Braude and Kapstein 92, n. 33.

relates this behavior of Abimelech when he razed the city of Shechem, and Deut 29:22 (Eng. 23) couples salt with sulphur, making the soil incapable of supporting any vegetation at all, like the region of Sodom and Gomorrah (cf. Gen 19:24–26). Elisha thus made his own field completely barren to exclude any second thoughts on his part of a later return. *Eliyyahu Rabbah* 5 undergirds this by quoting 1 Kgs 19:21, where Elisha then slaughters the yoke of oxen, boils the meat, feasts the people and follows Elijah. Without his own oxen, now dead and devoured, he could no longer plow.

The above imagery of Elisha's "leaving all that belonged to him / all his possessions" and "renouncing ownership of all that belonged to him / all his possessions" when he went off to serve Elijah as his disciple, strongly influenced the account of Jesus' calling his first disciples and the conditions of their discipleship found elsewhere in the Gospels.

B.

1) Mark 1:18 relates that after Jesus at the Sea of Galilee called the fishermen Simon and Andrew to be fishers of people, "they immediately 'left' (ἀφέντες) the[ir] nets and followed him." That is, they abandoned their trade, for they had been engaged in casting their nets in the Sea (v 16).

The same is true for James and John, whom Jesus then called while they were mending their nets (vv 19–20a). "'Having left' (ἀφέντες) their father Zebedee in the boat with the hired men, they followed [Jesus]" (v 20b).[55]

Both callings occur while those called are engaged in their trade, and both callings result in those called "leaving" the tools of their trade to follow Jesus. The model for this was Elisha's "leaving" the oxen with which he had been plowing in order to follow Elijah immediately.

2) In the Lukan parallel to Mark 1:16–20, the miraculous catch of fish in Luke 5:1–11, Jesus tells Simon that from then on he will be catching people (v 10). Verse 11 continues: "When they had brought their boats to shore, 'they left everything' (ἀφέντες πάντα) and followed [Jesus]." Here Simon, James and John (Andrew is not mentioned) are described as leaving their boats and nets, indeed "everything," in order to follow Jesus as his disciples.

---

[55] Although it is not expressly stated, it is also presumed in 2:14 that after Jesus called Levi to be his disciple, "he got up, [left the tax booth], and followed him."

The same emphasis on "leaving everything" is found in Mark 10:28, where Peter tells Jesus: "Look, 'we have left everything' (ἡμεῖς ἀφήκαμεν πάντα) and followed you."

Both Luke 5:11 and Mark 10:28, with their emphasis on the disciples' "leaving everything" when called by Jesus, reflect early Judaic tradition on 1 Kgs 19:20. There, at his call by Elijah, Elisha is also described as "leaving 'all' that belonged to him / 'all' his possessions," and as "renouncing ownership of 'all' that belonged to him / 'all' his possessions."

3) In Luke 14:33 Jesus tells the large crowds traveling with him: "none of you can become my disciple if he / she does not renounce / give up 'all his / her possessions' (πᾶσιν τοῖς ἑαυτοῦ ὑπάρχουσιν)." Here too the motif of "all" is emphasized as above in 2). Yet another important term is added.

"To renounce / give up" is the middle of ἀποτάσσω here.[56] This is the only occurrence of the verb in this sense in the NT. The Semitic background of it is פקר, hiphil or afel. It is precisely the term employed in *Eliyyahu Rabbah* 5 to describe Elisha at his call by Elijah as "'renouncing ownership of' (הפקיר) all that belonged to him / all his possessions." Here too early Judaic tradition on 1 Kgs 19:20 has influenced the terminology found in another discipleship text, Luke 14:33.

8. *Taking Farewell of One's Family.*

A.

After Elijah called Elisha to be his disciple by throwing his mantle over him, 1 Kgs 19:20 relates that the latter left the oxen with which he had been plowing, ran after Elijah and said: "Let me kiss my father and my mother, and then I will follow you." The cohortative form of נשׁק, to kiss, is employed here with the particle נא, meant as "I pray," or "please."[57] Before becoming Elijah's disciple, Elisha thus wishes to demonstrate filial piety as in the Fourth Commandment (Exod 20:12; Deut 5:16), which includes both father and mother. 3 Kgdms 19:20 omits

---

[56] BAGD 100; LSJ 222, IV. It can also mean to take farewell of a person.

[57] BDB 609. *Targum Jonathan* interprets it as "now" (כען, Jastrow 656): Sperber 2.262, Harrington and Saldarini 254.

the mother, showing very early interpretation of this verse in the Septuagint.

Elijah's response to Elisha's request is now enigmatic: "Go back again, for what have I done to you?" If Elisha intended to delay the beginning of his following Elijah, the latter's words could be represented as a "challenge that Elisha make up his mind." The fact that Elisha's farewell visit to his parents is then not mentioned in the text may indicate this.[58]

Eliyyahu Rabbah 5 appears to support the latter position. After quoting 1 Kgs 19:19, it states that "immediately Elisha left all that belonged to him / all his possessions and ran after [Elijah], as it is said: 'And he left the oxen,' etc. (v 20). Immediately he renounced all that belonged to him / all his possessions and sowed his entire field with salt, as it is said ... (v 21)."[59]

Since no mention of Elisha's request to kiss his parents, together with Elijah's reply, is made here, it is safe to assume that this strand of Judaic interpretation omitted the farewell motif altogether, emphasizing the other elements.

Many modern commentators, however, believe Elijah's enigmatic response to Elisha's request is meant positively: Elisha should have no compunction about first saying farewell to his parents. This view assumes that he in fact did so, although the biblical text does not explicitly mention it.[60]

Support for this interpretation is found in Josephus. In *Ant.* 8.354 the first century CE Jewish historian comments that after Elijah threw his mantle over Elisha, the latter immediately began to prophesy. Then he left his oxen and followed Elijah. However, when Elisha asked that (Elijah) assent to his kissing / taking farewell of [61] his parents, (Elijah) "commanded" him to do this. (Elisha) parted from them and then followed (Elijah).

Josephus employs the verb κελεύω at this point for Elijah's ordering / commanding / strongly bidding[62] Elisha to take leave of his parents before following him as his disciple.[63]

---

[58] S. De Vries, *1 Kings* 239. De Vries calls attention to Luke 9:61–62 here.

[59] Friedmann 23.

[60] Cf. C. Keil, *Die Bücher der Könige* 217, and R. Kittel, *Die Bücher der Könige* 155.

[61] The verb ἀσπάζομαι can mean both: LSJ 258. See also Str-B 1.995 for a rabbinic example of a farewell kiss.

[62] Cf. LSJ 936-937.

It thus appears that there were probably two different Judaic interpretations of 1 Kgs 19:20. One understood the enigmatic response of Elijah to Elisha's request to kiss / take farewell of his parents negatively, the other positively. While the interpretation found in Josephus is definitely from the first century CE, the other may be ultimately just as old. It is this alternative which is at issue in Jesus' calling his first disciples, and in the conditions of discipleship.

B.

After Peter and Andrew left their nets and began to follow Jesus as his disciples (Mark 1:18), the Gospel writer does not relate that they immediately took leave of their families. Instead, vv 29–31 recount Jesus' healing Simon's mother-in-law in Simon and Andrew's house in Capernaum.[64] This implies that no radical break with their family-ies took place at the point of their calling.

A different impression, however, is created in Mark 1:20. After Jesus called James and John to be his disciples, "they left their father Zebedee in the boat with the hired men, and followed him." The text implies that the two brothers did not even take farewell of their own father, not to speak of their mother at home, before following Jesus. Here a "hard" or radical interpretation of 1 Kgs 19:20 is implied, not like the "soft" interpretation reflected in Josephus, where Elijah even "orders" Elisha to first kiss / take leave of his parents before following him.

This "hard" interpretation may also be reflected in Mark 10:29. After Peter tells Jesus "we have left everything and followed you," the prophet from Nazareth replies: "Truly I tell you, there is no one who has left 'house' or brothers or sisters or mother or father or children or fields, for my sake and for the sake of the gospel...." Here "house" probably also implies one's wife, thought of as being at home.[65]

The "Q" tradition found in Matt 10:37 and Luke 14:26 also emphasizes the necessity of the disciple's having greater obedience to Jesus then to one's own relatives.

---

[63] The rabbinic censure of Elisha for not first reviving his own parents before reviving the son of the widow of Zarephath, however, is related to the period *after* Elijah's ascension. Cf. *Exod. Rab.* Shemoth 4/2 on Exod 4:18 (Soncino 3.78), with a parallel in *Tanh.* Shemoth 16 on the same biblical verse (Eshkol 222).

[64] In 1 Cor 9:5 Paul mentions that Cephas (Peter) was even later accompanied by his wife on missionary journeys.

[65] Cf. Jastrow 168, 5) on בַּיִת as "wife."

The Gospel passage most strongly influenced by the "hard" interpretation of 1 Kgs 19:20, however, is Luke 9:61–62. After an incident in vv 51–56 clearly reminiscent of Elijah's behavior in 2 Kgs 1:9–16, a third candidate expresses his wish to follow Jesus. "'But let me first say farewell to those at my home.' Jesus said to him, 'No one who puts a hand to the plow and looks back is fit for the kingdom of God.'"[66]

This scene, whether historical or not, is clearly based on a rigid interpretation of 1 Kgs 19:20.[67] Just as Elijah is there considered in one strand of Judaic interpretation to have denied Elisha's request to first kiss / bid farewell to his parents before following him, so Jesus here denies to someone who insists on the fulfillment of pre-conditions the possibility of following him. Instead, Jesus expects immediate and total commitment, even superseding the filial duty to bury one's own father (Luke 9:59–60; Matt 8:21–22).[68]

*   *   *

The above eight similarities between Elijah's calling Elisha while he was plowing, and Jesus' calling his first disciples while they were engaged in their trade of fishing, show that the narrative found in 1 Kgs 19:19–21, especially as employed in Judaic tradition, influenced the Palestinian Jewish Christian who composed the narrative now found in Mark 1:16–20 in major ways. While some of the eight similarities are certainly more convincing than others, cumulatively they speak very strongly for the major influence here of the Elijah / Elisha calling narrative. Other calling or commissioning stories could have been employed as a model by the author, such as Exodus 3 (Moses), Deut 31:23 and Joshua 1 (Joshua), Isaiah 6 (Isaiah), and Jeremiah 1 (Jeremiah).

Yet the Elijah / Elisha calling narrative, especially in Judaic tradition, provided the author with the most similarities to Jesus' calling of his first disciples while they were fishing, as Elisha was plowing. He therefore clothed the account now found in Mark 1:16–20 in terms of that narrative.

---

[66] This is special Lukan material, not found after Matt 8:22.

[67] The mention of a plow also recalls Elisha's plowing in 1 Kgs 19:19.

[68] The commentators in general note the relevance of Elisha's call by Elijah in Luke 9:61–62. See the discussion in Öhler, *Elia im Neuen Testament* 156 – 158.

II.   The Original Language.

In section I. above I suggested that there are numerous indications of a Semitic background to what is now found in the short narrative of Mark 1:16-20. This includes the following six factors.

1) The beginning of all five verses in the pericope with the loosely connecting καί (twice in v 20) results from the Semitic וְ.[69] The Hellenistic Jewish Christian who translated the account from Semitic into Greek retained the style of the original, and the Evangelist Mark appropriated it from him.

2) The παράγων of v 16 probably derives from the וַיַּעֲבֹר of 1 Kgs 19:19.[70] The LXX of that verse has instead ἐπῆλθεν, which the Hellenistic Jewish Christian author of the Gospel narrative did not borrow when he translated it from Semitic into Greek. Certainly recognizing the background of the account in 1 Kgs 19:19-21, he could have employed ἐπῆλθεν, but intentionally did not.

3) The ἀμφιβάλλοντες of Mark 1:16 is a translation of the Hebrew מַשְׁלִיכִים מְצוֹדָה or its Aramaic equivalent. If it was in Hebrew, the Palestinian Jewish Christian author of vv 16-20 employed precisely this verb because it appeared in his model at 1 Kgs 19:19 – וַיַּשְׁלֵךְ.

4) The δεῦτε ὀπίσω μου in Mark 1:17 is a literal translation of the phrase הלך אחרי (someone), or its Aramaic equivalent. As pointed out in section I. 1. above, the latter had become a technical term in early Judaism for (becoming and) being someone's disciple. Here the phrase is not merely a Septuagintism.[71]

5) The εὐθύς of Mark 1:18 derives from Palestinian Judaic interpretation of 1 Kgs 19:20-21. Josephus' Greek in *Ant.* 8.354 is εὐθέως, certainly based on his Aramaic original, and *Eliyyahu Rabbah* 5 at this point twice has מִיָּד, "immediately."

6) Other motifs such as "leaving all one's possessions," and being called to because a disciple while one is engaged in one's trade, are found only in Palestinian Judaic traditions on 1 Kgs 19:19-21. These are all now found only in Hebrew, as in *Eliyyahu Rabbah* 5, or in Josephus' translation Greek.

---

[69] For this as a Semitism, cf. BDF § 458 (p. 239).

[70] The LXX also translates the qal of עבר with παράγω in 2 Kgdms 15:18; Ps 128:8; and Ps 143:4. Lohmeyer (*Das Evangelium des Markus* 31) notes that παράγω with παρά is only found in Mark 1:16. Does it derive from an attempt to translate עַל after עבר? See BDB 717, 4.a.: pass along by.

[71] Cf. BDF § 215 (p. 115).

The above factors strengthen the generally accepted thesis that the first accounts of Jesus' individual sayings and deeds in Palestine were in a Semitic language. Later they were translated by Hellenistic Jewish Christians into Greek and only then became available to the Evangelist Mark, who shows no signs of knowing Aramaic or Hebrew. While the narrative of what is now Mark 1:16–20 may originally have been in Hebrew, it is just as possible that it was in Aramaic, the language most easily understood by the majority of Palestinian Jews and Jewish Christians. Only later was the account translated into Greek by a Hellenistic Jewish Christian, who, however, did not employ LXX terminology from 3 Kgdms 19:19–21, although he certainly recognized major similarities to that narrative. Whether the original narrative was in Hebrew or Aramaic, my main point here is that it was definitely in one of these Semitic languages.

III.   The Purposes of the Original Narrative.

Even before Mark inserted it into his Gospel,[72] the account of Jesus' calling his first four disciples at the Sea of Galilee had from the outset more than one purpose. The Palestinian Jewish Christian who composed it intended it to convey at least the following three meanings.

1) The narrative now found in Mark 1:16 – 20 legitimated within the earliest Palestinian Jewish Christian communities the later missionary activities of the two pairs of brothers, Peter and Andrew, and James and John.

    The author knew that already during his lifetime Jesus had sent out his disciples "two by two" in order to heal (Mark 6:7) and to proclaim the necessity of repentance (v 12; cf. 1:15 and 4). He then transferred this motif retroactively to the calling of Jesus' first four disciples, which he described as done in pairs (1:16–18 and 19–20).

    The special treatment of Simon (Peter / Cephas), named first in 1:16, was due to knowledge of Jesus' first Resurrection appearance to this disciple (1 Cor 15:5, before the "twelve"), and of Peter's leadership role already during Jesus' ministry (for example Mark 8:29).

    While on three occasions Jesus apparently preferred an inner circle of the disciples Peter, James and John (5:37 at the healing of Jairus' daughter; 9:2 at the transfiguration; and 14:33 in Gethsemane), the fourth disciple, Andrew, is mentioned together

---

[72] For its significance within the first Gospel, cf. Pesch, "Berufung" 25-31.

with these three in 1:29 and 13:3. He is also listed in the fourth position of the twelve disciples in 3:18.[73] This could simply be early Christian consideration of his being the brother of Jesus' main disciple.

Nevertheless, it may be assumed that Andrew continued his missionary activity after Jesus' death and Resurrection, as the members of the inner circle of three also did (Peter, James and John in Acts until James was killed in 12:2). Mark 1:16–20 traces this missionary activity all the way back to the calling of the four disciples at the Sea of Galilee. To this extent it is correct to speak of a missionary "aetiology" here.[74]

2) The Palestinian Jewish Christian who first composed Mark 1:16–20 also meant it as a paradigm of discipleship for his fellow Christians. Like the exemplary four first disciples at the Sea of Galilee, they too should "go after / follow" Jesus after his death and Resurrection. They should now seek to "catch people" (in the positive sense of the phrase), winning them over to Jesus' message of the necessity of repenting now. The kingdom of God is already breaking in, as evidenced in Jesus' miracles and healing ministry, but above all in God's having raising him from the dead. In the limited time still available to them, the original hearers of the narrative should abandon or take time off from their occupations and leave their immediate relatives in order to proclaim this good news of the kingdom and of Jesus' singular role in it.

To this extent the account now found in Mark 1:16 – 20 is early Palestinian Jewish Christian *motivation to mission*. It strongly calls for a decision now to practice one's discipleship by missionizing.

3. Finally, the narrative of Jesus' calling his first four disciples also demonstrates his authority as the Son of God and his superiority to the very popular prophet Elijah.

Before Elijah called Elisha to become his disciple by throwing his mantle over him (1 Kgs 19:19), he had been told to do so by the LORD (v 16). When Jesus called his first four disciples to follow him, he did this not by a symbolic action, but verbally: "Come after / follow me, and I will make you fishers of people" (Mark 1:17,

---

[73] Cf. also Acts 1:13. Matt 10:2 puts him after Simon, as does Luke 6:14. He is missing in Luke 5:1–11.

[74] Cf. Pesch, "Berufung" 13, 18 and 25.

presupposed also in v 20). Elijah's authority for calling derives from a divine commission, Jesus' from himself as the Son of God.

The latter is true because the Palestinian Jewish Christian author of the narrative now found in Mark 1:16–20 could presuppose that those who first heard his account also knew the story of Jesus' baptism by John the Baptist (in a pre-Markan form). When that took place, God spoke: "You are My beloved Son" (Mark 1:11). Jesus as the Son of God is thus represented as having his Father's broad authority to call his own disciples, while the prophet Elijah needed a specific commission from the LORD to call Elisha as his disciple.

The earliest Palestinian Jewish Christian communities also knew that Jesus was represented as indirectly referring to himself as a prophet at his visit in Nazareth (Mark 6:4). While some people apparently considered Jesus to be the prophet Elijah, thought to return at the end of the age (Mark 6:15 and 8:28; cf. Mal 4:5–6, Heb. 3:23–24), the earliest Gospel tradition has Jesus maintain that John the Baptist is Elijah (9:13). Indeed, at the transfiguration of Jesus, Elijah (and Moses) appeared to him and spoke to him (9:4). This scene, certainly already in its pre-Markan form, also expresses Jesus' superiority to Elijah, as indicated in God's again stating that Jesus is His beloved Son (v 7).

The narratives of Jesus' baptism and transfiguration, almost certainly known in their pre-Markan forms to the first hearers of 1:16–20, thus encouraged the latter to understand the authority with which Jesus called his first disciples to be greater than Elijah's, who called Elisha. This was because Jesus was the Son of God, already indicated at his baptism and transfiguration, but especially as confirmed when his heavenly Father resurrected Jesus from the dead.

*   *   *

These are the main three meanings of the narrative of Jesus' calling his first four disciples. They can be given an even sharper profile, however, by listing what the account does not mean.
1.   It is not an edifying paradigm for an early Christian sermon.[75] There are no indications of the account's being used homiletically.
2.   It is not in the style of an epiphany, reporting the appearance of Jesus as the Son of man.[76] No characteristics of an epiphany are found in

[75] Bultmann, *The History* 57.

[76] Lohmeyer, *Das Evangelium des Markus* 33.

the narrative, nor does the term "Son of man" stand in the background of it. Rather, Jesus' authority here comes from his being the Son of God.

3. It does not show that when Jesus calls fishermen, ostensibly looked down upon by the Pharisees, he is already on the way to the poor, tax collectors and sinners.[77] No early Judaic source views fishing as a negative trade.[78] Jesus called Simon, Andrew, James and John as his first disciples at the Sea of Galilee. They happened to be fishermen, but could just as well have been carpenters, cobblers, merchants, or something else.

4. Jesus' saying regarding "catching people" does not point to the coming Judgment, as the parable of the dragnet does.[79] The metaphor is meant positively, as in the final rabbinic examples I cited above in the Excursus. Those who previously caught fish in the Sea of Galilee should now try to catch or win over people for the good news of the inbreaking of God's kingdom, as particularly exemplified in the person and work of Jesus.

5. Although Diogenes Laertius, perhaps writing in the third century CE, has Socrates tell Xenophon: "Then follow me and learn," this saying is not "the closest parallel to Jesus' calling his first disciples...."[80] 1 Kgs 19:19–21 *in Palestinian Judaic tradition* rather provide the major part of the background, as shown above.

Greek sayings dealing with "catching someone" also do not point to Jesus' metaphor of "catching people" as belonging to the area of Hellenistic thought.[81] (Later) rabbinic examples of someone's "catching" another person or being a "catcher" (fisher), both meant positively, rather point to Palestinian Judaism as the background.

---

[77] Grundmann, *Das Evangelium nach Markus* 56.

[78] Cf. Str-B 1.186.

[79] J. Schniewind, *Das Evangelium nach Markus* 17, after first maintaining that it is a parable of "Dienst am Wort."

[80] Gundry, *Mark* 71. It is found in the *Lives of Eminent Philosophers* 2.48 (Long, *Diogenis Laertii* 77).

[81] Examples cited by the commentators are Diogenes Laertius, *Lives* 2.67 regarding Aristippus (Long 85; here he only gets a fish, not a human); 4.16 regarding Polemon, "caught" (ἐθηράθη) in a short time by Xenokrates' lectures (Long 173); 8.36, where Timon labels Pythagoras a "man-snarer" (θήρη ἐπ' ἀνθρώπων; Hicks 352, Long 408); and Aristaenetus 1.7, a fisherman's complaint about a girl he did not "catch" (ἤγρευσα; Mazal 18, Lesky 63).

Finally, Jesus is not presented as a Hellenistic "divine man" when he "predicts" that the four fishermen in the future will catch people.[82]   The Palestinian Jew Jesus does not make a superhuman "prediction" at this point.   Rather, he calls four men to be his disciples, promising them that they in the future will catch more than just fish if they follow him.

*   *   *

The above five negative statements, by means of contrast, aid in a better understanding of the original purposes of the narrative now found in Mark 1:16–20.

IV.   The Question of Historicity.

The narrative of Jesus' calling his first four disciples in Mark 1:16–20 is considered by S. Lachs to derive from the early church.[83]   Others like E. Haenchen[84] and W. Schmithals[85] believe Hellenistic tradition is found in the account.

Most commentators on the pericope, however, advocate its historicity, although for different reasons and in different forms.   R. Gundry asks whether "Mark heard the story from Simon Peter's own lips...,[86] and E. Klostermann as a first option maintains that it may go back to a remembrance of Peter.[87]

J. Schniewind argues that a number of things speak for the narrative as (historically) going back to the first disciples.[88]   R. Pesch speaks of it as deriving from circles around the four "apostles" named in the story.[89]

---

[82] Gundry, *Mark* 71, referring to A. Droge; see also 66.

[83] *A Rabbinic Commentary* 59, especially in regard to Jesus' saying regarding "fishers of people."   He relies on D. Nineham here.   Likewise, G. Klein in "Die Berufung des Petrus" in *ZNW* 58 (1967) 39 advocates the situation of Easter for the origin of the saying regarding fishers of people.

[84] *Der Weg Jesu* (Berlin: de Gruyter, 1968²) 81.

[85] *Das Evangelium nach Markus, Kapitel 1–9,1*, 105 in regard to the central logion. He also views the structure of the narrative as being borrowed from 2:13–14, and the other material to derive from Luke 5:1–11 in what he labels the "Grundschrift."

[86] *Mark* 70.

[87] *Das Markusevangelium* 12.

[88] *Das Evangelium nach Markus* 18.

Others concentrate their attention on Jesus' "fishers of people" saying in v 17. M. Hooker says regarding this that "there is no reason to deny it to Jesus himself...."[90] M. Hengel states that "One should concede to Jesus his own original turns of speech."[91] W. Grundmann, finally, considers the saying the most historical element in the entire narrative.[92]

While I agree that "I will make you into fishers of people" certainly goes back to the historical Jesus, I would maintain that the rest of the narrative was strongly influenced by the Palestinian Jewish Christian who composed it. R. Bultmann thinks for example that 1:16-20 "condenses into one symbolic moment what was in actuality a process...."[93] M. Hooker notes that the "fishers of people" saying "may perhaps have been spoken on a later occasion."[94] R. Pesch leaves the question open of whether or not the two pairs of brothers were called together, and concedes that an "ideal scene" is presented here in a schematic fashion.[95]

The Palestinian Jewish Christian author of Mark 1:16-20 had Jesus' historical "fishers of people" saying at his disposal. He also knew that the disciples were already sent out during Jesus' ministry two by two, and that Simon, (Andrew), James and John later played major roles among the twelve disciples. He then coupled this with knowledge of the occupation of the four: fishermen on the northern shore of the Sea of Galilee. Also cognizant of Jesus' later expectation that his closest followers should (at least temporarily) renounce family, possessions and their occupation, he created a vivid calling scene in light of a major calling scene in the Hebrew Bible: 1 Kgs 19:19-21. This was "imaginative

---

[89] "Berufung" 24.

[90] *The Gospel According to St Mark* 60.

[91] *Nachfolge und Charisma* 85.

[92] *Das Evangelium nach Markus* 54, dependent on R. Pesch, "Berufung."

[93] *The History* 57, where he also mentions 2:14. He is followed by E. Klostermann in *Das Markusevangelium* 12. J. Gnilka in *Das Evangelium nach Markus (Mk 1-8,26)* 75 aptly states regarding the calling of the first four disciples: " 'Historisch' wird sich der Anschluß dieser Männer an Jesus allmählicher und verwickelter vollzogen haben."

[94] *The Gospel According to St Mark* 60.

[95] "Berufung" 22 and 24. J. Gnilka in *Das Evangelium nach Markus (Mk 1-8,26)* 72 cites convincing arguments for vv 16-18 and 19-20 as belonging together from the outset.

dramatization," which J. Goldin labels one of the "familiar devices" of Judaic haggadic material.[96]

Simon and Andrew leave their nets "immediately" and follow Jesus in Mark 1:18. James and John's leaving their father in the boat after being called in v 20 also implicitly conveys the same motif. The Palestinian Jewish Christian author of the narrative borrowed the element "immediately" from Judaic tradition on 1 Kgs 19:19-21, as shown in Josephus and *Eliyyahu Rabbah* 5, described above. There Elisha at his calling "immediately" left all his possessions, followed Elijah and became his disciple / servant.

Historical reality will have been different, however, for Simon, Andrew, James and John. There was no "sudden summons from business to 'following,'"[97] no "miracle of sudden persuasion,"[98] and a "complete stranger" certainly did not call them to become disciples.[99] The Palestinian Jewish Christian author of the calling narrative rather wished to show Jesus' irresistible authority, and to indicate to his own fellow Christians how they should now put themselves in the service of their crucified and risen Lord, just as the first disciples did.

W. Schmithals writes concerning the above phenomenon of the four disciples' immediately following Jesus: "Of course, Jesus' proclamation is presupposed. There is no intention to describe a miracle."[100] F. Grant is also certainly correct in his assumption that "Evidently the fishers already knew him."[101] Both of these commentators are definitely close to the historical reality.

After leaving Nazareth and being baptized in the Jordan River by John the Baptist, Jesus appears to have made Capernaum on the NW shore of the Sea of Galilee his new home, the site from which he conducted the greater part of his ministry. Mark 2:1, for example, notes that when Jesus returned there once, "it was reported that he was at

---

[96] Cf. his remarks in *The Song at the Sea* 27. See also I. Heinemann's term, the "creative (re-)writing of history" ("schöpferische Geschichtsschreibung"), in Strack and Stemberger, *Einleitung* 225. The English in *Introduction* 260 employs "historiography," which is misleading here.

[97] Cf. R. Bultmann, *The History* 28, on this as the main motif of the story.

[98] R. Gundry, *Mark* 67.

[99] E. Lohmeyer, *Das Evangelium des Markus* 31; he calls this the point of the narrative.

[100] *Das Evangelium nach Markus, Kapitel 1–9,1*, 105.

[101] "The Gospel According to St. Mark" 658.

home" (cf. 7:17; 9:33). His family had apparently moved there with him (3:19-21), except for his sisters (6:3).

After the Evangelist Mark inserted into his Gospel the narrative of Jesus' calling his first four disciples at the Sea of Galilee (1:16-20), he noted that "they went to Capernaum" (v 21), assumed to be directly adjacent. There, after healing a man with an unclean spirit, Jesus together with James and John entered the house of Simon and Andrew, where he cured Simon's mother-in-law of a fever.

It seems very probable, therefore, that Jesus had first taught in Capernaum and the vicinity for some time before be made the decision to call disciples to follow and join him in the tasks of preaching the necessity of repentance, proclaiming the inbreaking of God's kingdom, and healing the sick. Only after having been exposed to Jesus' message for a length of time will the first four disciples have affirmatively answered Jesus' asking them to join him. This could very well have taken place on the north shore of the Sea of Galilee at or near Capernaum, where the four were perhaps fishing or mending their nets. Knowing that they were fishermen, Jesus then challenged the four to join him in catching not fish, but people for God's good news.

The narrative of Mark 1:16-20 is thus definitely historical in its core, yet strongly idealized and made paradigmatic in light of the needs of the earliest Palestinian Christian communities. In fashioning his account, the author employed Judaic tradition on Elijah's calling Elisha to produce what became a very vivid and meaningful model for Christian discipleship.

V.   Markan Editing, and the Date of the Original Narrative.

1.   Markan Editing.

R. Pesch has convincingly argued for Matt 4:18-22 and Luke 5:1-11 as later developments of Mark 1:16-20.[102] The latter is definitely the earliest form of the narrative of Jesus' calling his first four disciples which is available to us.

The Palestinian Jewish Christian's original Semitic account, now found in Mark 1:16-20, was later translated by a Hellenistic Jewish Christian into Greek. Only then did it become available to the Evangelist

---

[102] See his "Berufung," pp. 4-5 and 5-7, respectively.

Mark, who incorporated it into his Gospel. Fortunately, it is still in its original form, with possibly two exceptions.

1) It has been argued that the term "Galilee" in Mark 1:16a was added to "the Sea" by the Evangelist.[103] This is improbable. Even if the Palestinian Jewish Christian author of Mark 1:16–20 was from Galilee himself and composed the narrative primarily for Jewish Christians there, he would also have wanted his account to be understood in all the Jewish Christian communities of Palestine, including Jerusalem and Judea. Therefore he felt it necessary to designate "the Sea" that of Chinnereth, Genezareth or Tiberias, probably one of the latter two. He needed this further place name in order to differentiate "the Sea" (הים) from the Great Sea (ים הגדול = the Mediterranean), where there were also Jewish fishermen.[104] The term "Sea of Galilee" is found only in the Christian Gospels (1:16; 7:31; Matt 4:18 and 15:29; cf. John 6:1), and may be due to the Hellenistic Jewish Christian who first translated Mark 1:16–20 into Greek. There is no reason to attribute it to the Evangelist Mark.

2) R. Pesch also maintained that the term εὐθύς in Mark 1:20a may be attributed to the Evangelist Mark.[105] This is also improbable in light of the background of the narrative in Judaic tradition on 1 Kgs 19:19–21. Josephus in *Ant.* 8.354 also has εὐθέως, and *Eliyyahu Rabbah* 5 twice has מיד (see section I. 6 above). At the most it may be asked whether the Hellenistic Jewish Christian translator of the Semitic original by oversight transferred εὐθύς from Mark 1:20b to a, which originally would have read: "He called them, and 'immediately' they left their father...." This would be a better parallel to v 18, upon which v 20 is based structurally.

In light of the above, it seems probable that the calling narrative as now found in Mark 1:16–20 has preserved the Semitic original

---

[103] *Ibid.*, 7.

[104] There were obviously none at the ים המלח, the Salt Sea = Dead Sea. On the names in Hebrew and Aramaic for the "Sea of Galilee," cf. the discussion in Str-B 1.184–185.

[105] "Berufung" 7. E. Best in *Following Jesus: Discipleship in the Gospel of Mark* (JSNTSup 4; Sheffield: JSOT Press, 1981) 167-168 on Mark 1:16–20 even points to five expressions in the pericope which he considers Markan redaction. He is followed here by S. Barton, *Discipleship and Family Ties in Mark and Matthew* (SNTSMS 80; Cambridge: Cambridge University Press, 1994) 62. I discussed most of these above in section I. as belonging to the original narrative.

remarkably well and that there has been virtually no Markan editing of this pericope.

2. *The Date of the Original Narrative.*

The Semitic background of Mark 1:16-20 points to its Palestinian Jewish Christian origin. If, as seems very probable, the account is in part a legitimization of Simon, Andrew, James and John as missionaries in the early Palestinian church, it also points to their later return to Galilee and activity as missionaries there. The Gospel of Mark, for example, relates that Jesus first appeared to his disciples in Galilee after he was crucified in Jerusalem (16:7; 14:28; cf. John 21:1-14). Peter and the other three disciples will first have returned to their earlier occupation of fishing on the Sea of Galilee, and only after Jesus' Resurrection appearances to them will then have begun to win over or "catch" persons for Jesus' message, the gospel.[106] Mark 1:16-20 thus belongs to a very old layer of traditions now still found in the Synoptic Gospels.[107]

For the above reasons I see nothing which speaks against an early dating of the narrative in Mark 1:16-20. The Palestinian Jewish Christian who composed it may have already done so in the forties. It then took some time for the account to be translated into Greek by a Hellenistic Jewish Christian. Only in the latter form did it become available to the Evangelist Mark, who himself shows no knowledge of a Semitic language. Since his Gospel, the earliest we have, was probably composed shortly before or after the end of the Jewish-Roman War in 70 CE,[108] a date shortly before that is the latest possible. However, an earlier dating, even in the forties, seems much more probable.

---

[106] Peter only later returned from Galilee to Jerusalem, where he afterwards was entrusted with the gospel to the circumcised (Gal 2:7-8; for the "Jerusalem Council" see vv 1-14 and Acts 15:1-35).

[107] On this, cf. also Pesch, "Berufung" 25.

[108] See for example J. Marcus, "The Jewish War and the Sitz im Leben of Mark" in *JBL* 111 (1992) 460.

Chapter Three

The Road to Emmaus (Luke 24:13-35)

Introduction

Luke 24:13-35 is the longest Resurrection appearance narrative in the four Gospels. S. MacLean Gilmour calls it "a story of singular grace and charm,"[1] and I. H. Marshall notes that its literary quality is "exquisite."[2] C. Montefiore speaks of it as a "beautiful tale."[3] Others have remarked on its "great suspense,"[4] as well as its "rich use of detail" and "emotions subtly sketched."[5]

Nevertheless, as M. Goulder aptly states: "The Emmaus Road story has been a nest of problems."[6] Verse 13 states that on the same day (as

---

[1] "The Gospel According to St. Luke" in *IB* (1952) 8.421.

[2] *The Gospel of Luke* (NIGTC; Grand Rapids, Michigan: Eerdmans, 1992; reprint of 1978) 890. Cf. also W. Wiefel in *Das Evangelium nach Lukas* (THKNT 3; Berlin: Evangelische Verlagsanstalt, 1988) 408: its "kunstvolle, ja künstlerische Darstellungsweise."

[3] *The Synoptic Gospels*, 2 (New York: KTAV, 1968²) 637. Cf. also J. Schmid, *Das Evangelium nach Lukas* (RNT 3; Regensburg: Pustet, 1960) 355: "Die Erzählung ist wegen ihres wunderbaren Stimmungsgehalts und der Schönheit der Darstellung mit Recht berühmt."

[4] Cf. J. Wanke, *Die Emmauserzählung*. Eine redaktionsgeschichtliche Untersuchung zu Lk 24, 13-35 (ETS 31; Leipzig: St. Benno, 1973) 1. For secondary literature on the pericope, see his IX-X; J. Fitzmyer, *The Gospel According to Luke X-XXIV* (AB 28A; Garden City, New York: Doubleday, 1985) 1571-1572; and J. Nolland, *Luke 18:35-24:53* (WBC 35c; Dallas: Word Books, 1993) 1194-1196. Fitzmyer at 1559 speaks of "the suspense and the excitement of the account ...."

[5] L. Johnson in *The Gospel of Luke* (Sacra Pagina 3; Collegeville, Minnesota: The Liturgical Press, 1991) 398.

[6] *Luke, A New Paradigm*, II (JSNTSS 20; Sheffield: JSOT Press, 1989) 779.

Jesus' Resurrection in vv 1-12) "two of them" were going to a village called Emmaus. The antecedent of "them" is unclear. Does the term refer to other disciples, or to followers of Jesus from "all the rest" beyond the eleven (v 9)? Is Emmaus presented here as the actual home of at least one of the two men, or is it merely an intermediate station on their way back to Galilee? Where is the site located, so that after their encounter with Jesus there Cleopas and his companion could easily return to Jerusalem the same day, although this was nearly over (v 29)? If the two were close followers of Jesus, why were they incapable of recognizing him when he joined them on the road in v 16? What does the term "stranger" in v 18 mean? Why does Jesus scold the two men so severely in v 25, and why does he walk ahead of them after approaching Emmaus, as if he were going on? How should one imagine Jesus' sudden vanishing from their presence in v 31?

These many questions can be supplemented by a great deal of vocabulary peculiar to the pericope. The following expressions occur only here in the NT: ἀντιβάλλω in v 17; ὀρθρινός in v 22; προσποιέω in v 28; παραβιάζομαι in v 29; ἄφαντος in v 31; and ἀθροίζω in v 33. Other expressions are only found here in the four Gospels: ὁμιλέω in vv 14-15; σκυθρωπός in v 17 (elsewhere only Matt 6:16); παροικέω in v 18; ἀνόητος in v 25; and διερμηνεύω in v 27. While every longer pericope can be expected to have some peculiar vocabulary, the very large amount here is impressive. It is thus legitimate to ask whether the Evangelist Luke borrowed most of vv 13-35 from a source, perhaps "Special L," and whether the original narrative was in a Semitic language, as I shall argue below.

While J. Warnke wrote a monograph on the Emmaus narrative in 1973, and much secondary literature on the pericope has appeared since then,[7] major problems have not yet been resolved. The following study attempts to clarify a number of them by showing that the narrative derives primarily from early Palestinian Judaic traditions on the figure of Elijah, just before his own ascension in 2 Kings 2 (section I.), and on the incident of the Levite's concubine in Judges 19 (section II.). Section III. then deals with the original language, provenance and genre of the account, section IV. with the historicity of the narrative, section V. with the extent and purposes of the original account, section VI. with the dating of the original narrative, and in conclusion, section VII. with the location of Emmaus.

---

[7] Cf. n. 4.

I. Elijah Motifs

The Sources.

L. Ginzberg, the master of Judaic haggada *par excellence*, once wrote that Elijah "has been glorified in Jewish legend more than any other biblical personage."[8] This was not only due to his colorful earthly exploits as described in 1 Kings 17-19, 21 and 2 Kings 1.[9] It was primarily based on his ascension without dying at the end of his life (2 Kings 2),[10] and on Malachi's description of him as the Lord's messenger / angel who is to prepare the way before Him (3:1), and as the prophet the Lord will send at the end of time with a special function (3:23-24 = Eng. 4:5-6).

Haggadic amplification of the figure Elijah is already attested in Sir 48:1-12, originally written in Hebrew between 198-175 BCE in Jerusalem.[11] 1 Macc 2:58 states that "Elijah, because of great zeal for the law, was taken up into heaven." This writing was also composed in Hebrew, between 104-63 BCE.[12] "The Lives of the Prophets," a Palestinian writing from the first half of the first century CE and thought

---

[8] Cf. his art. "Elijah," "In Rabbinical Literature" in *JE* (1903) 5. 122-127, quotation p. 122. See also P. Billerbeck's statement in Str-B 4. 764: "Von den Großen des AT.s hat keiner eine solche Popularität in der alten Synagoge erlangt wie der Prophet Elias." See also his entire excursus on Elijah on pp. 764-798. J. Jeremias agreed with him in his art Ἠλ(ε)ίας in *TDNT* 2. 928-941, p. 928: "No biblical figure so exercised the religious thinking of post-biblical Judaism as that of the prophet Elijah ..." (original 1935). See also M. Aberbach, art. "Elijah," "In the Aggadah," in *EJ* (1971) 6. 635-638, as well as A. Wiener, *The Prophet Elijah in the Development of Judaism* (London: Routledge and Kegan Paul, 1978), especially 43-77.

[9] Cf. also 2 Chr 21:12-15.

[10] The only other figure in the Hebrew Bible who does not die is Enoch (Gen 5:24 – "then he was no more, because God took him"). Yet he does not "ascend" to heaven here, as does Elijah. Josephus in *Ant.* 9. 28 mentions the two figures together. R. Yose b. Ḥalafta, a third generation Tanna (Strack and Stemberger, *Introduction* 84), may already be polemicizing against Jesus' ascension in *b. Sukk.* 5a, where he maintains that neither Moses nor Elijah ever ascended to heaven. 2 Kgs 2:11 is then quoted (Soncino 15, with n. 3). On this and other similar texts see, however, Ginzberg, *Legends* 6. 322-323.

[11] Cf. G. Nickelsburg, *Jewish Literature Between the Bible and the Mishnah* 64 and 55.

[12] *Ibid.*, 117.

by many scholars to have been composed in a Semitic language,[13] also includes a chapter on Elijah (21) with much haggadic material.[14]

Mark 6:15 par. attests Palestinian Jewish belief at the time of Jesus' ministry that he might be Elijah, who had returned to earth (see also 8:28 par.). The Transfiguration scene, with Elijah, Moses and Jesus and the ensuing discussion of the necessity of Elijah's returning before the "rising from the dead" (9:2-13 par.), also confirms the imminent expectation of Elijah in the first half of the first century CE.   Finally, Jesus' words on the Cross ("Eloi, Eloi") are represented as possibly referring to Elijah, and a bystander then says: "Wait, let us see whether Elijah will come to take him down" (15:34-36 par.). Matt 27:49 modifies the latter to read: "will come to save him," pointing to the popular belief in Elijah's sudden appearance to rescue an imperiled person (see section 14. B. below).

Several of the above passages from Mark may go back to the time of Jesus' public ministry. All of them can be dated at the latest to when Mark composed his Gospel, generally thought to be shortly before or after 70 CE.[15] Dependent on Mark, Matthew wrote only decades later.[16]

The Jewish historian Josephus, a native of Jerusalem whose mother tongue was Aramaic, included much Palestinian haggadic material on Elijah in his description of the prophet's exploits in *Ant.* 8. 319 – 9. 28. He completed the *Antiquities* in 93-94 CE.[17]

The above sources, from the early second century BCE to the end of the first century CE, show that the prophet Elijah was already then very popular in Palestinian Jewish (and Jewish Christian) circles. This means that the relevance of rabbinic traditions on Elijah should not be rejected out of hand because their *present* form is often quite late. Some, especially those found in Tannaitic sources, may ultimately be as old as

---

[13] Cf. D. Hare in *OTP* 2.380-382.

[14] *Ibid.*, 2.396-397.

[15] Cf. J. Marcus, "The Jewish War and the Sitz im Leben of Mark" in *JBL* 111 (1992) 460, and D. Lührmann, *Das Markus-Evangelium* 6.

[16] Cf. U. Luz, *Das Evangelium nach Matthäus* (Mt 1-7) (EKKNT 1/1; Zurich: Benziger; Neukirchen-Vluyn: Neukirchener, 1992³) 76: "lange nach dem Jahre 80 wird man das Matthäusevangelium nicht ansetzen können." W. Davies and D. Allison in *The Gospel According to Saint Matthew*, I (Edinburgh: Clark, 1988) 138: "Matthew was almost certainly written between A.D. 70 and A.D. 100, in all probability between A.D. 80 and 95."

[17] Cf. *Ant.* 20.267 and Feldman's note "c."

those reflected in Sirach, First Maccabees, the Lives of the Prophets, the Gospels and Josephus.

Secondary Literature on Elijah in the Gospel of Luke.

A number of special studies have recognized the importance of Elijah traditions for the Gospel of Luke.[18] A 1996 Vienna dissertation by M. Öhler deals in a major way with them.[19] A. Zwiep has also analyzed the ascension motif in Luke and Acts in a monograph.[20] Yet no one up to now has recognized and described the importance of Palestinian Judaic traditions on the account of the walk on the road just before the ascension of Elijah in 2 Kings 2 for the narrative of the road to Emmaus in Luke 24:13-35. This is strange, for directly afterwards Jesus' ascension takes place, in part clearly based on Elijah's. The following analysis of nineteen motifs in the Lukan Emmaus narrative seeks to fill this gap.

*   *   *

1.   Walking on the Road and Returning.

A.

The Emmaus narrative strongly emphasizes the motif of walking on the road and returning to the place from which one set out. Luke 24:13 begins the account by stating: "Now on that same day two of them *were going* (ἦσαν πορευόμενοι) to a village called Emmaus ...."   Verse 15 continues: Jesus approached them and "*went with* (συνεπορεύετο) them." In v 17 he asks the two: "What are you discussing with each other *while you walk along* (περιπατοῦντες) ?"   Verse 28 later notes: "As they came near the village to which *they were going* (ἐπορεύοντο), [Jesus] acted as though *he were going* (πορεύεσθαι) further."   Verse 32 then has the two ask each other: "Wasn't our heart burning [within us] while he was speaking to us *on the road* (ἐν τῇ ὁδῷ) ....?"   Finally, v 35 repeats the last

---

[18] Cf. for example the works cited by C.A. Evans in "Luke's Use of the Elijah / Elisha Narratives and the Ethic of Election" in *JBL* 106 (1987) 77, n. 16.

[19] *Elia im Neuen Testament.* The chart on p. 233 gives an overview for Luke and Acts. Secondary literature is listed on pp. 308-339.

[20] Cf. his *The Ascension of the Messiah in Lukan Christology* (NovTSup 87; Leiden: Brill, 1997).

phrase: Having returned to Jerusalem, the two "told what had happened *on the road* (ἐν τῇ ὁδῷ) ...."

Here the verb πορεύομαι, "to go, walk," is employed three times; συμπορεύομαι, "to go (along) with (someone)" once; περιπατέω, "to walk / go" with someone, once; and the expression ἐν τῇ ὁδῷ, "on the road," twice. I suggest that this seven-fold emphasis on "walking on the road," plus returning to the place from which one set out, is due to the author's dependence on a model, 2 Kings 2.

B.   *2 Kings 2.*

Just before a chariot of fire and horses of fire separated Elijah and his disciple Elisha, and Elijah "ascended" (וַיַּעַל) in a whirlwind into heaven (v 11), the two are described five times as walking together (on the road). 2 Kgs 2:1 opens the narrative by stating that "when the Lord was about to take Elijah up to heaven by a whirlwind, Elijah and Elisha *were on their way* (וַיֵּלֶךְ) from Gilgal." Verse 2 then notes that "*they went down*" (וַיֵּרְדוּ) to Bethel." Verse 4 relates that "*they came* (וַיָּבֹאוּ) to Jericho." Verse 6 states that "the two of them *went on* (וַיֵּלְכוּ)." Finally, v 11 notes that as Elijah and Elisha "*continued walking* (וַיְהִי הֹלְכִים הָלוֹךְ) and talking," Elijah ascended into heaven.

Here the term "to walk / to be on one's way" (הלך) is employed three times, "to go down" (ירד) once, and "to come" (בוא) once. This fivefold concentration within eleven verses, describing a walk from Gilgal above Bethel down to the Jordan and beyond it, provides the background for the walk to Emmaus, just before Jesus' ascension. My proposal is confirmed by the frequent mention here of "the two of them," to be analyzed next in section 2. below.

In addition, after Elijah's ascension, his disciple Elisha retraces the road back to Bethel alone (2 Kgs 2:23).[21] The Palestinian Jewish Christian author of the Emmaus narrative appropriated this general pattern for his

---

[21] This may somehow be connected to the strange reading of MS D for "Emmaus" in Luke 24:13, ονοματι Ουλαμμαους. LXX Gen 28:19 A has Ουλαμμαυς for the MT's אוּלָם לוּז, "howbeit Luz" (was its [Bethel's] name earlier). For the many variations in the LXX, see the apparatus in the Göttingen edition by J. Wevers, *Genesis*, pp. 18-19. Above Moṣa, a village just west of Jerusalem, which Josephus calls Emmaus (*Bell.* 7.217) and I identify in section VII. below as the Emmaus of Luke 24:13, there was a Naḥal Luz. It may have triggered the strange reading in MS "D" above. On Naḥal Luz, see M. Fischer, B. Isaac and I. Roll, *Roman Roads in Judaea, II. The Jaffa-Jerusalem Roads* (BAR International Series 628; Oxford: Tempus Reparatum, 1996) 227, as well as the ʿēn lōze noted by G. Dalman in *Jerusalem und sein Gelände* (Gütersloh: Mohn, 1930) 215, n. 4.

own account. After Jesus and his two adherents (Cleopas and his companion) walk together to Emmaus, he "vanishes / disappears," and they return alone to Jerusalem. The general pattern is very similar.

*   *   *

One could imagine that the Evangelist Luke himself borrowed the motif of "walking on the road" and returning to Jerusalem in the Emmaus narrative from 2 Kings 2, especially since Luke's special section 9:57 - 19:27 begins: "As they were going along the road..." (cf. also 13:22 and 17:11). Indeed, T. Brodie even maintains that 9:51-56 is modeled on 2 Kgs 1:1 - 2:6.[22]

Yet as I will show below, it is very improbable that Luke himself composed the basic narrative of what is now found in 24:13-35. Rather, its Palestinian Jewish Christian author employed early Judaic traditions on 2 Kings 2 as his primary model, a walk on the road just before and after Elijah vanished / disappeared from his disciple Elisha.[23]

2. *Two of Them.*

A.

The pericope Luke 24:13-35 begins in v 13 abruptly with the statement: "And behold, *two of them* (δύο ἐξ αὐτῶν) on the same day were going to a village...." As noted in the Introduction, the antecedent of "them" is at first unclear. Only in v 33 does it become apparent that these two do not belong to the remaining eleven disciples of Jesus nor to "those with them" in Jerusalem, but are other Judean Christians on their way home after participating in the Passover festival in Jerusalem (see section VII. below on Emmaus).

---

[22] Cf. his "The Departure for Jerusalem (Luke 9, 51-56) as a Rhetorical Imitation of Elijah's Departure for the Jordan (2 Kgs 1, 1 - 2,6)" in *Bib* 70 (1989) 96-109. He contends that Luke is dependent on the LXX here (p.96), and he does not analyze any Semitic sources.

[23] Jesus' being "on the way / road" with the disciples was already a major motif in the materials which later entered the earliest Gospel, that of Mark (cf. especially 8:27 [omitted in Matthew and Luke]; 9:33-34; 10:32 and 52). See also the later designation "the Way" for belief in Jesus as the Christ (Acts 9:2; 18:25-26; 19:9, 23; 22:4; 24:14 and 22). W. Michaelis in his art. ὁδός etc. in *TDNT* 5. 67 points out in regard to Luke 24:32 and 35 that it is "the only account which depicts the exalted Christ as a traveller." Mark 16:12-13, part of the longer ending of Mark, is clearly based on the Emmaus account in the Gospel of Luke.

J. Ernst asks whether the number two possibly has to do with the men's task as witnesses, as in Deut 19:15.[24]   J. Nolland, in contrast, believes that two is "a Lukan touch; the original would have envisaged a larger group."[25]   Yet he does not explain what motivation the Evangelist would have had for reducing a larger number to two.   Finally, the number two has nothing to do with Jesus' sending his disciples out in pairs.[26] Cleopas and his unnamed companion have no commission from Jesus at the outset. Rather, C.F. Evans is certainly in part correct when he remarks that the number two "is so that a conversation, upon which everything hangs, may take place."[27] As will be pointed out in the next section (3. below), the two are "talking and discussing" when Jesus joins them (24:15). Such an intense conversation is much easier for the hearer (and later reader) to imagine between two travelers on the road than among a larger group. It is thus part of the author's narrative artistry to employ two persons.

Yet the main reason for the Emmaus road narrative's beginning abruptly with "two of them" is due to the Palestinian Jewish Christian's model for his account, 2 Kings 2, just before Elijah's ascension.

B.

2 Kings 2:1-11 describe Elijah and his disciple Elisha's walk from Gilgal north of Bethel[28] via Bethel to the Jordan, where Elijah's ascension takes place. It emphasizes the expression "the two of them" by repeating it four times.

Verse 6 states: "So *the two of them* (שְׁנֵיהֶם) went on." Verse 7 says of Elijah and Elisha: "*they both* (שְׁנֵיהֶם) were standing by the Jordan." The next verse (8) speaks of the water's parting "until *the two of them* (שְׁנֵיהֶם) crossed on dry ground." Finally, v 11 notes that "As they continued walking and talking, a chariot of fire and horses of fire separated *the two of them* (שְׁנֵיהֶם), and Elijah ascended in a whirlwind into heaven." As will be pointed out in the next section (3.), Judaic interpretation of the

---

[24] *Das Evangelium nach Lukas* (RNT 3; Regensburg: Pustet, 1977) 658.

[25] *Luke 18:35 - 24:53*, 1200.

[26] Cf. Mark 6:7; 11:1; 14:13 and their parallels.

[27] *Saint Luke* (TPI New Testament Commentaries; London: SCM Press; Philadelphia: Trinity Press International, 1990) 904.

[28] For this Gilgal as north of Bethel, cf. for example N. Snaith, "II Kings" in *IB* (1954) 3.193, and M. Cogan and H. Tadmor, *II Kings* (AB 11; New York: Doubleday, 1988) 31.

latter verse provides the major background to the two Emmaus Christians' "talking and discussing" on the road on the same day as Jesus' later ascension.

The concentration of the expression "the two of them" (שְׁנֵיהֶם) four times within very few verses argues for its appropriation by the Palestinian Jewish Christian author of the Emmaus narrative, even if the latter thus begins somewhat abruptly. The Hebrew of the MT[29] could be translated literally as δύο ἐξ αὐτῶν, as in Luke 24:13. The Aramaic form in Targum Jonathan is always similar: תַּרְוֵיהוֹן, "both" or "the two of them".[30] It should be noted that the LXX always employs ἀμφότεροι in 4 Kgdms 4:6-8 and 11, and not the term δύο. This is one argument for a Semitic background to the original Emmaus narrative.

3. Talking and Discussing on the Road.

A.

The Emmaus pericope has as one of its main motifs Cleopas and his companion's "talking and discussing" with each other on the road. Verse 14 begins by stating that the two "*were talking* (ὡμίλουν) with each other about all these things that had happened." Verse 15 continues: "While *they were talking and discussing* (ἐν τῷ ὁμιλεῖν αὐτοὺς καὶ συζητεῖν), Jesus himself came near and went with them." In v 17 he asks them: "What *are you discussing* (οἱ λόγοι οὗτοι οὓς ἀντιβάλλετε) with each other while you walk along?" After their encounter with Jesus in Emmaus, the two ask themselves in v 32: "Were not our hearts burning within us while *he was talking* (ἐλάλει) to us on the road ... ?"[31]

Here four different verbs are employed five times for talking and discussing: 1) ὁμιλέω (twice), found only here in the Gospels: to speak, converse, talk with someone.[32] 2) συζητέω means to discuss or carry on a discussion, to debate about something with someone.[33] 3) ἀντιβάλλω,

---

[29] If the Emmaus account was originally in Hebrew, as I argue below, the form could have either been שְׁנֵיהֶם, or שְׁנֵי מֵהֶם, as in the Hebrew New Testaments of Delitzsch (160) and the United Bible Societies (230).

[30] Cf. Sperber 2.274, and the English in Harrington and Saldarini 266-267, as well as Jastrow 1698.

[31] On Jesus' "interpreting" and "opening" the Scriptures to his followers, cf. section 4. below.

[32] BAGD 565.

[33] BAGD 775.

found only here in the NT and in 2 Macc 11:13 in the LXX, is literally to put or place (something) against. Here it means "exchanging" words in conversation.[34]   4) λαλέω simply means to speak, talk, converse.[35] The use of the Greek imperfect tense for 1) and 4) in vv 14 and 32, respectively, emphasizes the ongoing, prolonged nature of the conversation.

This fivefold accentuation of "talking and discussing on the road" is due to the Palestinian Jewish Christian author of the account, who borrowed it from his source, 2 Kings 2, just before Elijah's ascension.

B.

Elijah and his disciple Elisha's walk from Gilgal via Bethel to the east side of the Jordan River is described in 2 Kgs 2:1-11. Before Elijah's ascension in v 11b, "the two of them" have four discussions on the road, the last being the most important for the Emmaus pericope.

Verses 2, 4, 6 and 9-10 describe the contents of Elijah and Elisha's conversations on the road. Verse 11 comments on the last one: "*As they continued walking and talking*, a chariot of fire and horses of fire separated the two of them, and Elijah ascended into heaven."

The Hebrew of the italicized phrase is: וַיְהִי הֵמָּה הֹלְכִים הָלוֹךְ וְדַבֵּר. This unusual grammatical construction, especially the הָלוֹךְ, attracted the attention of early Judaic commentators, who made it into a standard proof text for the necessity of disciples' discussing a piece of *halakah* or legal matter (thus a wordplay is involved) on the road before departing from each other. Commentators also expressed interest in exactly what Elijah and Elisha were "talking about" (וְדַבֵּר). The best text to illustrate this is the continuation of *Eliyyahu Rabbah 5*, the first part of which was so important for the narrative of Jesus' calling his first disciples, as Elijah called Elisha, described above in chapter two.

Directly after the description of Elijah's calling Elisha as his disciple, *Eliyyahu Rabbah 5* continues:

> From here [the conversation between Elijah and Elisha] it is said[36]
> that one should not take leave of one's companion without

---

[34] BAGD 74; LSJ 153-154.

[35] BAGD 463.

[36] Braude and Kapstein, whom I modify here, translate "But it is also said [in connection with the discourse between Elijah and Elisha]..." (p. 92, referring to L. Ginzberg's interpretation in n. 35). See his remarks in M. Kadushin, *Organic Thinking. A Study in Rabbinic Thought* (New York: The Jewish Theological Seminary of America, 1938) 284, n. 306. The Hebrew is in Friedmann 23. In his

discussing "a matter of Halakah" (דבר הלכה). [This is] so that the companion can say: "May so-and-so be remembered for good, for he fixed a halakah in my memory." [In this respect] Scripture states: ויהי הם הולכים הלוך ודבר, "And it came to pass, as they went on walking, they kept on talking" (2 Kgs 2:11).[37] And their "talk" [דִּבּוּר][38] consisted only of "words" [דברי] of Torah, as it is said: " 'Is not My word [דְבָרִי] like fire?' says the Lord" (Jer 23:29). [Therefore] when an angel was sent to Elijah and Elisha to destroy them,[39] he came and found them "discussing words" [היו עסוקין בדברי] of Torah. He thereupon said to the Master of the Universe: "They 'are discussing words' [עוסקין בדברי] of Torah, so I cannot seize them." Thus [to explain the angel's inability at this point] Scripture states: "And behold, a chariot of fire and horses of fire, and the two of them were separated" (2 Kgs 2:11). "Chariots of fire": These are the Torah, the Prophets and the Writings. "And horses of fire": Mishnah, [including] Halakoth and Aggadoth. "Fire": This is Torah, for Scripture states: "The Torah of the Lord is perfect, reviving the soul" (Ps 19:8, Eng. 7). Now what is meant by "and the two of them were separated"? Only that [the angel] returned and stood before the Holy One, blessed be He, and said before Him: "Master of the Universe, I have provided spiritual satisfactions for You in the world. The degradation which I caused them when I knocked them all about [Elijah and Elisha while discussing the Scriptures on the road] is sufficient." Thus [the Lord decreed that Elijah should not die, but] "the two of them were separated from each other" (2 Kgs 2:11).

On the basis of the above incident it is said: "Two men who are walking along on the road and 'are discussing words' [עוסקין בדברי] of Torah, no evil thing [דבר] can have power over

---

n. 26 he maintains that the text is defective at the beginning. Braude and Kapstein in general are very periphrastic. I thank N. Oswald of Berlin for discussing this text with me.

[37] The MT has המה instead of הם here. Braude and Kapstein (92, n. 37) note that the author of *Eliyyahu Rabbah* at this point "seems to find an indication of Halakah" in הלוך.

[38] Jastrow 294-295.

[39] "Them" should probably be "him," Elijah. Cf. Braude and Kapstein 93, n. 39. See also Friedmann's n. 29 on p. 23, where one MS has "to dissolve 'him,'" yet this is corrupt. Yalquṭ Shem'oni omits the verb. Friedmann maintains the angel is the whirlwind.

them." Thus Scripture says: "And as they went on walking, they kept on talking" (*ibid.*).

The above account in its present form is Amoraic. Nevertheless, it certainly contains very old elements. This is shown in the Tannaitic passage *t. Ber.* 3:21, which states in regard to *m. Ber.* 5:1 : "one should not take leave of his fellow while conversing, while laughing, nor out of levity, but rather 'after words [דברים] of wisdom.' "[40] This is quoted in *y. Ber.* 5:1, 8d before a discussion of Elijah's only taking leave of Elisha after speaking words of Torah, as וידבר in 2 Kgs 2:11 is interpreted. Then four explanations are given of what the two were "talking about."[41] Similar comment on the necessity of speaking of and discussing some matter of Scripture before parting from one another on a journey is found in *b. Ber.* 31a,[42] *b. Ta'an.* 10b,[43] and *b. Sotah* 49a.[44]

Eliyyahu Rabbah 5 thus points to the OT (2 Kgs 2:11) and Judaic background of the activity of Jesus' followers on the road to Emmaus: they were "talking and discussing" with each other, and Jesus "spoke" to them on the road. The Semitic behind "talking" (ὁμιλέω) and "speaking" (λαλέω) is the piel of the verb דבר,[45] found in the base text 2 Kgs 2:11 (וידבר). "Discussing" (συζητέω) renders the Semitic ב עסק: "to be engaged in,"[46] or as I translated it above, "to discuss."[47] The term עסק ב also appears to stand behind the Greek of "these words which *you are exchanging* with each other while walking" in Luke 24:17 - ἀντιβάλλω, a very rare expression.[48]

---

[40] Zuckermandel / Liebermann 8; Neusner 1.18.

[41] Neusner / Zahavy 1.192-193.

[42] Soncino 189, also dealing with the Tosephta passage.

[43] Soncino 46-47, with 2 Kgs 2:11.

[44] Soncino 263, also with 2 Kgs 2:11. Some of the details in this and the above passages help to illuminate details in *Eliyyahu Rabbah* 5. Cf. also *b. 'Erub.* 64a (Soncino 447-448) for the basic point.

[45] Jastrow 278.

[46] Jastrow 1098. Cf. the hithpa. and nithpa. 4) as to dispute, argue. The Aramaic is similar (p. 1099).

[47] Braude and Kapstein translate similarly: "engaged in discussion on," "engaged in discourse on" (p. 93).

[48] If דברים is behind the λόγοι of v 17, the original may have meant "matters," "things" (Jastrow 278,2): "What are these matters which you are comparing with each other?" (cf. also LSJ 154, II., on ἀντιβάλλω).

4. Interpreting and Opening the Scriptures.

A.

In Luke 24:25-26 Jesus severely chides his followers whom he has joined on the road to Emmaus. He tells them: "Oh, how foolish you are, and how slow of heart to believe all that the prophets have declared! Was it not necessary that the Messiah should suffer these things and then enter into his glory?" That is, his own adherents should have already realized that the prophets in the Hebrew Bible had spoken precisely about him. "Then beginning with Moses and all the prophets,[49] *he interpreted* (διερμήνευσεν) to them the things about himself in all the Scriptures" (v 27).

Later, after their meal together with Jesus in Emmaus and his disappearance, the two ask: "Were not our hearts burning within us while he was talking to us on the road, while *he was opening* (διήνοιγεν) the Scriptures to us?" (v 32).

The verb διερμηνεύω in v 27 means to "explain" or "interpret" here.[50] If the Semitic באר stands behind it,[51] it may be a wordplay with בער for the hearts of Jesus' followers as "burning" in v 32 (see section 6.B. below).

The verb διανοίγω in v 32 literally means to "open," but it too can mean to "explain, interpret."[52] It repeats the motif of the "opening" of the eyes of Jesus' followers in v 31, just before. The Semitic פתח lies behind the Greek here.[53] A good example of the verb in the sense of explaining or interpreting is *m. Šeq.* 5:1, where the person in charge of

---

[49] These include both the former (Joshua through Second Kings) and the latter prophets (Isaiah through Malachi). For Moses as a prophet, cf. the end of *Seder 'Olam* 20 (Milikowsky 353, Eng. 509), Philo (see *Mut.* 125 - "the chief of the prophets" and the many other references cited in the index of the LCL edition, 10.386-387), and Josephus, *Ap.* 1. 40, as well as Str-B 3.12-13 for the 48 male and 7 female prophets of Israel.

[50] BAGD 194, 2. The variant in D, ἑρμηνεύω, means the same (BAGD 310,1.).

[51] Cf. the Hebrew New Testaments of Delitzsch (161) and the United Bible Societies (231). On the piel of the verb as to "explain," see Jastrow 135; the Aramaic is the same.

[52] BAGD 187, 2. (cf. Acts 17:3). For the same verb, see also Luke 24:45.

[53] Cf. the Hebrew New Testament of Delitzsch (161), as well as Jastrow 1251 for the Hebrew and Aramaic as meaning both to "open" and to "explain."

the bird-offerings at the end of the Second Temple, Petaḥiah, is called so "because he was able to 'open' matters and expound them."[54]

In the Emmaus narrative Jesus is portrayed as "interpreting" and "opening" the Hebrew Scriptures to his followers on the road to Emmaus. This is because precisely this task was one of the main activities of Elijah on earth after his ascension in 2 Kgs 2:11.

B.

Several rabbinic examples of Elijah's appearing on earth and interpreting the proper meaning of a Scriptural passage are the following.

In *b. Ḥag.* 9b Elijah asks either Bar Hé-Hé, a proselyte at the time of Jesus, or R. Eleazar, probably ben Pedat, a third generation Palestinian Amora[55]: "What is the meaning of the verse: 'Behold, I have refined thee but not as silver; I have tried thee in the furnace of affliction (עֹנִי)' (Isa 48:10)? It teaches that the Holy One, blessed be He, went through all the qualities in order to give [them] to Israel, and He found only poverty (עֹנִי)."[56]

In *Midr. Pss.* 104/25 on Ps 104:32, Elijah explains to R. Nehorai on the basis of Jer 25:30 and the psalm verse why earthquakes occur.[57] Elsewhere Elijah also interprets to various individuals the following Scriptural verses: Gen 2:18;[58] 4:7;[59] Lev 18:19;[60] 27:8 and 25:35;[61] and Deut 23:14.[62]

---

[54] Albeck 2.199; Neusner 258; Danby 157, with notes 6-7. A parallel is found in *b. Menaḥ.* 65a (Soncino 383).

[55] Cf. Str-B 4.773 for the first, and Strack and Stemberger, *Introduction* 98 for the second.

[56] Soncino 48; cf. n. 9 for the Hebrew as meaning both affliction and poverty.

[57] Buber 447; Braude 2.177.

[58] Cf. *b. Yebam.* 63a (Soncino 420).

[59] Cf. *b. Yoma* 19b-20a (Soncino 87).

[60] Cf. *b. Šabb.* 13b (Soncino 53).

[61] Cf. *b. B. Meṣ.* 114a (Soncino 651, without noting the Scriptural references).

[62] Cf. *y. Ter.* 1:6, 40d (Neusner / Avery-Peck 6.90). For other examples, with parallels, see also Str-B 4.773-774.

Elsewhere Elijah is described as being "engaged in the study of the Torah" with R. Joshua b. Levi, a first generation Palestinian Amora.[63] The Hebrew of this is: היה עוסק בדברי תורה, "He was engaged in matters / words of the Torah." The same verb, עסק, is employed here as in *Eliyyahu Rabbah* 5, cited in section 3. B. above in regard to Elijah and Elisha's "discussing" matters / words of the Torah on the road before Elijah's ascension. I suggested there that this Semitic term lies behind the verb συζητέω in Luke 24:15 and the phrase with ἀντιβάλλω in v 17.

While the above passages in their present form are not Tannaitic, the motif of Elijah's correctly interpreting legal aspects of the Scriptures to others is very old. This is for example shown in *b. Pesaḥ.* 70 b, where a Baraitha states in regard to Judah b. Durtai, active in Jerusalem ca. 20 BCE[64]: "Judah the son of Durtai separated himself [from the Sages], he and his son Durtai, and went and dwelt in the South. '[For,]' said he, 'if Elijah should come and say to Israel, 'Why did you not sacrifice the *hagigah* on the Sabbath?' what can they answer him? I am astonished at the two greatest men of our generation, Shemaiah and Abṭalyon, who are great Sages and great interpreters [of the Torah], yet they have not told Israel, 'The *hagigah* overrides the Sabbath.'"[65]

It was also thought that when Elijah later appeared on earth for the final time, he would settle all legal disputes.[66] A concrete example of this early attitude is found in *m. Šeq.* 2:5, where the third generation Tanna[67] R. Meir states: "The surplus of [money collected to pay for the burial of] one dead person must be left until Elijah comes."[68] The third generation Tannaim Rabban Simeon b. Gamaliel (II) and R. Yose (b. Ḥalafta) employ the same expression, "until Elijah comes," in *m. B. Meṣ.* 1:8 and 3:4-5.[69]

* * *

---

[63] Cf. *Midr. Pss.* 36/8 on Ps 36:11 (Buber 252 or 136b; Braude 1.420), and Strack and Stemberger, *Introduction* 92-93. For Elijah as teaching Eleazar Torah for thirteen years, see *Pesiq. Rav Kah.* 11/22 (Braude and Kapstein 220).

[64] Cf. Str-B 6.174.

[65] Soncino 360-361; cf. notes 11 and 1 and 2, as well as Str-B 4.795.

[66] Cf. the general statement in *Cant. Rab.* 4:13 § 5 (Soncino 9.224), as well as Str-B 4.794-796.

[67] Strack and Stemberger, *Introduction* 84.

[68] Albeck 2.193; Danby 154; Neusner 255.

[69] Cf. Albeck 4.68 and 75 respectively, as well as Danby 348 and 351, and Neusner 530 and 535. See also *m. B. Meṣ.* 2:8.

The above discussion makes it very probable that Jesus is also portrayed in terms of Elijah when he appears to his two followers on the road to Emmaus and both "interprets" and "opens" the Scriptures to them.

5. *Asking a Question and Answering it Oneself.*

A.

After joining two of his followers on the road to Emmaus, Jesus asks them in Luke 24:17: "What are you discussing with each other while you walk along?" They had been "talking with each other about all these things that had happened" (v 14) and "discussing" them (v 15). The one wayfarer, Cleopas, thereupon asks Jesus if he is "the only stranger in Jerusalem who doesn't know the things that have taken place there in these days" (v 18). Jesus then intensifies his questioning by asking, "What things?" (v 19). Cleopas and his companion react by giving a thumbnail sketch in vv 19-24 as their answer to Jesus' question. After severely chiding the two, Jesus then interprets to them from "all the Scriptures" the things about himself contained in them (vv 25-27).

This twofold questioning on the part of Jesus, and answering on the part of the two followers, is not only dramatic irony: the hearer (and later the reader) of the narrative knows that the stranger is Jesus, and that Jesus of course is aware of "the things that have happened" in Jerusalem in regard to himself. After the preliminary twofold questioning and answering, which review the most important events of the day, the Palestinian Jewish Christian author of the account then has Jesus interpret and open the Scriptures to his two followers.

Jesus' posing a question, receiving a preliminary reply, and then himself giving the correct interpretation of Scriptural passages is due here to the author's Judaic model, Elijah's discussions with others about Scriptural passages or halakhic rulings dependent on them.

B.

As pointed out in the previous section, one of the major tasks of Elijah after he had ascended to heaven was to appear on earth and to give the proper interpretation of Scripture to others. Often these instances are also introduced by his asking a question.

One good example of this procedure is *b. Ḥag.* 9b, discussed above in section 4., where Elijah asks either Bar Hé-Hé or Eleazar what Isa 48:10 means. Then Elijah interprets it himself.

A favorite interlocutor of Elijah was thought to be R. Nehorai, a third generation Tanna.[70]   One example is *Midr. Pss.* 104/25 on Ps 104:32, "Who looks on the earth and it trembles." Elijah first asks this rabbi why earthquakes occur. After listening to his answer, Elijah tells him: "Although things appear to be as thou sayest, yet this is not the reason. The reason is that the Holy One, blessed be He, looks upon the circuses of the nations of the earth, they sitting unperturbed and the Temple in ruins – looks upon His earth and wishes to lay it waste," as Elijah interprets Jer 25:30 and Ps 104:32.[71]

Other examples with R. Nehorai are *Ruth Rab.* 4/1 in regard to 1 Chr 8:8,[72] and *Midr. Pss.* 18/12 on Ps 18:8 regarding animals and reptiles forbidden as food.[73]

Elsewhere Elijah is portrayed as also appearing and then asking questions of Eliezer b. Hyrcanos,[74] R. Yose,[75] and R. Ishmael b. Yose.[76]

The above rabbinic accounts are not historical, and the majority are not Tannaitic.[77] Nevertheless, it is very probable that especially the first go back to a long established pattern: Elijah appears, asks a question, receives an answer, and then himself proceeds to give the proper interpretation. Because this is exactly the same pattern found in the Emmaus narrative, it is also very probable that in this regard Jesus is also portrayed here as Elijah.

---

[70] Strack and Stemberger, *Introduction* 86.

[71] Buber 447 or 224a; Braude 2.177. Parallels are found in *Midr. Pss.* 18/12 on Ps 18:8 (Buber 141 or 71a, Braude 1. 241), and *y. Ber.* 9:2, 13c (Neusner / Zahavy 1.323-324).

[72] Soncino 8.49. Elijah's own answer is either lacking here, or, less probably, the answer given is Elijah's.

[73] Buber 142 or 71b, Braude 1.242. A parallel is found in *y. Ber.* 9:2, 13c (Neusner / Zahavy 1. 324).

[74] Cf. *Pirq. R. El.* 1 (Eshkol 5, Friedlander 2): "Why do you weep?"

[75] Cf. *b. Ber.* 3a (Soncino 6-7: "My son, why did you go into this ruin...?" within a Baraitha).

[76] Cf. *b. B. Meṣ.* 84a (Soncino 479: "How long will you deliver the people of our God to execution?").

[77] Cf. n. 65, however, for a Tannaitic tradition.

6. Burning of the Heart at the Interpretation of the Tripartite Scripture.

A.

Jesus joined two of his followers on the road to Emmaus and, "beginning with Moses and all the prophets, he interpreted to them all the things about himself in all the Scriptures" (Luke 24:27). Then he ate with them in the village of Emmaus, where they finally recognized him, after which he vanished.

At this point Cleopas and his companion ask: "Were not our hearts burning within us while he was talking to us on the road, while he was opening the Scriptures to us?" (v 32). "Our hearts" is literally the singular, "our heart" (ἡ καρδία ἡμῶν). "Was burning" is καιομένη ἦν. This imagery is also due to the Palestinian Jewish Christian author of the Emmaus narrative, who portrays Jesus here as Elijah, *the* prophet of fire, especially in regard to 2 Kgs 2:11, just before his ascension.

B.

Fire is associated with Elijah at three points in the Hebrew Bible. 1 Kgs 18:23-25 and 38 deal with the fire of the Lord which will consume Elijah's wet offering on Mount Carmel at his contest with the prophets of Baal. 2 Kgs 1:10, 12 and 14 concern Elijah's use of fire in his denunciation of Ahaziah.[78] Finally, 2 Kgs 2:11 states regarding Elijah and Elisha: "As they continued walking and talking, a chariot of *fire* and horses of *fire* separated the two of them, and Elijah ascended in a whirlwind into heaven." Before I discuss this biblical verse in Judaic interpretation, so important for the Emmaus narrative, several remarks on Elijah in the Book of Sirach from the beginning to the second century BCE in Jerusalem are appropriate.

Sir 48:1 begins: "Then Elijah arose, a prophet like fire, and his word burned like a torch." "Like fire" in the available Hebrew MSS is כאש; the LXX has ὡς πῦρ. The verb "burned" is the present participle of the Hebrew: בוער;[79] the LXX renders it with ἐκαίετο, the same verb as in Luke 24:32. In Sir 48:3 it is related that Elijah brought down "fire" three times, a reference to the occasions enumerated above. Then v 9

---

[78] Cf. in this regard Luke 9:54, peculiar to Luke.

[79] Cf. *Lev. Rab.* Vayyikra 1/1 on Lev 1:1, where the face of Phinehas (=Elijah in Judaic tradition) "burned like a torch" when the Holy Spirit rested on him (Margulies 3; Soncino 4.2).

emphasizes regarding Elijah: "You were taken up by a whirlwind of *fire*, in a chariot with horses of *fire*," a paraphrase of 2 Kgs 2:11.[80]

Sirach 48 shows how, at a very early time in Judaic tradition, Elijah's word was considered to "burn" like a torch, for he was *the* prophet of fire. Above all, the motif of fire emphasized in 2 Kgs 2:11 in Sirach was later interpreted further in *Eliyyahu Rabbah* 5, so important for the Emmaus narrative.

This haggadic work on Elijah first cites 2 Kgs 2:11, "As they went on walking, they kept on talking (וידבר)." It then comments:

> And their "talk" [דִּיבּוּר] consisted only of "words / matters" [דברי] of Torah, as it is said: " 'Is not My word [דברי] *like fire* [כָּאֵשׁ]?' says the Lord (Jer 23:29). [Therefore] when an angel was sent to Elijah and Elisha to destroy them, he came and found them discussing words [דברי] of Torah. He thereupon said to the Master of the Universe: "They are discussing words [דברי] of Torah, so I cannot seize them." Thus [to explain the angel's inability at this point] Scripture states: "And behold, a chariot 'of fire' [אשׁ] and horses 'of fire' [אשׁ], and the two of them were separated" (2 Kgs 2:11). "Chariots of fire": These are the Torah, the Prophets and the Writings. "And horses of fire": Mishnah, [including] Halakoth and Aggadoth. "Fire": This is Torah, for Scripture states: "The Torah is perfect, reviving the soul" (Ps 19:8, Eng. 7).[81]

Here the reference to the Mishnah is obviously a further development of the basic, earlier tradition. What is important to note, however, is that the content of the "talking" of 2 Kgs 2:11, where Elijah and Elisha walk along on the road from Gilgal via Bethel to the Jordan, is considered to consist of words / matters of the Torah, which is like "fire" (אשׁ). Here "Torah" signifies the five books of Moses as the first division of Scripture. It is then mentioned together with the other two divisions, the Prophets and the Writings (Hagiographa), in regard to the "fire" of 2 Kgs 2:11.

Eliyyahu Rabbah 5, with Jer 23:29, reflects very old Judaic tradition at this point. The Tannaitic midrash *Mek. R. Ish.* Baḥodesh 4 on Exod 19:18,

---

[80] Cf. Ben Ḥayyim, *The Book of Ben Sira* 60 for the Hebrew, and Ziegler, *Sapientia Iesu Filii Sirach* 350-351 for the Greek.

[81] Cf. above, section 3.B., with notes 34-36 on this. Braude and Kapstein, *Tanna debe Eliyyahu* 93, n. 40, call attention to a parallel in *Yalquṭ Shem'oni* Psalms § 674, which cites here Ps 19:7, "Nothing is hid from the heat of judgment's sun," and comments on it before citing v 8.

"because the Lord had descended upon it [Mount Sinai] in fire," states for example: "This tells that the Torah is fire, was given from the midst of fire, and is comparable to fire." Shortly after this Deut 4:11 is cited: "the mountain [Sinai] *burned* with fire to the *heart* of heaven."[82]

Deut 4:11 was interpreted at a very early time in regard to the tripartite division of Scripture, and to fire as appearing when scholars occupied themselves with its exposition. *Ruth Rab.* on Ruth 3:13, "Remain this night," for example, has Elisha b. Abuya, a second generation Tanna,[83] relate that at his circumcision in Jerusalem his father

> invited all the notables of the city, including R. Eliezer and R. Joshua. And when they had eaten and drunk, they sang, some ordinary songs, and others alphabetical acrostics. R. Eliezer said to R. Joshua, "They are occupied with [אילין עסקין ב'] their matters (profane amusements), while we neglect to be occupied with [אנן עסקין ב'] our matters (exposition of the Torah)." They therefore began with [התחילו ב'] (the exposition of) the Torah, and from the Torah (they went on) to the Prophets, and from the Prophets (they went on) to the Writings. The words then rejoiced as when they were given on Sinai, and the fire [האש] shone / glowed[84] around them. For were they not originally given on Sinai in fire [באש], as Scripture states: "And the mountain 'was burning with fire' [בּוֹעֵר בָּאֵשׁ] to the 'heart' [לֵב] of heaven' " (Deut 4:11)?[85]

This narrative is found in several parallel traditions, showing its popularity.[86] Other accounts also describe fire as burning around those who engage in and expound the Scriptures, also in connection with Deut 4:11.[87]

---

[82] Lauterbach 2.220-221, with the RSV translation of Deut 4:11. Cf. also *Sifre* Deut. Wezot hab-berakah § 343 on Deut 33:2, "And His right hand was a fiery law unto them." It comments: "This shows that the words of Torah are likened to fire" (Finkelstein 399; Hammer 355).

[83] Strack and Stemberger, *Introduction* 82.

[84] Cf. Jastrow 693 on להט.

[85] Cf. the Vilna edition of *Ruth Rabbah*, p. 21. I have modified the translation of L. Rabinowitz in Soncino 8.77, incorporating his notes 5-6. The rest of the story is irrelevant here.

[86] Cf. *Eccl. Rab.* 7:8 § 1 (Vilna, p. 38; Soncino 8.184); and *y. Ḥag.* 2:1, 77b (Neusner 20.47).

[87] Cf. *Lev. Rab.* Meṣora 16/4 on Lev 14:2 (Margulies 254; Soncino 4.205); *Cant. Rab.* 1:10 § 2 (Donsqi 41-42; Soncino 9.74); and *b. Ḥag.* 14b (Soncino 88-89). In their

I suggest that early Judaic traditions connected to Deut 4:11 influenced the Emmaus narrative via 2 Kgs 2:11 (as seen in *Eliyyahu Rabbah* 5) in three ways.

1) "Beginning with."

Luke 24:27 states: "Then *beginning with* Moses and all the prophets, [Jesus] interpreted to [Cleopas and his companion] the things about himself in all the Scriptures." The Greek of "beginning with", ἀρξάμενος ἀπό, corresponds exactly to the Hebrew verb בְּ הִתְחִיל[88] employed in the *Ruth Rabbah* passage above. There "the Torah" means the five books of Moses, signified by "Moses" in the Lukan passage.

2) The Tripartite Division of Scripture.

Luke 24:25 has Jesus speak of "all that the prophets have declared" concerning himself. Verse 27 follows with: "Then beginning with Moses and all the prophets, he interpreted to them the things about himself in all the Scriptures." If Jesus began with the five books of Moses and all (the former and the latter) prophets, he must have proceeded on to the Writings. This is also meant by "all" the Scriptures. Verse 32 then speaks of "the Scriptures" in general, including all three divisions. (Later on in the same chapter, the Evangelist himself has Jesus speak of everything written about himself "in the law of Moses, the prophets and the psalms" [v 44].)

This tripartite division of Scripture found in the Emmaus account also owes its origin to early Judaic interpretation of Deut 4:11, as shown in *Ruth Rabbah* above. There one began with the Torah and went on to the Prophets, and from there to the Writings. This constellation influenced the early Judaic interpretation of 2 Kgs 2:11, with "chariots of fire" as the Torah, the Prophets and the Writings as seen in *Eliyyahu Rabbah* 5, so important for the Emmaus narrative.

---

exposition of the first text, P. Lenhardt and P. von der Osten-Sacken in *Rabbi Akiva. Texte und Interpretationen zum rabbinischen Judentum und Neuen Testament* (ANTZ 1; Berlin: Institut Kirche und Judentum, 1987) 151 also call attention to Luke 24:32, 27 and 44. Yet they do not interpret Deut 4:11 in regard to 24:32, the heart's burning. They also mention Luke 24:27, 32 and 44 in regard to the practice of drawing parallels between biblical passages by stringing them as beads (חרז, Jastrow 500).

[88] Cf. Jastrow 1661 on תחל, hiphil. The Aramaic is similar. In their Hebrew New Testaments, both Delitzsch (161) and the United Bible Societies (231) have the same root.

3) *Burning of the Heart.*

Luke 24:32 has Cleopas and his companion ask each other: "Were not our hearts burning within us while [Jesus] was talking to us on the road, while he was opening the Scriptures to us?" Here "our hearts" is literally the singular, ἡ καρδία ἡμῶν. "Was burning" is καιομένη ἦν. Both "heart" and "burning" derive from the base verse behind the early Judaic tradition dealing with fire accompanying the interpretation of the Torah, the Prophets and the Writings, as shown in the *Ruth Rabbah* passage above.

Deut 4:11 reads: "And the mountain was burning with fire to the heart of heaven." "Burning" is the verb בּעֵר here,[89] used to describe Mount Sinai / Horeb, from which the Lord spoke to Israel out of fire at the giving of the Torah.[90] This verb, via the early Judaic tradition still found in *Ruth Rabbah* and elsewhere, and developed in regard to 2 Kgs 2:11 in *Eliyyahu Rabbah* 5, formed the background for the expression in Luke 24:32, "our heart was 'burning.'"[91] This burning also took place when Jesus, the Son of God through his Resurrection from the dead, on the same day interpreted and opened the Scriptures anew to two of his followers on the road to Emmaus.

The verb בּעֵר here could very well be a wordplay with the verb בָּאֵר, which I proposed above in section 4.A as standing behind διερμηνεύω in 24:27.

The Palestinian Jewish Christian author of the Emmaus narrative then borrowed the term "heart," לֵב, from the same verse, Deut 4:11. This is one of the few occasions in the Hebrew Scriptures where it is closely associated with "burning."[92] The use of "heart" in Luke 24:32

---

[89] Cf. BDB 128-129, and Jastrow 182 with an example of burning fire.

[90] Cf. Deut 4:10, 12, 15, 33 and 36; 5:4-5; and Exod 19:18.

[91] The verb בּעֵר is translated in the LXX twenty-one times by καίω. In their Hebrew New Testaments, both Delitzsch (p. 161) and the United Bible Societies (p. 231) have בּעֵר here.

[92] Cf. also Hos 7:6, "their heart burns," yet this is in regard to anger and / or passion. See also Ps 39:4 (Eng. 3): "my heart became hot within me. While I mused, the fire burned...." This expresses the psalmist's distress. In spite of its negative character, the verse is cited in the margin of the Nestle-Aland NT (1990[26]) at Luke 24:32. Other commentators (Lightfoot, Gilmour, Rengstorf) cite Jer 20:9 here: "there is in my heart as it were a burning fire" (RSV). The latter is due to the psalmist's inability to mention the Lord or speak in His name (v 9a), also a negative phenomenon. Rejecting Ps 39:4 (3) and Jer 20:9 as irrelevant to Luke 24:32 because of their "inner turmoil and distress," C.F. Evans in *Saint Luke* 914 states: "Here 'heart' is likely to have the Semitic sense of 'mind,' and the burning may be that of a mind set on fire by understanding." The latter is

also recalls the "slow of 'heart'" (καρδία) in v 25. Here too it is a part of the narrator's skill to repeat a term in a different way later on in his account.

7. *Jesus' Sudden Appearing and Disappearing / Vanishing.*

A.

Luke 24:15 relates that while two of his adherents on Easter Sunday were going to a village called Emmaus, they were talking and discussing on the road. "Jesus himself 'came near' and went with them," yet they did not recognize him. The verb "to come near" or "approach" here is ἐγγίζω.[93] Jesus is presented as suddenly appearing out of nowhere.[94]

The same is true for his disappearance. Only after Jesus walked to Emmaus and ate with Cleopas and his companion did they finally recognize him. Then "he vanished from their sight" (v 31). The latter in Greek is: καὶ αὐτὸς ἄφαντος ἐγένετο ἀπ' αὐτῶν. The very rare term ἄφαντος, "invisible,"[95] occurs only here in the NT. Nor is it found in the LXX, Philo or Josephus. This justifies the question of whether the Semitic original derives from a specific Judaic motif complex, and was then translated as ἄφαντος ἐγένετο into Greek.

I suggest that Jesus' sudden "appearing" in Luke 24:15 is due to the Palestinian Jewish Christian author of the Emmaus narrative as describing him here in terms of Elijah. After his ascension into heaven, this prophet was considered capable of appearing suddenly wherever he desired, even coming from long distances to do so. Jesus' "disappearing" in v 31 also derives from Elijah's "disappearing."

---

correct, especially in light of early Judaic interpretation of Deut 4:11. P. Billerbeck's reference to *Test. Naphtali* 7:4 (Str-B 2. 299) is also irrelevant here: "I was burning inwardly with compassion to tell him that..." (*OTP* 1. 813).

[93] BAGD 213.

[94] Cf. the similar phenomenon in Luke 24:36 in Jerusalem, where his followers are startled and terrified, considering him a ghost (because he can walk through doors). See also the account in John 20:19, also on Easter Sunday in Jerusalem; locked doors are explicitly mentioned. The same phenomenon occurs a week later for the disciples, this time with Thomas (v 26).

[95] BAGD 124.

B.

Elijah is already presented in the Hebrew Bible as appearing and disappearing suddenly. In 1 Kgs 18:7 the prophet simply "meets" (קְרָא) Obadiah on the road. Obadiah tells Elijah: "As soon as I am gone from you, the spirit of the Lord will carry you I know not where." That is, God is thought to transport the prophet from one place to another even while he is still on the earth. Elijah then tells Obadiah: "I will surely appear / show myself (אֵרָאֶה)[96] to [Ahab] today" (v 15), and their encounter takes place shortly thereafter (vv 16-19). When Elijah ascends in a whirlwind into heaven (2 Kgs 2:11), the company of prophets at Jericho also suggest to his successor Elisha that they should send fifty men to seek Elijah: "it may be that the spirit of the Lord has caught him up and thrown him down on some mountain or into some valley" (v 16). This also attests belief in the Lord's transporting Elijah from one place to another, where he then suddenly appears out of nowhere.

The above passages from First and Second Kings show that already in the Hebrew Bible, Elijah was thought of as suddenly appearing and disappearing. In later Judaic tradition this was intensified, primarily due to the interpretation of Elijah as an angel. The latter in turn was based on Mal 3:1 as read in light of v 23 (Eng. 4:5).

1) Appearing.

Mal 3:23 has God state: "Lo, I will send you the prophet Elijah before the great and terrible day of the Lord comes." Verse one of the same chapter was then interpreted in Judaic tradition of Elijah:[97] "See, I am sending My מַלְאָךְ to prepare the way before Me, and the Lord whom you seek will suddenly come to His Temple. The מַלְאָךְ of the covenant in whom you (pl.) delight – indeed, he is coming, says the Lord of hosts." The Hebrew noun מַלְאָךְ can mean either "messenger," as in the NRSV, or "angel."[98]

Considered an angel in Judaic tradition, Elijah was thought to have all the special abilities of angels. One of these was to suddenly fly from one section of the earth to another in order to fulfill a specific task. This

---

[96] BDB 908, niph., 1.b. of רָאָה: appear = present oneself.

[97] Cf. J. Smith in *Haggai, Zechariah, Malachi and Jonah* (ICC 30; Edinburgh: Clark, 1951) 62, and P. Verhoef, *The Books of Haggai and Malachi* (NICOT 37; Grand Rapids, Michigan: Eerdmans, 1987) 287-288. See also *Deut. Rab.* Re'eh 4/11 on Deut 12:20 (Mirqin 11.80-81; Soncino 7.101), where Mal 3:23-24 are followed immediately by v 1.

[98] BDB 521.

is based on the phrase צִפּוֹר שָׁמַיִם in Ps 8:9 (Eng. 8), "the bird of the heavens / air."[99] *Midr. Pss.* 8/7 on the verse says it alludes to Elijah, "who flies about the world like a bird."[100] A Tannaitic teaching found in *b. Ber.* 4b states: "Michael [reaches his goal] in one [flight], Gabriel in two, Elijah in four, and the Angel of Death in eight."[101] This early passage clearly considers Elijah to be an angel, who can cover great distances very quickly. An example of this is found in *b. Qidd.* 40a, where Elijah suddenly travels 400 parasangs in order to save R. Kahana from death, for the rabbi out of desperation had hurled himself down from a roof.[102]

The above materials help to explain how Jesus, portrayed in terms of Elijah, can suddenly approach and join two of his adherents on the road to Emmaus in Luke 24:15. The first hearers (and later readers) of the narrative know Jesus has not come from Jerusalem and, walking faster than Cleopas and his companion, simply overtakes them. Instead, Jesus as the Resurrected One can suddenly appear in their midst because he is described in terms of the angel Elijah. It is thus thoroughly justifiable to speak of an angel christology for Jesus at this point, mediated through early Judaic tradition on the ascended prophet Elijah.

In the Emmaus account, although Jesus has already risen from the dead, he appears to his two adherents on the road in human form (Luke 24:15). Elijah as an angel was thought to make earthly appearances in the guise of an Arab merchant, Harbonah, an old man, a horseman, a rabbi, a Roman, a bear and a harlot.[103] Yet he also very frequently appeared just as he was, i.e., he was recognizable as Elijah.[104] Jesus also appeared to Cleopas and his companion in his usual human form, in

---

[99] Cf. BDB 861-862. Originally meant collectively, the singular noun צִפּוֹר is interpreted in the following as one person.

[100] Buber 78 or 39b; Braude 1. 128.

[101] Soncino 15.

[102] Soncino 197. See also *Targ. Eccl* 10:20 (Sperber IV A, 166; Levine 45): "Elijah the high priest continually hovers in the air like an angel, the king of the winged tribe, and discloses the things that are done in secret to all the inhabitants of the earth." This Targum, read publicly in the synagogues, shows how popular the idea was of Elijah as an angel with wings, flying all about.

[103] Cf. the examples cited in Str-B 4.769-773; Ginzberg, *Legends* 4.203-211 and the sources in the relevant notes; and Friedmann, *Seder Eliyyahu* 27-38.

[104] Cf. for example *Gen. Rab.* Vayetze 71/9 on Gen 30:11 (Theodor and Albeck 834-835; Soncino 2.660); *b. Qidd.* 40a (Soncino 197); *Pesiq. Rav Kah.* 18/5 (Mandelbaum 1.296; Braude and Kapstein 318); and *Pirq. R. El.* 1 (Eshkol 5; Friedlander 2).

spite of the fact that his Resurrection had already taken place. The two do not recognize him (v 16; cf. v 31), however, for other reasons (see below, section 18.).

In Luke 24:15 the risen Jesus appears to his two adherents simply by "approaching" and "walking along with" them. That is, he "comes" or "appears" to them. Various verbs are employed in Judaic sources for Elijah's sudden appearances to mortals: "to come" (בּוֹא);[1] "to come" (אָתָא),[2] and "to come in the guise of" ('אתא אידמי כ);[3] "to appear in the guise of" ('נדמה כ);[4] "to appear" (נגלה);[5] "to meet" (פגע);[6] and "to meet," "to join oneself to" (נזדמן).[7] The latter Semitic verb may stand behind the Greek of Luke 24:15, ἐγγίζω, "to approach." Jesus is pictured as "joining up with" or overtaking Cleopas and his companion on the road.[8]

In light of the above discussion it seems very probable that Jesus' approaching his adherents in Luke 24:15 is described in terms of Elijah, who also came to, appeared to, or joined himself to others unexpectedly.

---

[1] Cf. *Gen. Rab.* Vayetze 71/9 on Gen 30:11 (Theodor and Albeck 834-835; Soncino 2.660); *b. Ber.* 3a (Soncino 6); and *Midr. Prov.* 9 on Prov 9:2 (Buber 62; Visotzky 49).

[2] Cf. *Gen. Rab.* Vayyigash 94/9 on Gen 46:26-27 (Theodor and Albeck 1185; Soncino 2.879); *b. Šabb.* 13b (Soncino 53); and *b. Sukk.* 52a (Soncino 249).

[3] Cf. *b. Ber.* 58a (Soncino 361); *b. Šabb.* 109b (Soncino 534); *Pesiq. Rav Kah.* 11/22 (Mandelbaum 1.196; Braude and Kapstein 219), with בדמות; and *Gen. Rab.* Noach 33/3 on Gen 8:1 (Theodor and Albeck 306; Soncino 1.262), with בדמותיה ד'. See Jastrow 313 on the niphal, 2, of דמי, דמה as "to appear in the disguise of." The ithpe., 2., of דמי, דמא means the same (*ibid.*). The noun דְמוּת derives from this verb (*ibid.*).

[4] Cf. *Esth. Rab.* 10/9 on Esth 7:7 (Vilna 29; Soncino 9. 119); *Pirq. R. El.* 50 (Eshkol 203; Friedlander 407); and the Aramaic in *b. Ber.* 6b (Soncino 28).

[5] The niphal of גלי, גלה means "to reveal oneself," "to appear" (Jastrow 247). The Aramaic ithp. is the same (p. 248). Cf. *Exod. Rab.* Mishpaṭim 32/9 on Exod 23:20 (Mirqin 6.86; Soncino 3.413); *Pesiq. R.* 22/5 (Aramaic in Friedmann 111b; Braude 459); and *Pirq. R. El.* 1 (Eshkol 5; Friedlander 2).

[6] For the Hebrew and Aramaic of פגע as "to meet," cf. Jastrow 1135. See *b. B. Meṣ.* 84a (Soncino 479).

[7] Cf. Jastrow 404 on the nithpa. of זמן: "to meet," "to join oneself to." See *'Avot R. Nat.* A 2 (Schechter 8; Goldin 17; Neusner 19). A parallel is found in *b. Šabb.* 13a (Soncino 53). The above verbal examples are only selected instances and are not meant to be inclusive.

[8] Cf. *b. 'Avoda Zara* 25b (Soncino 128): "If a Jew happens to be overtaken by an idolater while on the road...."

2)   "Vanishing" / "Disappearing."

The very rare term for Jesus' "vanishing" or "disappearing" from his two adherents in v 31, ἄφαντος ἐγένετο ἀπό, probably also derives from Elijah's "disappearing." In none of the rabbinic examples of Elijah's appearing on earth and holding a conversation with mortal(s) is a specific verb to my knowledge employed for his disappearing at the end. After the encounter is finished, it is simply assumed that Elijah disappears in order to appear to someone else on another occasion elsewhere.[9]

Yet a special Semitic term is used in Judaic tradition for Elijah's being "taken away" into heaven at his ascension in 2 Kings 2. From here the same term was probably transferred to Jesus' "vanishing" or "disappearing" from Cleopas and his companion before his own ascension (later described by the Evangelist Luke in 24:51). Before Elijah "ascended" (עלה) into heaven in 2 Kgs 2:11 (cf. the same verb in v 1), the Hebrew text emphasizes twice in vv 3 and 5 that the Lord will "take" (לקח) Elijah from Elisha. The same verb is employed in the passive in vv 9 and 10 for Elijah's being "taken away." I suggest that this verb, "to be taken away," informed Josephus' paraphrase of Elijah's ascension, the terminology found regarding this incident in the *Tosefta* and *Seder 'Olam*, and Jesus' "vanishing" in Luke 24:31.

Paraphrasing and rationalizing the contents of 2 Kgs 2:1-11, Josephus reports in *Ant.* 9. 28 that "about that time Elijah 'disappeared' from among men, and to this day no one knows his end." Both he and Enoch " 'became invisible,' and no one knows of their death."[10] The Greek of "disappeared" here is ἠφανίσθη, and "invisible" is ἀφανεῖς. The root of this verb is ἀφανίζω, "to make unseen," "to hide"; the passive, as here, means "to disappear." The adjective ἀφανής alone means "unseen," but together with γίγνεσθαι it is equivalent to ἀφανίζεσθαι, "to disappear."[11] The terminology Josephus employs of Elijah's "disappearing" at this point is very close to that used of the "vanishing" or "disappearing" of Jesus, described in terms of Elijah in Luke 24:31 - αὐτὸς ἄφαντος ἐγένετο ἀπ' αὐτῶν.

The Semitic verb for Elijah's "vanishing" or "disappearing" in Josephus and for Jesus' "disappearing" in the Emmaus narrative is

[9] Cf. the statement by L. Ginzberg in *Legends* 6.333, n. 93: Some mortals "were not aware of the great distinction conferred upon them until [Elijah] had disappeared from them...."

[10] LCL translation by R. Marcus.

[11] Cf. LSJ 286 for both. See also 2 Macc 3:34 for the "vanishing" of angels.

probably the niphal or ithpe. of גנז: "to disappear," "to be hidden."[12] This is shown in the Tannaitic *Tosefta*, and in what is most probably a Tannaitic section of *Seder 'Olam*.[13]

In reference to 2 Kgs 2:2-3, *t. Soṭah* 12:5 states that before Elijah "disappeared" (נגנז), the Holy Spirit was commonplace in Israel.[14] The whole passage refers to 2 Kgs 2:2, 3, 4, 5, 6, 7, 16 and 17. It is thus a kind of early midrash on 2 Kings 2, showing a development similar to the employment of the same chapter in Jewish Christian tradition as part of the background for the Emmaus narrative.

Seder 'Olam 17, part of the oldest Jewish chronology, states that "in the second year of Ahaziah Elijah 'disappeared' (נגניז) and will not appear until the Messiah comes."[15] The same section notes that seven years after Elijah "disappeared" (נגנז), a letter from him arrived for King Jehoram (2 Chr 21:12).[16] This shows Elijah's further activity after he "disappeared" from the earth.

The combination of *t. Sota* 12:5 and *Seder 'Olam* 17, which both employ גנז of Elijah's "disappearing," makes it probable that this Semitic verb stands behind the similar Greek terminology of Elijah's "disappearing" in Josephus, and Jesus' "disappearing" or "vanishing" in Luke 24:31. There he is also portrayed in terms of the angel Elijah.[17]

---

[12] Jastrow 258.

[13] On the *Tosefta* as close chronologically to the *Mishnah*, cf. Strack and Stemberger, *Introduction* 175 (this has nothing to do with the dating of the *final* form of the text). On *Seder 'Olam*, see *ibid.*, p. 354, especially Milikowsky's remarks, which, however, may be too positive for the dating of the whole work.

[14] Zuckermandel / Liebermann 317. Neusner in 3.199 has "was hidden away." While this is also possible, "disappeared" is better because Judaic tradition considered Elijah to be active after his ascension or "disappearance."

[15] Milikowsky 323-324. I modify his "was hidden away" (497) for the reason stated in the previous note. The passage goes on to relate that in the days of the Messiah, Elijah will appear and disappear again. This view is singular in early Judaism.

[16] Milikowsky 326 and 498-499.

[17] Against for example commentators like W. Wiefel, who believe Jesus' "vanishing" derives from the Greek world of language and thought. Cf. his *Das Evangelium nach Lukas* 412.

8. The Resurrected Jesus' Eating.

A.

When Cleopas and his companion approached the goal of their journey, Emmaus, they strongly urged Jesus to "stay" with them because of the lateness of the day. Thus he went in to "stay" with them (at the home of one of them): Luke 24:29. The Greek verb μένω employed here twice means to "lodge" with someone, including partaking in the meals of the home.[18] The latter was standard Jewish hospitality at the time of Jesus. If one stayed overnight, one was automatically invited to eat with the host.

For this reason v 30 continues: "When [Jesus] reclined at table with them, he took bread, blessed and broke it, and gave it to them." That is, Jesus actually ate with Cleopas and his companion.[19] At this point they recognized Jesus, and he vanished from their sight (v 31). During their common meal, Jesus' two adherents are pictured here as being reminded of the regular meal fellowship they enjoyed with him while he was still alive, although they themselves did not belong to the inner circle of twelve disciples (cf. v 33). It was standard practice for the person whose house it was to play the role of host at the meal, i.e. to take bread, bless, break and distribute it. Yet here Jesus takes the initiative and takes over the role of host, as he always had as leader of his followers. His taking the initiative thus also pointed to him as Jesus, for a stranger's doing so would have been a major affront to the real host (בעל הבית).

Yet in what corporeal state did the already resurrected Jesus eat with his two adherents in Emmaus? S. MacLean Gilmour, for example, notes in regard to the narrative that "the risen Christ appeared to his followers in a spiritual, noncorporeal form...."[20] I suggest that the portrayal of the resurrected Jesus' eating with Cleopas and his companion in Emmaus is based on his being described in terms of Elijah, thought of as an angel after he was taken up to heaven.

---

[18] BAGD 503; LSJ 1103, 2.b.

[19] J. Fitzmyer's statement in this regard is too subtle: "We do not even learn whether he ate anything at table in Emmaus..." (*The Gospel According to Luke X-XXIV* 1557). Reclining at table, Jesus is simply assumed to eat with the two.

[20] "The Gospel According to St. Luke" in *IB* (1952) 8.430. He contrasts the account to 24:36-43, which "presupposes a physical resurrection and an appearance in the material body that had been buried in the sepulcher" (*ibid.*).

B.

In Judaic sources it is usually thought that before God in heaven there is no eating or drinking.[21] *Pesiq. R.* 43/3 on 1 Sam 1:11, "O Lord of hosts," for example, has Hannah say to God about the angels, the heavenly host: "The host above do not eat, nor drink...."[22] Yet there were exceptions to this rule such as the angel Elijah and the angels who visited Abraham in Genesis 18.

In *Pesiq. Rav Kah.* 11/22, for example, Elijah appeared to Eleazar b. R. Simeon in the guise of an old man. Eleazar gave the prophet something to eat and drink, and "after Elijah ate and drank," he encouraged the man to become a rabbi. Then Eleazar studied thirteen years with Elijah in order to do so.[23] Another account in *b. Šabb.* 13b has the wife of a scholar who had died in middle age complain everywhere of this. When she received no answer, Elijah came to her and explained the true cause. The narrative has him begin by saying: "On one occasion 'I was a guest' at her house...."[24] The expression for "I was a guest" here is נתארחתי, the nithpael of ארה, meaning "to be received," "to be the guest of," "to lodge with."[25] This included meals, as in the biblical account of Elijah and the widow of Zarephath (cf. 1 Kgs 17:8-16).[26]

The above examples suffice to make it probable that Jesus, although already resurrected, could share a meal with Cleopas and his companion in Luke 24:30 because he is portrayed as the angel Elijah here. The prophet was also thought to suddenly appear and eat and drink with mortals.

The angels who visited Abraham in Genesis 18 did the same (v 8).[27] *Num. Rab.* Naso 10/5 asks why these angels ate. It answers: "Because those angels, when they first appeared to Abraham, did so in the form of 'wayfarers.' When he brought them into his house, as was his wont, and

---

[21] Cf. on this issue *Sifre* Num § 143 on Num 28:8 (Horowitz 191; Kuhn 591).

[22] Friedmann 179b; Braude 757. Cf. also the other sources cited in Str-B 1. 891.

[23] Mandelbaum 197; Braude and Kapstein 220.

[24] Soncino 53. The story is said to derive from *Tanna debe Eliyyahu.*

[25] Jastrow 118.

[26] Cf. also Elijah's remark to R. Yose in regard to R. Judah b. Bathyra in *b. Yebam.* 102a (Soncino 701): "he in fact always sits at my table." This probably refers to meals.

[27] Cf. also 19:3. "Eating" included drinking, indicated by the curds and milk of 18:8.

invited them to eat, they did not want to deprive him of the exercise of hospitality, and so they ate with him."[28]

The term for "wayfarers" here is עוֹבְרֵי דֶרֶךְ.[29] It recalls the "wayfarer" Jesus who, after being urged by Cleopas and his companion, accepted their hospitality and ate (and drank) with them in Emmaus.

The expression "to pass on," עבר, employed by Abraham of the angels twice in the account (18:3 and 5), may provide part of the thought background for Jesus' somewhat strange behavior in Luke 24:28. There he acts as if he wants to "go on further" (πορρώτερον πορεύεσθαι), but then after much urging allows himself to be persuaded to stay and eat with his two adherents. Abraham also asks the angels not to "pass by," but to stay and eat and drink.

9. Jesus' Acting as if he Would go Further.

A.

As just noted, when the three wayfarers approached the village of Emmaus, Jesus in Luke 24:28 "pretended" or "acted" as if he were going further. The Greek of the first verb is the middle of προσποιέω, which occurs only here in the NT.[30] The motivation for Jesus' behavior is not easily discernible, for Cleopas and his companion have not yet recognized the wayfarer as Jesus. One reason may lie in the literary art of the Palestinian Jewish Christian author of the narrative. By having his main figure act in such a way, he provided a reason for the two adherents' strongly urging Jesus to stay and eat with them (vv 29-30). Although the angels' wanting to "pass on" in Gen 18:3 and 5 may provide part of the background to this motif (see section 8. above), the main reason for Jesus' strange behavior is found in Elijah's behavior towards his main disciple, Elisha, while on the road.

B.

2 Kgs 2:1 relates: "Now when the Lord was about to take Elijah up to heaven by a whirlwind, Elijah and Elisha were on their way from Gilgal." Then the prophet said to his disciple: "Stay here, for the Lord

---

[28] Mirqin 9. 254; Soncino 5. 367-368. Cf. Ginzberg, *Legends* 5. 236, n. 143 on the older conception that angels could sometimes eat human food. Later this became the minority view.

[29] Cf. Jastrow 1047.

[30] BAGD 718; LSJ 1524, II. 4.

has sent me as far as Bethel" (v 2). That is, during the first segment of their common journey, Elijah expresses the desire to continue on the road alone to Bethel.

This motif is repeated at the beginning of the second segment of their common journey, from Bethel to Jericho (v 4), and at the beginning of the third and final segment, from Jericho to the Jordan (v 6). Elijah each time accedes to Elisha's urging or request to accompany him further. Thus v 6 states: "So the two of them went on."

As indicated numerous times above, Jesus in the Emmaus account is portrayed in terms of Elijah. I suggest that the Palestinian Jewish Christian author of the narrative transferred here the threefold motif of Elijah's wanting to continue on the road without his disciple Elisha, to Jesus. He is described as "acting" as if he wanted to continue or go further on the road when he was approaching Emmaus with "the two of them," Cleopas and his companion. This borrowing from 2 Kgs 2:1-6 would explain the very rare προσεποιήσατο in Luke 24:28, "he acted as if," as well as the following πορρώτερον πορεύεσθαι, "to go on further" (on the road).[31]

10. *Stay.*

A.

When they were approaching Emmaus, Jesus acted as if he would continue on the road alone, without Cleopas and his companion. Yet they urged him strongly with the words: " 'Stay with us, because it is almost evening and the day is now nearly over.' So he went in to *stay* with them" (Luke 24:29). The first occurrence of "stay" here, μεῖνον, is the masculine singular aorist imperative of μένω, to stay, lodge, spend the night with someone.[32] The second occurrence is the aorist infinitive of the same verb: μεῖναι. I suggest that the motif of "staying," here emphasized by repetition, is due first of all to its repeated occurrence in the Elijah – Elisha narrative of 2 Kings 2.

---

[31] The first expression was thus composed *ad hoc* by the author of the narrative. As pointed out at the end of section 8.B., the angel's wanting to "pass by" Abraham in Genesis 18 may have exerted a minor influence on the second expression. The phrase מתחמי הלך, "he pretended to go on," may lie behind προσεποιήσατο πορρώτερον πορεύεσθαι. See Jastrow 476-477, ithpa. and ithpe., and 352-353 on הלך, as well as *Gen. Rab.* Vayyishlach 78/12 on Gen 33:11, "And [Jacob] urged [Esau], and he took it." The midrash comments: "*he pretended* [מתחמין] to draw back, but his hands were stretched out" (Theodor and Albeck 931; Soncino 2. 723).

[32] BAGD 503, 1.α.

B.

Elijah tells Elisha on their way from Gilgal: "*Stay here;* for the Lord has sent me as far as Bethel" (2 Kgs 2:2). The same phrase is repeated in v 4 in regard to going on to Jericho, and in v 6 in regard to going on to the Jordan. All three occurrences are שֵׁב־נָא פֹּה in Hebrew. The verb יָשַׁב means not only to sit,[33] but also to "remain, *stay, tarry.*"[34]

Here the disciple Elisha does not asks his master Elijah to "stay" with him and not proceed on the road. Rather, before they reach the end of their journey, it is Elijah who requests Elisha to "stay" here. Nevertheless, I suggest that this motif, repeated three times, was the main inspiration for the Palestinian Jewish Christian author of the Emmaus narrative to have Cleopas and his companion ask Jesus to "stay" with them shortly before reaching Emmaus, which he then did (Luke 24:29).

The motif of "staying" in 2 Kings 2 also occurs numerous times in Judges 19 together with the verb for "spending the night." I shall point out the influence of that chapter on the Emmaus narrative, especially v 29, in section II. 3. below.

11. A Prophet Mighty in Deed and Word.

When Jesus asks Cleopas and his companion on the road to Emmaus what things had taken place in Jerusalem recently, they answer in Luke 24:19, "The things about Jesus of Nazareth, who was 'a prophet mighty in deed and word' before God and all the people...."

The term Ναζαρηνός, "coming from Nazareth," only occurs here in the Gospel of Luke, apart from 4:34, which is taken over from Mark 1:24. The Evangelist himself prefers the term Ναζωραῖος, "Nazarene," as in 18:37, where he modified the Ναζαρηνός of Mark 10:48. Throughout Acts, Luke consistently uses Ναζωραῖος.[35] This means that "Jesus Ναζαρηνός" in Luke 24:19 ultimately goes back to a source, which I consider to be the Palestinian Jewish Christian author of the original Semitic narrative.

---

[33] So the LXX at this point: κάθου, from κάθημαι (LSJ 853). Yet see BAGD 389, 1.b.

[34] BDB 442, 2.a. *Seder 'Olam* 21 repeats all three of Elijah's requests to Elisha to "stay" here (Milikowsky 358 and 511).

[35] Cf. Acts 2:22; 3:6; 4:10; 6:14; 22:8; 26:9, as well as 24:5. See also the remarks in BAGD 532 *ad verbum.*

The expression "a prophet mighty in deed and word" in Greek is ἀνὴρ προφήτης δύνατος ἐν ἔργῳ καὶ λόγῳ. The pleonastic expression ἀνὴρ προφήτης occurs only here in the NT. It is based on the Hebrew נְבִיא אִ"שׁ, as in Judg 6:8. There both the A and B versions of the LXX have a literal translation, ἄνδρα προφήτην. The very rare form ἀνὴρ προφήτης in Luke 24:19 thus probably also points to a Semitic background to the original Emmaus narrative.[36]

Jesus may have considered himself a prophet, as indicated in Luke 4:24 (cf. Mark 6:4) and 13:33 (only Luke). Some of the people definitely thought he was one: Luke 7:16 (only Luke), 39 (only Luke); 9:8 (cf. Mark 6:15) and 19 (cf. Mark 8:28). The mocking of Jesus as a prophet by the Temple police at his interrogation in the high priest's house in Jerusalem in 22:64 (cf. Mark 14:65) also attests this view of Jesus.

Numerous commentators think Jesus is described in Luke 24:19 as the prophet like Moses whom God will raise up for Israel according to Deut 18:15. This view is based on Acts 7:37, as well as v 22, where the expression "powerful in his words and deeds"[37] is very similar to that in Luke 24:19.[38]

Yet the Palestinian Jewish Christian author of the Emmaus narrative portrayed Jesus as a mighty prophet in Luke 24:19 rather in terms of Elijah. One major indication of this is found in the scene of Jesus' rejection at Nazareth (4:16-30). After Jesus states of himself in 24, "Truly I tell you, no prophet is accepted in the prophet's hometown" (borrowed from Mark 6:4), Luke's special source[39] adds two examples of such prophets. The first one mentioned is Elijah in vv 25-26. He is followed by his successor Elisha in v 27. This is another indication that Elijah was held in very high esteem as a prophet by the Palestinian Jewish Christian community in which "Special Luke" arose.

Another sign of this is the account of Jesus' raising the widow's son at Nain in Luke 7:11-17. It too belongs to "Special Luke," and one of its purposes is to portray Jesus as the modern-day Elijah. That prophet in 1 Kgs 17:17-24 had revived the dead son of the widow of Zarephath.

---

[36] A. Schlatter in *Das Evangelium des Lukas* (Stuttgart: Calwer, 1960²) 458 points to this expression as a Palestinian feature in the narrative. The term אִ"שׁ נְבִיא is also found twice of Jonah in Yalquṭ Jonah § 550. See a very similar expression in Gen 20:7.

[37] Cf. also 2:22.

[38] Perhaps the strongest proponent of this view is J. Green in his *The Gospel of Luke* (NICNT 3; Grand Rapids, Michigan: Eerdmans, 1997) 846, where he also points to Deut 34:10-12.

[39] I consider it improbable that the Evangelist himself added all this material.

"And gave him to his mother" regarding Elijah in v 23 is even quoted in Luke 7:15. After Jesus' great deed, v 16 states: "Fear seized all of them; and they glorified God, saying, 'A great prophet has risen among us!' and 'God has looked favorably on His people!' " Here "a great prophet" (προφήτης μέγας) and God and His people are somewhat similar to the imagery found in Luke 24:19. Just as Jesus is portrayed in the incident of 7:17-24 in Special Luke in terms of Elijah, so he is described in 24:19 in terms of Elijah, also in material from Special Luke.

B.

At the beginning of section I., I quoted L. Ginzberg to the effect that the prophet Elijah "has been glorified in Jewish legend more than any other biblical personage." This was because of his words and deeds, not only while he lived on the earth before his ascension into heaven, but also afterwards, and because of the prophet's predominant role in the final events. Two Judaic sources, one very early and the other from much later, attest this.

Sir 48:1-12a, from the beginning of the second century BCE in Jerusalem and originally in Hebrew, deals with the prophet Elijah. It praises both his word(s) and deeds. The first verse says the prophet's " 'word' burned like a torch." This is ὁ λόγος αὐτοῦ in the Greek, and ודבריו in the extant Hebrew.[40] An example of this is then given in v 2, which relates that Elijah brought a famine upon (Israel by his word – 1 Kgs 17:1). Numerous instances of Elijah's miraculous deeds are then given. They are already summarized in v 4: "How glorious you were, Elijah, 'in your wonderful deeds'! Whose glory is equal to yours?" The phrase "in your wonderful deeds" is ἐν θαυμασίοις σου in Greek, which is lacking in the present Hebrew text, but was probably original.[41] Even if not, Elijah is described here in Sirach 48 as a prophet famous both for his word(s) and miraculous deeds, exactly as Jesus is described in Luke 24:19.

Pesiq. R. 4/2 comments on 1 Kgs 18:31, "And Elijah took twelve stones...." R. Tanḥuma Berabbi Abba, a fifth generation Palestinian Amora,[42] opened his lecture on this text by quoting Hos 12:14 (Eng. 13). " 'By a prophet the Lord brought Israel up from Egypt' – this is Moses; 'and by a prophet he [Israel] was preserved' – this is Elijah. You find that two prophets rose up for Israel from the tribe of Levi, Moses being the

---

[40] Cf. Ziegler 350 and Ben Ḥayyim 60, respectively.

[41] *Ibid.*

[42] Strack and Stemberger, *Introduction* 106.

first of all the prophets and Elijah the last of all the prophets. The two of them redeem Israel with a commission (from God)." These acts of redemption are then elucidated, Mal 3:23 being employed for Elijah, the prophet who will reappear in the time-to-come.[43]

While the latter text is Amoraic, it certainly reflects much of earlier Judaic tradition on Elijah as the last of the prophets. This is buttressed by the quotation of Mal 3:23, "Lo, I will send you the prophet Elijah before the great and terrible day of the Lord comes." He is the Lord's messenger / angel, to be sent to prepare the way before Him (v 1). I suggest that Jesus is labeled "a prophet mighty in deed and word" in Luke 24:19 because the Palestinian Jewish Christian author of the Emmaus narrative wished to describe him in terms of Elijah, the Lord's final messenger.

12. *The Messiah.*

A.

In Luke 24:25-26 Jesus severely scolds Cleopas and his companion on the road to Emmaus with the words: "Oh, how foolish you are, and how slow of heart to believe all that the prophets have declared! 26) Was it not necessary that the Messiah should suffer these things and then enter into his glory?" In the latter verse Jesus speaks of himself as "the Messiah," ὁ χριστός.[44] One major reason the Palestinian Jewish Christian author of the narrative equates Jesus with the Messiah here is that in at least one strand of early Judaism Elijah was considered to carry out messianic functions, and even to be called the Messiah. The following four units attest this.

B.

1) *Gathering in the Exiles.*

One standard function of the Messiah, the son of David, in Judaic thought was to gather in the dispersed, the exiles, at the end of time.[45] Yet one segment of very early and later Judaic tradition attributed this to Elijah. Already at the beginning of the second century BCE in Jerusalem,

---

[43] Friedmann 13a; Braude 84-85. Braude prefers the Parma MS at this point (his n. 9), which has "of all the prophets" twice, lacking in Friedmann's main text.

[44] Cf. v 46, where Luke also has Jesus refer to himself as the Messiah.

[45] This is found in Pss Sol 17:26 and 28 (*OTP* 2.667). See also other sources cited in Str-B 4. 907-908.

Sir 48:10 notes in a free rendering of Mal 3:23-24 that "at the appointed time" Elijah will also "restore the tribes of Jacob." The Greek of the latter is καταστῆσαι φυλὰς Ιακωβ.[46] The extant Hebrew of this verb is ולהכין.[47] It is the hiphil of כון, meaning to [re-]establish, restore.[48] P. Billerbeck correctly points out that the Hebrew phrase "to [re-]establish the tribes of Jacob" here goes back to Isa 49:6. This verse has the Lord ask His servant: "Is it too light a thing that you should be My servant 'to raise up (להקים)[49] the tribes of Jacob' and to restore the survivors of Israel? I will give you as a light to the nations, that My salvation may reach to the end of the earth."[50] Since 2 Kgs 10:10 states: "the Lord has done what He said through 'His servant Elijah,'" it is understandable that Elijah as the servant of the Lord can be thought of as taking over a particular task of the Servant of the Lord, also considered the Messiah in many Judaic sources.[51]

For the above reasons L. Ginzberg could state in regard to Sir 48:10 that "to the author of Ecclus. Elijah is very likely the promised Messiah."[52]

A targumic passage also notes Elijah's task of gathering the Jewish exiles at the end of time. *Targ. Pal.* Deut 30:4 reads: "Even though your dispersal will be to the ends of the heavens, from there will the Memra of the Lord gather you through the mediation of Elijah, the great priest, and from there he [God] will bring you near through the mediation of the King Messiah."[53] It is quite possible that the latter clause was added

---

[46] Ziegler 351. Cf. similar imagery in Acts 1:6, where Jesus is asked if he will "restore" the kingdom to Israel at that time.

[47] Ben Ḥayyim 60.

[48] BDB 466.

[49] BDB 878 on the hiphil of קום.

[50] Cf. Str-B 4.780.

[51] Cf. the art. παῖς θεοῦ by J. Jeremias in *TDNT* 5. 681-700. For Elijah as the servant of the Lord in liturgical usage, see *Soferim* 13:13, "Gladden us, O Lord our God, with Elijah the prophet, Thy servant..." (Soncino, *Minor Tractates* 274).

[52] *Legends* 6. 339, n. 105.

[53] Aramaic in Rieder 2. 298; English by E. Clarke, *Targum Pseudo-Jonathan: Deuteronomy* 83, with n. 10 on Elijah. Cf. also *Eliyyahu Zuṭa* 1 (Friedmann 169; Braude and Kapstein 403): "because the Ten Tribes had been absorbed by the heathen Cutheans, proselytes will not be accepted from the Cutheans until Elijah and the Messiah come and clear up their ancestry," after which Mal 3:23-24 are quoted. It is assumed here that Elijah and the Messiah will "separate" Jewish proselytes from the heathens when these two gather in the exiles at the end of the age.

later to make the earlier belief in Elijah's gathering in the exiles conform with "standard" or majority thought, which attributed this task to the Messiah, the son of David.

2) *Comforting Israel.*

Another messianic prerogative taken over by Elijah in at least one segment of early Judaism was the comforting of Israel at the end of time. Usually this too was considered the task of the Messiah, the son of David. Indeed, one of the latter's names was Menaḥem, (מְנַחֵם), "Comforter."[54]

Deut. Rab. 'Eqeb 3/17 on Deut 10:1, for example, first relates a parable by R. Yoḥanan b. Zakkai, a first generation Tanna.[55] The section continues by having God promise to Moses that when He brings the prophet Elijah in the time to come, Mose will come with him. Here 2 Kgs 2:11-12 are quoted of Elijah. Then the midrash concludes by stating regarding Elijah: "At that time he will come and 'comfort' (וְנִחֵם) you (pl.), as Scripture states": Mal 3:23-24.[56] Here Elijah is to comfort Israel in the final time.

The same motif is found in *Deut. Rab.* Ki Thetze 6/7 on Deut 22:7. Here R. Tanḥuma quotes Mal 3:23 concerning Elijah and then states that "he will come and 'comfort' (וְנִחֵם) you (pl.)," as in Mal 3:24.[57]

The above passages suffice to illustrate how Elijah in one segment of early Judaism took over another prerogative of the Messiah in the final time: comforting Israel.

3) *Resurrecting the Dead.*

In early Judaic writings it was expected that in the days of the Messiah all sicknesses, including death, would be healed.[58] For this reason Jesus is portrayed in the Gospels as healing the blind, deaf, lame and speechless.[59] Yet as the Messiah he is also reported to have raised

---

[54] Cf. Str-B 1.66, and Jastrow 799, 2).

[55] Strack and Stemberger, *Introduction* 74-75.

[56] Mirqin 11.69; Soncino 7.88. It seems probable that Yoḥanan b. Zakkai is still expounding here, yet the final section could also be later.

[57] Mirqin 11.102; Soncino 7.125. Cf. also *Pirq. R. El.* 29 in Friedlander 214, n. 2, and Luria's comments there on Mal 3:24. It may be that the Messiah was originally interpreted here in terms of Mal 3:24 regarding Elijah.

[58] Cf. examples given in Str-B 1.593-594.

[59] This in part is the fulfillment of texts such as Isa 29:18 and 35:5-6.

the dead daughter of Jairus (Mark 5:21-24, 35-43 par.), the widow's son at Nain (Luke 7:11-17), and Lazarus (John 11:28-44); to have instructed his disciples to raise the dead (Matt 10:8); and to have answered John the Baptist's question of whether he is "he who is to come" (the Messiah) by pointing out that the dead are already raised up (Matt 11:5 and Luke 7:22). These Gospel references show that the Messiah was associated with resurrecting the dead in first century CE Palestinian Judaism, even though rabbinic sources on the Messiah's effecting the general resurrection of the dead are very rare.[60]

Yet it was a firm Tannaitic teaching that Elijah would effect the resurrection of the dead, for he had already done so in 1 Kgs 17:17-24. This incident is certainly alluded to in Sir 48:5, "You raised a corpse from death and from Hades...." The Mishnah at *Soṭah* 9:15, for example, concludes this tractate with a statement by R. Pinḥas b. Yair, a fourth generation Tanna:[61] "the Holy Spirit leads to the resurrection of the dead, and the resurrection of the dead shall come through (עַל יְדֵי) Elijah, blessed be his memory, Amen."[62] This tradition is found in a variety of forms, showing its popularity.[63]

It thus appears that when Elijah is described as effecting the resurrection of the dead, he may have appropriated another task of the Messiah, especially as indicated in the Gospels of the NT. Or to phrase it differently: When Jesus the Messiah is described as raising the dead, he is portrayed in terms of Elijah (cf. Luke 7:11-17).

4) *Judging Israel.*

In Ethiopian Enoch, Qumran and rabbinic sources, one of the functions of the Elect One / Son of man, the shoot of David, and the Messiah is to hold or help hold judgment. This is often associated with Isa 11:3-4.[64]

---

[60] *Pirq. R. El.* 32 for example interprets Ps 72:17 of the messianic king, who will awaken those sleeping in the dust (Eshkol 109; Friedlander 233 with a variant). Cf. Str-B 1.524.

[61] Strack and Stemberger, *Introduction* 87.

[62] Albeck 3.262; Danby 307; Neusner 466.

[63] Cf. *Midr. Pss.* 3/7 on Ps 3:6 with Mal 3:23 (Buber 39; Braude 59; the rest of the verse is interpreted of the messianic king); *Midr. Prov.* 15:33 (Buber 81; not in Visotzky 80); *y. Šabb.* 1:3, 3c (Neusner 11.57); *y. Šeq.* 3:3, 47c (Neusner 15.69); *Cant. Rab.* 1:1, § 9 (Soncino 9.12, with both the resurrection leading to Elijah, and its being through the agency of Elijah). See also Str-B 1.194.

[64] See the specific references I note in my article "Gericht Gottes. II. Judentum" in *TRE* 12, pp. 466-469. Precisely in the area of the eschatological events there were

Yet in many other Judaic sources it is Elijah who presently prepares the final judgment, or even effects it. The early Judaic chronography *Seder 'Olam* 21, for example, states regarding Elijah's heavenly activity: "At present he records the deeds of all the generations."[65] A Tannaitic teaching found in *b. Qidd.* 70a notes regarding the three classes of Jews (priests, Levites and Israelites) who marry a woman inappropriate to them: "Concerning all these Elijah writes and the Holy One, blessed be He, attests...." Then Elijah is represented as binding the person involved, while God flagellates him.[66] Here Elijah writes down the deed and aids in the process of judgment.

Elijah's "writing down" human deeds is based on Judaic interpretation of Mal 3:16, "The Lord took note and listened, and a book of remembrance 'was written' before Him of those who revered the Lord and thought on His name." On the day (of judgment) when God acts (v 17), the difference between the righteous and the wicked will be seen (v 18). The first verse is quoted in *Lev. Rab.* Behar 34/8 on Lev 25:25. There R. Levi, a third generation Palestinian Amora,[67] asks: "now if a man does a good deed, who records it? Elijah and the King Messiah, the Holy One, blessed be He, signing beside them," as Mal 3:16 is interpreted.[68] In a parallel tradition "Elijah records it, and the messianic king and the Holy One, blessed be He, subscribe their seal to it," also with Mal 3:16.[69] Here Elijah performs preliminary work, very important for the final judgment.

Finally, in the section on Elijah in the *Lives of the Prophets*, a Palestinian writing probably from the beginning of the first century CE,[70] the author in 21:2 describes Elijah's father at the prophet's birth ("when he was to be born") as receiving a vision of angels, who greeted (Elijah),

---

very diverse opinions in early Judaism, some held by only certain communities at certain times. Generalization is difficult. On Jesus the Messiah as judging, cf. for example Matt 19:28 and 25:31-46.

[65] Milikowsky 324 and 498. Cf. also the expression "Elijah and his Court" in *b. 'Abodah Zara* 36a (Soncino 175).

[66] Soncino 354, with n. 5.

[67] Strack and Stemberger, *Introduction* 98.

[68] Margulies 790-791; Soncino 4.435, with n. 1.

[69] Cf. *Ruth Rab.* 5/6 on Ruth 2:14 (Vilna 19 or 10a; Soncino 8.66). The Hebrew is basically the same, for חתם can mean both to sign (as a witness or judge) and to seal (Jastrow 513-514). Both *Ruth Rabbah* and *Leviticus Rabbah* mention the prophet (Elijah's) also writing down good things in the past.

[70] Cf. D. Hare in *OTP* 2.380-381.

wrapped him in fire, and "gave him flames to eat." In order to understand this vision, the father went to Jerusalem, where he was told in an oracle: "Do not be afraid, for his dwelling will be light and his word judgment, and he will judge Israel" (v 3).[71] Here Elijah is depicted as acting as the eschatological judge.[72] At least in this early source, Elijah assumes a prerogative, that of judging Israel, usually given to the Messiah, and to God.

The above discussion of Elijah as gathering in the exiles, comforting Israel, resurrecting the dead, and judging Israel, all prerogatives usually attributed to the Messiah in Judaic sources (or in early Jewish Christian sources: the resurrection of the dead), makes the statement now found in *Midr. Prov.* 19:21 very understandable: Elijah is one of the seven names of the Messiah, for which Mal 3:23 is adduced.[73] L. Ginzberg maintains that this statement demonstrates that "even later this biblical passage was taken to refer to the Messiah."[74] That is, Elijah as described in Mal 3:23 was the Messiah for a certain segment of early Judaism, which could even maintain itself against the majority view which regarded the son of David as the Messiah.

*   *   *

On the basis of the Judaic sources cited above, I suggest that when the Palestinian Jewish Christian author of the Emmaus narrative has Jesus speak of himself as the "Messiah" to Cleopas and his companion in Luke 24:26, he is also describing Jesus at this point in terms of Elijah.

13. "Hoping" for the Redeeming of Israel.

A.

Cleopas and his companion on the way to Emmaus tell the stranger who has joined up with them how their chief priests and leaders handed Jesus over to be condemned to death and crucified him. Then they add: "But 'we had hoped' that he was the one to redeem Israel" (NRSV of Luke 24:21). The Greek at this point is ἠλπίζομεν, the imperfect of

---

[71] *OTP* 2.396.

[72] Cf. Hare's remarks in *OTP* 2.383. Elijah's activity at the final judgment is also indicated in *Eccl. Rab.* on 4:1 (Soncino 8.110).

[73] Buber 87; Visotzky 90. It is transmitted in the name of R. Huna, perhaps a fourth generation Palestinian Amora (Strack and Stemberger, *Introduction* 103).

[74] *Legends* 6.339, n. 105.

ἐλπίζω, to hope. Perhaps a better translation would be: "But we had been hoping...," indicating a longer period of time, not just the last events of Jesus' life in Jerusalem.

I suggest that the motif of "hoping for" the redeeming of Israel is influenced at this point by Judaic thought on "hoping for" Elijah. He also was considered to be the final redeemer of Israel (see the next section, 14.).

B.

The Tannaitic midrash *Sifre* Deut. 'Eqeb 41 on Deut 11:13 comments on various expressions found in Cant 7:5 (Eng. 4). It asks: "What is meant by 'Thy nose is like the tower of Lebanon, which *looketh toward* Damascus' (v 5c)?" The Hebrew verb of "looketh toward" is צֹפָה, which not only means to "look out or about, spy, watch," but also to "look out (expectantly)."[75] In rabbinic Hebrew it means in the piel to "look forward to, wait, hope,"[76] which then influenced the following comment in the midrash. "If you perform the Torah, 'you may hope for' (the final coming of) Elijah, to whom I had said, 'Go, return on thy way to the wilderness of Damascus' (1 Kgs 19:15), and I had also said, 'Remember the Torah of Moses, My servant...,' and 'Behold, I will send (you Elijah the prophet before the coming of the great and terrible day of the Lord' [Mal 3:22-23])."[77]

Here Elijah is associated with Damascus in Cant 7:5 because of the same catchword in 1 Kgs 19:15 regarding the prophet. The Hebrew of "You may hope for (the final coming of) Elijah" is: קַוּוּ לְאֵלִיָּהוּ.

I suggest that this Semitic expression, "hoping for" the final coming of Elijah, also thought to be the final redeemer of Israel, stands behind the statement by Cleopas and his companion regarding Jesus in Luke 24:21 – "But 'we had been hoping' that he was the one to redeem Israel." The United Bible Societies' Hebrew New Testament has here, for example: ... וַאֲנַחְנוּ קִוִּינוּ.[78]

---

[75] BDB 859.

[76] Jastrow 1296.

[77] Finkelstein 87; I have slightly modified the translation of Hammer, 84-85. A parallel tradition is found in *Num. Rab.* Naso 14/4 on Num 7:48 (Soncino 6.583; Mirqin 10.99). Another text dealing with hope and Elijah is found at the beginning of the next section, 14. B.

[78] P. 231.

14. *The One About to Redeem Israel.*

A.

As remarked in section 13. A. above, Cleopas and his companion on the way to Emmaus tell the stranger who has joined them in regard to Jesus: "But we had been hoping that he was the one to redeem Israel" (Luke 24:21). The Greek for "that he was the one to redeem" is ὅτι αὐτός ἐστιν ὁ μέλλων λυτροῦσθαι. The verb μέλλω with the infinitive can express certainty ("that he would certainly redeem Israel"). Yet its more probable meaning here is "to be about to, be on the point of doing" something.[79]   That is, the Greek phrase should more probably be translated here: "But we had been hoping that he was about to redeem Israel." Jesus' two followers express here their hope that the redemption of Israel is imminent, to be brought about by Jesus himself. Because of his crucifixion (v 29), however, their hopes for this act of redemption for all of Israel (the Jewish people) were dashed.

The verb for "to redeem" here is λυτρόομαι, which means to free by paying a ransom, to set free, rescue, but above all to "redeem."[80] Of the 98 occurrences of this Greek verb in the LXX with a Hebrew equivalent, almost half (43) translate an original גְּאֻלָּה or גָּאַל. The latter verb primarily means to "redeem" in biblical Hebrew,[81] but also in rabbinic Hebrew.[82] The term גּוֹאֵל is "redeemer," and גְּאוּלָּה "redemption."[83] It is therefore very probable that the Semitic original of "to redeem" in Luke 24:21 is the same verb, גָּאַל.[84]

I suggest that the Palestinian Jewish Christian author of the Emmaus narrative described Jesus as him who was thought to be about to "redeem" Israel, because the prophet Elijah in Judaic sources was considered to be the final "redeemer" of Israel.

---

[79] BAGD 500-501:1.a-c.α. The NRSV follows c.β., which considers it a substitute for the disappearing forms in Koine Greek.

[80] BAGD 482-483.

[81] BDB 145.

[82] Jastrow 202. The Aramaic is the same.

[83] Jastrow 216 and 201.

[84] It is employed, for example, in the Hebrew New Testaments both of Delitzsch (p. 160) and the United Bible Societies (p. 231).

B.

Numerous Judaic sources speak of the "redemption" which Elijah is to bring in the future, of this as the "last redemption," of Elijah's "redeeming" Israel, and the prophet as "the redeemer." Many of these traditions are connected to Mal 3:23. Several examples are the following.

Gen. Rab. Vayechi 99/11 on Gen 49:18, "I wait for / hope for (קִוִּיתִי) Your salvation, O Lord," has Jacob state that not Samson is the one who will bring "the redemption" (הַגְאוּלֹה), but one from (the tribe of) Gad. Gad's raiding at others' "heel" in v 19 is then interpreted to mean (Elijah), for he will come at the "heel" (end). For this Mal 3:23 is cited: "Behold, I send you Elijah the prophet."[85] Here Elijah is he who at the end of time will bring the redemption, for which others had hoped.

Exod. Rab. Shemoth 3/4 on Exod 3:12, "that I (*anoki*) have sent you (Moses)," has "our Sages" maintain that this term was a sign of the first deliverance, that from Egypt. "It is also symbolic of 'the latter redemption' (גְּאֻלָּה הָאַחֲרוֹנָה), for with an *anoki* are they healed, and in the future 'they will be redeemed' (לְהִגָּאֵל)." To buttress the latter assertion, the midrash then cites Mal 3:23, with "Behold, I (*anoki*) will send you Elijah the prophet."[86] Here the first deliverance, that from Egypt under Moses, is set alongside the last "redemption," that which will take place in the future under Elijah.

A variant of the latter midrash is found in *Pesiq. R.* 33/8 on the "I" (*anoki*) of Isa 51:12. It states of God: "With *anoki* I will bring 'the redeemer' (גּוֹאֵל): 'Behold, *anoki* will send you Elijah the prophet' (Mal 3:23)."[87] Here Elijah is labeled the future "redeemer."

I cited *Pesiq. R.* 4/2 on 1 Kgs 18:31 above in section 11. B. on Elijah as the last of the prophets. This midrash also states that both Moses and Elijah had / have a commission "to redeem" (גּוֹאֲלִים) Israel. Moses with his commission "redeemed them" from Egypt. "And Elijah 'will redeem them' (גָּאַל) in the time to come through his commission / sending. [It is:] 'Behold, I send you Elijah the prophet,' etc." After Elijah will have redeemed Israel from the fourth enslavement, from Edom (= Rome), the Israelites will no longer return and become enslaved again. Rather, it will be an eternal deliverance.[88] Here too the redemption to come about through Elijah will be the final one. According to *Exod. Rab.* Mishpaṭim

---

85 Theodor and Albeck 1282; Soncino 2.985-986.

86 Mirqin 5.71; Soncino 3.63.

87 Friedmann 153b; Braude 645.

88 Friedmann 13a; Braude 84-85.

32/9 on Exod 23:20, "Behold, I send an angel before you," in the time to come when [the angel – Elijah] will reveal himself, "the redemption" (הַגְּאֻלָּה) will come to Israel.   Mal 3:1, "Behold, I send My angel / messenger..." on Elijah is then cited to buttress this.[89]

The above Judaic sources suffice to show that at least in one segment of Palestinian Judaism, Elijah was thought to effect the final redemption, to "redeem" Israel at the end of time.   Influenced by this thought, the Palestinian Jewish Christian author of the Emmaus narrative described Jesus in terms of Elijah in Luke 24:21.   There Cleopas and his companion state: "But we had been hoping that he was about to 'redeem' Israel."

15. Jesus as Alive.

A.

Cleopas and his companion also relate to Jesus on the road to Emmaus that certain women from their group astounded them.   These were at (Jesus') grave early in the morning (of Easter Sunday), but did not find his body.   Thereupon they returned and reported they had seen a vision of angels, who said that he "was alive" (Luke 24:23).[90]   The latter in Greek is ζῆν, the present infinitive of ζάω, to live, to be living, to be alive.[91]

I suggest that Jesus, resurrected from the dead, is referred to here as "living / alive" primarily because he is described in terms of Elijah. Judaic tradition emphasizes that even after the prophet was taken up to heaven, Elijah remained "alive."

B.

Already at the beginning of the second century BCE in Jerusalem, Sirach 48 points to Elijah as "alive" after being taken up into heaven by a whirlwind of fire.   The Greek version of v 11 reads: "Blessed are those

---

[89] Mirqin 6.86; Soncino 3.413. *Midr. Pss.* 42-43/5 on Ps 43:1-2 (Buber 267; Braude 1.445) compares the two redeemers of the generation of the exodus, Moses and Aaron, with the two redeemers of this generation, Elijah and the Messiah, the son of David.   Usually, however, the comparison is simply between Moses and Elijah.

[90] Cf. also 24:5, where the angels ask the women: "Why do you seek 'the living one' (τὸν ζῶντα) among the dead?"   The Evangelist Luke may have borrowed this motif from v 23, part of a narrative he appropriated from elsewhere.

[91] BAGD 336.   The reference to Melchizedek in Heb 7:8 as alive is relevant here (l.ε.).

who saw you, and those who have fallen asleep (= died) in affection (for you). 'And we too shall live!'" The latter phrase is: καὶ γὰρ ἡμεῖς ζωῇ ζησόμεθα.[92] While the Hebrew at this point is only partially extant, it may have read: כי חיה תחיה, "for you shall surely live."[93] At least the Greek translation by ben Sira's grandson,[94] however, attests popular Palestinian belief in Elijah's continuing to live after his being taken up or ascending to heaven in 2 Kgs 2:11.

This is corroborated by R. Judah (b. Ilai), a third generation Tanna,[95] who comments on Eccl 3:15 in the sense of "That which has been is now." He asks in regard to Elijah, who never sinned: "Is he not alive, does he not endure even now?" (אינו חי וקיים עד עכשיו).[96] Here an early Tanna not only emphasizes that Elijah is still alive. He is also sinless, as the Messiah is in the pre-Christian writing originally in Hebrew from Jerusalem, the Psalms of Solomon (17:36).[97]

The early Judaic chronography *Seder 'Olam* 1 also notes that there were seven people whose lives spanned all of time. The first person is Adam, and the last is Elijah, "and he is still alive" (ואדיין הוא קיים).[98] This is also found in variants in *b. B. Bat.* 121b[99] and *'Avot R. Nat.* B 38.[100]

Finally, *Pirq. R. El.* 47, although often considered late, may well contain the Scriptural basis (beyond 2 Kgs 2:11) for Elijah's continuing to "live." Here R. Eliezer maintains God gave Elijah "the life of this world and the life of the world to come, as it is said, 'My covenant was with him of life (הַחַיִּים – Mal 2:5).'"[101]

---

[92] Ziegler 351. The NRSV follows another MS tradition at the beginning of the verse (see the textual evidence in Ziegler's footnote).

[93] This is I. Lévi's proposal on p. 67, n. "q." Only the final two letters are attested. Ben Hayyim makes no emendation (p. 60).

[94] Cf. the prologue to Sirach, as well as Nickelsburg, *Jewish Literature* 55.

[95] Strack and Stemberger, *Introduction* 84-85.

[96] Mandelbaum 152; Braude and Kapstein 175. Cf. similar comment on Eccl 3:15 in *Pesiq. R.* 48/2 (Friedmann 192b; Braude 814). Friedmann's text reads: "Does he not live forever?" Braude follows instead the Parma MS 1240 (see his p. 28, n. 41).

[97] Cf. *OTP* 2.668, and R. Wright's remarks on pp. 640-641. See also 2 Cor 5:21 and Heb 4:15.

[98] Milikowsky 215, which has a typing mistake (בוא for הוא), and 451.

[99] Soncino 500, with "Our Rabbis taught."

[100] Schechter 103; Saldarini 231.

[101] Cf. Friedlander 371, who translates the A. Epstein MS (xiv). See also M. Higger in *Horeb* 10 (1948) 292, n. 63, which has a similar reading from MS א.

Other Judaic sources also emphasize Elijah's living now.[1] The above references suffice to make it probable that the Palestinian Jewish Christian author of the Emmaus narrative also describes Jesus in terms of Elijah when he has the angels at Jesus' grave tell the women who had gone there: he is "alive" (Luke 24:23). (I shall briefly address the question of the relation between Jesus' Crucifixion, Resurrection and Ascension in section VI. below.)

16. The Third Day.

A.

When Cleopas and his companion tell Jesus, who has joined them on the road to Emmaus, that their chief priests and leaders had handed Jesus over to death and had crucified him, they add that "it is now the third day since these things took place" (Luke 24:21). That is, it is now Easter Sunday afternoon (v 29).

This motif of "the third day" derives primarily from Hos 6:2, which reads: "After two days He will receive us; on the third day He will raise us up." Early Judaic tradition maintained on the basis of this verse that "Israel are never left in dire distress more than three days," and this third day is also interpreted as the day of resurrection.[2]

Nevertheless, one major impetus for the specific mention of the third day in Luke 24:21 is its occurrence in 2 Kings 2 in regard to Elijah's being taken up to heaven.

B.

After Elijah ascended in a whirlwind into heaven in 2 Kgs 2:11, his disciple Elisha recrossed the Jordan River to the west. There the company of prophets at Jericho saw Elisha again, maintaining that Elijah's spirit now rested on him. They then asked Elisha for permission to go and seek Elijah, for "it may be that the spirit of the Lord has caught

---

[1] Cf. *b. Mo'ed Qaṭ.* 26a (Soncino 164) in connection with 2 Kgs 2:11-12, and *Der. Er. Zuṭ.* 1.18 (Soncino, *Minor Tractates* 571) for Elijah as one of the nine who entered the Garden of Eden (Paradise) *alive*.

[2] Cf. the discussion below in section VI. The mention of the third day in Luke 24:21 has nothing at all to do with the idea proposed by some commentators that the soul hovers over the grave for three days after death in the hope of returning to the body. Cf. *Gen. Rab.* Vayechi 100/7 on Gen 50:10 (Theodor and Albeck 1290; Soncino 2.995) in the name of Bar Qappara, a fifth generation Tanna (Strack and Stemberger, *Introduction* 90-91), and parallels cited in Str-B 2.545. The idea may, however, influence John 11:39 – Lazarus has already been dead four days.

him up and thrown him down on some mountain or into some valley"
(v 16). Elisha, knowing that it was the Lord who had taken up Elijah
(vv 1, 3, 5, 9 = his "ascending" in v 11), at first refused their request.
When they continued to ask until he became ashamed, however, he
finally relented. Thereupon the company of prophets at Jericho sent fifty
men who searched for "three days," but could not find Elijah (v 17).

I suggest that this motif of "three days" after the taking up /
ascension of Elijah into heaven strongly encouraged the Palestinian
Jewish Christian author of the Emmaus narrative to have Cleopas and
his companion say: "it is now 'the third day' since these things took
place" (Luke 24:21).

17. *Severe Scolding.*

A.

After Cleopas and his companion relate to Jesus on the road to
Emmaus "the things about Jesus of Nazareth," including the women's
visit to the empty tomb and their vision of angels there, Jesus severely
scolds them with the words: "Oh, how foolish you are, and how slow of
heart to believe all that the prophets have declared!   26) Was it not
necessary that the Messiah should suffer these things and then enter into
his glory?" (Luke 24:25-26). "Oh, how foolish [you are]" in v 25 is in
Greek: ὦ ἀνόητοι. The term ἀνόητος means "unintelligent," "foolish,"
"not understanding," "senseless."[3]   A Semitic expression such as
"without knowledge," בְּלִי דַעַת,[4] could lie behind the Greek.[5]

The second expression in v 25, "slow of heart," is in Greek: βραδεῖς
τῇ καρδίᾳ. Except for James 1:19, the adjective βραδύς, "slow," only
occurs here in the NT. "Slow of heart" is meant as "dull."[6] The term
"slow" does not occur in the LXX, but a related expression is very
instructive. Exod 4:10 has Moses protest to the Lord that he is "slow of
tongue." The Hebrew כְּבַד לָשׁוֹן here is translated in the LXX as
βραδύγλωσσος, with the same Greek stem for slow or dull. The
adjective כָּבֵד in the MT basically means "heavy," but of the tongue
"dull." In Exod 7:14 it is employed with "heart" when the Lord tells

---

[3] BAGD 70; LSJ 145.

[4] On בלי, cf. BDB 115, and on דעת 395, as well as Jastrow 316. For examples of
the expression, see Job 42:3 and, with 'ד, בְּבְלִי, Job 35:16 and 36:12.

[5] Both the Hebrew New Testaments of Delitzsch (p. 160) and the United Bible
Societies (p. 231) have here: "'lacking in' knowledge," חַסְרֵי דַעַת.

[6] BAGD 147. Cf. LSJ 327, 2. of the mind: dull, sluggish.

Moses that Pharaoh's heart is "hardened" (כָּבֵד לֵב).[7] That is, the Semitic expression behind βραδεῖς τῇ καρδίᾳ in Luke 24:25 may imply that Cleopas and his companion were not only "slow / dull of heart." The two may also be portrayed here as "hard of heart," an even sharper rebuke or scolding on the part of Jesus. Both the Hebrew New Testaments of Delitzsch and the United Bible Societies have here: כבדי לב.[8]

The latter Semitic adjective is definitely a wordplay with the background of the Greek for "glory," δόξα, in the very next verse, Luke 24:26. It is כָּבוֹד.[9] The Palestinian Jewish Christian author of the Emmaus account here exhibits his narrative artistry, which would have appealed to his original hearers (and later readers).

Jesus' severe scolding of Cleopas and his companion in v 25 is rare in the Gospels.[10] I suggest that it is due here to the Palestinian Jewish Christian author's portrayal of Jesus as Elijah, a "hot-tempered" man.

B.

In 1 Kgs 19:10 and 14 Elijah states: "I have been very jealous for the Lord, the God of hosts."[11] Elijah's "being jealous" (קָנֹא) for the Lord was demonstrated, for example, when he killed the 450 prophets of Baal in 1 Kgs 18:40, and had 102 soldiers of King Ahaziah destroyed by fire from heaven in 2 Kgs 1:9-12. A later example of this is found in *b. Ber.* 6b.[12] There Elijah, disguised as an Arab merchant, draws his sword and kills a man praying at the rear of a synagogue for standing with his back towards God. Such behavior on the part of the prophet led to the statements in Sir 48:2, "by his zeal he made them few in number," and in 1 Macc 2:58, "Elijah, because of great zeal for the law, was taken up into heaven."

---

[7] BDB 458. Cf. the expression σκληροκαρδία in Mark 10:5 and Matt 19:8.

[8] Cf. pp. 160 and 231 respectively.

[9] Cf. *ibid.*, 161 and 231, which both have כְּבוֹדוֹ for "his glory"; and BDB 458-459 on the noun. It is interesting to note that Sir 48:4 asks concerning Elijah: "Whose glory is equal to yours?"

[10] The only incident which comes close to it might be Jesus' rebuke of Peter as Satan in Mark 8:33 par.

[11] In *Pirq. R. El.* 29 (Friedlander 213) the first verse is quoted to associate Elijah's zeal with that of Phinehas in Num 25:11. He in his great zeal had killed Zimri. Here Elijah and Phinehas are equated, as so often in Judaic sources.

[12] Soncino 28.

All encounters with the prophet, however, did not end so drastically. In *b. 'Aboda Zara* 17b Elijah disguises himself as one of the dignitaries of Rome and hurls an accuser of R. Eleazar b. Peraṭa 400 parasangs, making further proceedings against the rabbi impossible.[13]   Elsewhere he upbraids a ruler in Rome for squandering his father's treasures, (destined in the time to come for the Messiah).[14] In *b. B. Meṣ.* 84a Elijah is described as meeting R. Ishmael b. R. Yose, a fourth generation Tanna,[15] and reproving him with the words: "How long will you deliver the people of our God to execution?"[16]

Elijah's hot temper is labeled so and demonstrated in *b. Sanh.* 113a-b. There it is related that R. Yose (b. Ḥalafta), a third generation Tanna,[17] taught in Sepphoris: "Father Elijah was 'a hot tempered man.'" As a result Elijah did not visit him for three days. On the fourth day R. Yose stated that before them (in the academy) Elijah had displayed his temper.[18]   The term for "hot tempered" here is קְפֵדָן: hot tempered, impetuous, impatient.[19]

An example of Elijah's hot tempered name-calling is found in *Eliyyahu Zuṭa* 8. It describes how Elijah once "was filled with great wrath at Ahab (1 Kgs 17:1) and said to him: 'You good-for-nothing wretch!' You spurned Him who created the entire world...." Then the prophet imposes upon him the punishment of severe drought.[20]   The Hebrew for "good-for-nothing wretch" here is רֵיקָה, which literally means empty or void, but also a worthless person.   It is especially employed as an expression of contempt to mean "good-for-nothing."[21]

Especially the last two passages help to explain the unusual, severe scolding Jesus employs in Luke 24:25.   He tells Cleopas and his

---

[13] Soncino 90.

[14] Cf. *Gen. Rab.* Vayyishlach 83/4 on Gen 36:43 (Theodor and Albeck 1000; Soncino 2.768).

[15] Strack and Stemberger, *Introduction* 87.

[16] Soncino 479. Cf. a similar incident in *y. Ter.* 8:10, 46b (Neusner / Avery-Peck 6. 418-419) with R. Joshua b. Levi. There Elijah scolds him with the words: "Should I reveal myself to informers?"

[17] Strack and Stemberger, *Introduction* 84.

[18] Soncino 780-781.

[19] Jastrow 1398.

[20] Friedmann 185; Braude and Kapstein 436.

[21] Jastrow 1476. Cf. the term ῥακά in Matt 5:22, and the numerous examples in Str-B 1.278-279.

companion they are "foolish and slow / hard of heart" precisely because he is described here in terms of Elijah, the hot tempered prophet who appeared to men and severely scolded them.

18. *The Opening of Closed Eyes, and Recognizing Someone.*

Although Jesus joined Cleopas and his companion on the road to Emmaus and walked along with them, "their eyes were kept from recognizing him" (Luke 24:16). Only after he "opened" the Scriptures to them on the road (v 32) and ate together with them in Emmaus (v 30), "were their eyes opened, and they recognized him" (v 31). Later, back in Jerusalem, the two reported to the eleven (disciples) and those assembled with them what had happened on the road, and how Jesus "had been made known" to them in the breaking of the bread (v 35).

The motifs of closed and open eyes, as well as recognition, play major roles in the Emmaus account. I suggest that they both derive from OT passages dealing with Elijah and his successor Elisha.

1) *Opening Closed Eyes.*

The phrase "their eyes were kept from recognizing [Jesus]" in Luke 24:16 is in Greek: οἱ δὲ ὀφθαλμοὶ αὐτῶν ἐκρατοῦντο τοῦ μὴ ἐπιγνῶναι αὐτόν. The two adherents of Jesus do not fail to recognize him because he is wearing different clothes on this day, or because his resurrected body is somehow different from his previous earthly one. Rather, the passive is employed here to avoid express mention of the divine name.[22] God "keeps" or "holds shut" the disciples' eyes at this point because His Son Jesus has not yet "opened" the Scriptures to them about himself.

The verb κρατέω, to take hold of, grasp, seize, means here to hold back, restrain from, hinder, in the passive "to be prevented from."[23] In the LXX it translates the Hebrew verb אחז thirteen times, and this is the probable Semitic background here.[24] In regard to a sorcerer in *m. Sanh.* 7:11, it is stated that one is not culpable who only "holds shut (הָאוֹחֵז) the eyes."[25] This is commented upon in *b. Sanh.* 65b[26] and *y. Sanh.* 7,

---

[22] Cf. BDF §§ 130.1 (p. 72), 313 (pp. 164-165), and 342.1 (p. 176).

[23] BAGD 448.

[24] Cf. the Hebrew New Testaments of Delitzsch (p. 160) and the United Bible Societies (p. 230). For the verb, see Jastrow 39, who cites *b. Sanh.* 65b.

[25] Albeck 4.194; Danby 393 ("deceives the eyes"); Neusner 599 ("creates an illusion").

[26] Cf. Soncino 447, with Rashi's remark in n. 2.

25d.[27] Here the active form of the verb is employed for a sorcerer who practices magic. In Luke 24:16 the passive form is used, pointing to God as the cause of Jesus' two adherents' inability to recognize him.

The Greek for "'Then their eyes were opened,' and they recognized him" in Luke 24:31 is αὐτῶν δὲ διηνοίχθησαν οἱ ὀφθαλμοί. The verb διανοίγω, to open,[28] is employed in LXX Gen 3:5 and 7 of Adam and Eve's eyes being "opened" to know good and evil. Yet the "opening" occurs here as a result of human volition.[29]

Another OT passage with eyes being opened, already noted by the commentators,[30] is 4 Kingdoms (2 Kings) 6. There Elisha prays that the Lord "open" the eyes of his servant that he might see. So the Lord "opened" his eyes and he saw (v 17). Later in the city of Samaria, Elisha prays to the Lord to "open" the eyes of the enemy's men he has brought there. Thereupon He "opened" their eyes, and they saw that they were within the city (v 20). All occurrences of "open" here are with διανοίγω, and it is always the Lord who is behind this action, also after He had struck the latter men with temporary blindness (v 18).[31]

The Hebrew verb behind διανοίγω in all four cases here is פָּקַח, the most frequent verb in the MT for "opening" eyes.[32] I suggest that the Palestinian Jewish Christian author of the Emmaus narrative selected it in the Semitic original of Luke 24:31 first of all because of its association with Elisha, Elijah's disciple. Secondly, 2 Kgs 6:17 states that "the mountain was full of horses and chariots of fire all around Elisha." This imagery caused him to think of the present passage on the basis of 2 Kgs 2:11, only four chapters before, where at Elijah's ascension in Elisha's presence there were also chariot(s) and horses of fire. As pointed out numerous times above, 2 Kgs 2:11, especially in Judaic tradition, is a key verse for many of the expressions and motifs in the Emmaus narrative. When a Hellenistic Jewish Christian translated the Emmaus account into

---

[27] Neusner 31.261. This passage was noted by A. Schlatter in *Das Evangelium des Lukas* 458 as a Palestinian feature in the Emmaus narrative.

[28] BAGD 187.

[29] Against L. Johnson, *The Gospel of Luke* 397, who cites this passage as being echoed in Luke 24:31.

[30] Cf. J. Fitzmyer, *The Gospel According to Luke X-XXIV* 1568; M. Goulder, *Luke, A New Paradigm*, II 788; and R. Stein, *Luke* (The New American Commentary 24; Nashville: Broadman Press, 1992) 613.

[31] The Targum specifically notes that this is "temporary blindness." Cf. Sperber 2.285 and Harrington and Saldarini 276, as well as Jastrow 1518 on שברירא.

[32] BDB 824.

Greek, he employed διανοίγω at Luke 24:31, recognizing the background in 2 Kings 6, where the LXX has the same verb four times.

When the redeemed return to Zion / Jerusalem, Isa 35:5 states that "the eyes of the blind shall be opened" (פָּקַח).[33] One of the tasks of the Servant of the Lord is to perform precisely this task, "to open the eyes that are blind" (42:7). While the blind are literally to have their eyes opened, and therefore the Messiah heals the blind, the "opening" of closed eyes can be meant in a metaphorical sense, as in Luke 24:31.[34] It is Jesus, the Messiah (v 26), who as the Servant of the Lord "opens" the Scriptures to Cleopas and his companion while walking with them on the road (v 32).[35] This, in addition to Jesus' eating with them in Emmaus (v 30), led to their eyes' being "opened" (v 32) and their recognizing him.

Finally, it should be noted that a part of the original author's literary art consists in his employing the Semitic verb פָּקַח in v 31, and פָּתַח directly afterwards in v 32. The great similarity in sound would have been appreciated by the hearers (and later the readers).[36]

2) Recognizing Someone.

The Greek of the latter phrase in Luke 24:16, "but their eyes were kept 'from recognizing him,'" is: τοῦ μὴ ἐπιγνῶναι αὐτόν. Verse 31 is similar, which states, "Then their eyes were opened, 'and they recognized him'": καὶ ἐπέγνωσαν αὐτόν. Finally, v 35 has, "'and how he had been made known to them' in the breaking of bread": καὶ ὡς ἐγνώσθη αὐτοῖς.

The form ἐπιγνῶναι is the 2 aor. act. infin. of ἐπιγινώσκω, to recognize, know τινά someone again.[37] The form ἐπέγνωσαν is also 2 aor. act. indic., the third pers. pl. of the same verb. The third form,

---

[33] In *Pesiq. Rav Kah.* 9/4 (Braude and Kapstein 176) God says He will open the eyes of the blind (in the messianic future; Braude in n. 34 refers to Isa 35:5) just as He had already opened someone's eyes in 2 Kgs 6:17. Parallels are found in *Lev. Rab.* 'Emor 27/4 on Lev 22:27 (Soncino 4.347), and *Eccl. Rab.* 3:15 § 1 (Soncino 8.98-99).

[34] Isa 43:8 for example speaks of "people who are blind, yet have eyes."

[35] Cf. *Targ. Isa.* 42:7 on the Servant of the Lord (v 1; see also 43:10 for "My servant the Messiah"), whom the Lord appoints "to open the eyes of the house of Israel who are as it were blind to the law..." (Stenning 140-141). On Elijah, the Lord's servant (2 Kgs 10:10), as described in Sir 48:10 in terms of the Servant of the Lord passage Isa 49:6, see section 12. B.1) above.

[36] While פָּקַח can also be employed of eyes being opened (Gen 3: 5 and 7; Isa 35:5), in light of 2 Kings 6 פָּתַח is much more probable here.

[37] BAGD 291.

ἐγνώσθη, is the 1 aor. pass. indic., third per. sing. of the simple verb γινώσκω, "knowing" here in the sense of recognizing.[38]

I suggest that the Palestinian Jewish Christian author of the Emmaus narrative appropriated the imagery of "recognizing" from another OT passage dealing with Elijah. Only five chapters before Elijah and Elisha's walk together on the road before the former was taken up / ascended into heaven in 2 Kgs 2:11, there is another account of a meeting on the road. Because of the severe drought caused by Elijah, King Ahab of Samaria asked Obadiah, in charge of his palace, to go through the land in one direction looking for springs of water with grass in order to keep the horses and mules alive. 1 Kgs 18:7 then relates: "As Obadiah was on the way, Elijah 'met' him." Then "[Obadiah] 'recognized him,' fell on his face, and said: 'Is it you, my lord Elijah?'" Verse 8 continues by having Elijah reply positively.

The Hebrew for Elijah's "meeting" Obadiah in v 7 is לִקְרָאתוֹ, from קְרָא, to meet, encounter.[39] As a catchword it linked this verse to 2 Kings 1-2 (1:3, 6, 7 and 2:15), dealing with Elijah and Elisha. The expression "on the road" (בַּדֶּרֶךְ) also caused the Palestinian Jewish Christian author to relate 1 Kgs 18:7 to Judaic interpretation of 2 Kings 2, where Elijah and Elisha are also described as "walking" (on the road) from Gilgal to Jericho. In his own Emmaus narrative, the author has Cleopas and his companion "walk" towards the village in v 1, which motif is then repeated in vv 17 and 28, along with "on the road" in vv 32 and 35.

"And he [Obadiah] recognized him [Elijah]" in 1 Kgs 18:7 is the Hebrew וַיַּכִּרֵהוּ.[40] This verb is the hiphil of נכר, to recognize (as formerly known).[41] It is used of recognizing persons seven other times in the MT.[42] Both Delitzsch and the United Bible Societies in their Hebrew New Testaments employ the hiphil of נכר in Luke 24:16, 31 and 35.[43] "They recognized him" is הִכִּירוּהוּ.[44]

---

[38] *Ibid.*, 161, 1.b.

[39] BDB 896.

[40] Strangely, the LXX has the verb σπεύδω at this point: to press on, hasten (LSJ 1627).

[41] BDB 647-648.

[42] Gen 27:23; 42:7, 8 (twice); 1 Kgs 20:41; Job 2:12; and the proverbial phrase in Ruth 3:14.

[43] Cf. pp. 160-162 and 230-232, respectively.

[44] The Hellenistic Jewish Christian translator of the original Semitic narrative may have employed the passive of the simple verb γινώσκω in v 35 in order to vary the style. The meanings of "how he had been made known to them" (NRSV; "how he was known to them," RSV) and "they recognized him" are very

19. The Place-Name Emmaus.

A.

The Emmaus narrative begins by stating that on the same day (as Jesus' Resurrection) two of his adherents were going to a village named Emmaus (Ἐμμαοῦς), sixty stadia from Jerusalem (Luke 24:13). After Jesus joined them on the road, they urged him to lodge with them because it was already so late in the day. When he entered (one of their homes) to stay (overnight) with them, they first reclined at table for a common meal. Finally being recognized by them, Jesus then disappeared. Verse 33 relates: "That same hour they got up and returned to Jerusalem." In other words, the locality Emmaus, expressly labeled a village twice (vv 13 and 28), must have been close enough to the city in order to return there relatively easily in the evening. While I shall describe the site Emmaus extensively below in section VII., here I would simply like to point out the source of the Palestinian Jewish Christian author's inspiration for the name of the village, a passage in 2 Kings 2, so important for the entire Emmaus narrative.

B.

Before Elijah was taken up / ascended into heaven in 2 Kgs 2:11, he was on his way with his disciple Elisha from Gilgal (north of Bethel) to Bethel, to Jericho, and the Jordan. That is, the common journey on the road was downwards, a drop of at least 1131 meters (3711 feet).[45] As I shall point out in section VII. below, the NT road from Jerusalem to Emmaus also descended, although much less. Later Elijah's disciple Elisha then retraced the way up to Bethel (2 Kgs 2:23) alone, as Cleopas and his companion made their ascent back to Jerusalem alone, without Jesus.

After Elijah's ascent to heaven, Elisha recrossed the Jordan to the west and was met there by the company of prophets at Jericho. In addition, he was met by the people of the city, who maintained that its

---

similar. I doubt whether *Targ. Jon.* 1 Kgs 18:7 was influential at this point. It reads: "and he recognized him" (וְאִשְׁתְּמוֹדְעֵיהּ – Sperber 2.57; Harrington and Saldarini 251). The verb אִשְׁתְּמוֹדַע can mean to recognize or to be recognized (Jastrow 131, 2.3.), and it ultimately derives from the root יְדַע, to recognize, know (Jastrow 564-565).

[45] Jericho lies 250 m. below sea level, and Beitin (Arabic for Bethel) 881 m above sea level. Cf. F.-M. Abel, *Géographie de la Palestine* (Études Bibliques; Paris: Gabalda, 1967³), map VI at the end of volume I.

water was bad. Performing a miracle for them, he first asked for a new bowl into which salt should be put. When they brought this to him, Elisha went to "the spring of water," threw the salt into it, and spoke a blessing over it, thus purifying it (2 Kgs 2:19-22). The spring is now known as Elisha's spring by Jews and Christians, and 'Ayn al-Sultan by Moslems. It still today produces 4500 liters of excellent water per minute.[46]

The Hebrew for "the spring of water" in 2 Kgs 2:21 is מוֹצָא הַמַּיִם. Deriving from the root יצא, to go or come out,[47] מוֹצָא means a place or act of going forth, "source" or "spring."[48] In the latter sense it occurs only six times in the MT, one of them being here.[49]

I suggest that the term מוֹצָא, found in the chapter so important to the Palestinian Jewish Christian author of the Emmaus narrative, 2 Kings 2, caused him to think of the village of his own time near Jerusalem also called מוֹצָא.[50] It lay only 7 km or 4.2 miles west of the city, and one could easily return from it within a short period of time, as Cleopas and his companion are portrayed as doing in Luke 24:33. Josephus in *Bell.* 7.217 calls this village "Emmaus": Ἀμμαοῦς.

The association of the "spring" מוֹצָא in 2 Kgs 2:21 and the village מוֹצָא near Jerusalem may seem farfetched to a modern person. At the time, however, it was a frequent method of associating two quantities. One good example of this is *Sifre* Deut. 'Eqeb 41 on Deut 11:13, noted above in section 13. The "Damascus" of Cant 7:5 is interpreted there of Elijah because in 1 Kgs 19:15 the prophet is told to return to "Damascus." While not employing two biblical verses at this point, the Palestinian Jewish Christian author of the Emmaus narrative used the same basic method of association for מוֹצָא / מוֹצָא.

I shall describe the site of the village מוֹצָא – Emmaus just west of Jerusalem more extensively below in section VII. The above suffices to point out that the author of the Emmaus account thought of it because of

---

[46] Cf. O. Keel and M. Küchler, *Orte und Landschaften der Bibel*, 2 (Zurich: Benziger; Göttingen: Vandenhoeck & Ruprecht, 1982) 494. The exact location of Jericho is shown on the map on p. 495. See also the article "Jericho" by N. Avigad and the editors in *EJ* (1971) 9.1365 and 1370.

[47] Cf. BDB 422-425. Water "goes out," for example, in Gen 2:10; Exod 17:6; Num 20:11; and Judg 15:19.

[48] BDB 425, 3.a. as source or spring of water.

[49] Cf. also Isa 41:18; 58:11; Ps 107:33 and 35; and 2 Chr 32:30. It does not occur in rabbinic Hebrew. The more usual designations in both biblical and rabbinic Hebrew are עַיִן and מַעְיָן.

[50] Cf. Jastrow 746.

the occurrence of the same term, מוֹצָא, in 2 Kings 2, a chapter so important for the background of his narrative.

*   *   *

The above nineteen expressions and motifs were associated with Elijah and his disciple Elisha, and 2 Kings 2, mostly in Judaic tradition. They form the main background to the Emmaus narrative. Yet the Palestinian Jewish Christian author also drew upon Judaic interpretation of another biblical chapter, Judges 19, in order to fill out several details of his narrative.

II. Motifs from Judges 19

The incident of the Levite's concubine in Judges 19 deals with homosexuality, gang rape and murder. Yet its relevance to Luke 24:29 is noted, for example, in the margin of the Nestle-Aland Greek New Testament[26].   C. Montefiore remarks on this verse: "It is odd to find in this beautiful tale a verbal reminiscence of the ugly story in Judges xix.9."[51]   Nevertheless, this biblical chapter appears to have also influenced the lovely Christmas story in Luke 2:1-20,[52] as well as the Emmaus narrative.

One reason for the author's association of the incident of the Levite's concubine in Judges 19 and Elijah, especially in 2 Kings 2, is that these two passages were already connected in early Judaic tradition. This is shown in *Pseudo-Philo*, a Palestinian writing originally in Hebrew from the beginning of the first century CE.[53] Chapter 45 deals with the Levite and his concubine, and 46-48 are concerned with the rest of the incident in Judges 20-21. Here in *Pseudo-Philo* the Phinehas of Judg 20:28 is consulted as priest in order to determine the further behavior of the Israelites (chapter 46), and he speaks of himself in terms of the zealot Phinehas in Numbers 25 (chapter 47). Because Phinehas is equated in this writing with Elijah, he is portrayed in terms of the prophet,

---

[51] *The Synoptic Gospels*, 2.637.

[52] Cf. "but no one took them in to spend the night" in Judg 19:15 (and 18) and Luke 2:7; the journey from northern Israel to Bethlehem and back in both narratives; as well as the Levite's "concubine" in Judges 19 and Mary as not yet fully married in Luke 2:5.

[53] Cf. D. Harrington's remarks in *OTP* 2.299-300.

including his ascension (48; see 2 Kgs 2:11).[54] In *Pseudo-Philo* the author intentionally changes the city Gibeah, to which the Levite and his concubine go, to Nob, showing his artistic freedom. The Palestinian Jewish Christian author of the account now found in Luke 24:13-35 applied the following five motifs and expressions from Judges 19 to his own artistic creation, the Emmaus narrative.[55]

1. A Stranger.

A.

When Cleopas and his companion were walking from Jerusalem to Emmaus, talking to each other about "all these things that had happened" (Luke 24:14), Jesus, (coming from the direction of Jerusalem), caught up and walked with them. When he asked them what they were discussing while walking along, Cleopas answered with a counter question in v 18: "Are you the only stranger in Jerusalem who does not know the things that have taken place there in these days?"

Jesus' two adherents are described later on as urging him to stay overnight (in the home of one of them) and to eat with them, for the day was nearly over. This he then did (vv 29-30). Here Cleopas and his companion are presented as residents of the village of Emmaus near Jerusalem.

The Evangelist Luke notes in 4:44 that Jesus proclaimed his message in the synagogues of Judea. According to 5:17, Pharisees and teachers of the law had come from the villages of Judea and from Jerusalem to hear him teach in Galilee. From all of Judea and Jerusalem many people came to hear Jesus and to be healed by him (6:17). When he raised the son of the widow at Nain from the dead, the news of this event "spread throughout Judea" (7:17). Finally, at Jesus' hearing before Pilate in Jerusalem, the chief priests and the crowds maintain: "He stirs up the people by teaching throughout all Judea, from Galilee where he began even to this place" (23:5).

While some these passages are certainly from the hand of the Evangelist, there is good reason to believe that Jesus not only had a

---

[54] Cf. *OTP* 2.359-362, with n. "a." Harrington labels chapter 48 "The ascension of Phinehas." L. Ginzberg in *Legends* 6.316, n. 3, maintains this is the earliest known attestation of the identification of Elijah and Phinehas.

[55] It may also be noted that the expression "the two of them" (שְׁנֵיהֶם) connects 2 Kings 2 and Judges 19 (verses 6 and 8), it reappearing in Luke 24:13. Interestingly, in *b. Giṭ.* 6b (Soncino 20-21) on Judges 19, Elijah appears and settles a dispute regarding the correct interpretation of this biblical passage.

Galilean ministry, but also, as indicated above, a Judean one, even if shorter. The various pilgrimages to Jerusalem mentioned in the Gospel of John also presuppose this,[56] as do the Apostle Paul's statements about the churches, plural, in Judea (1 Thess 2:14; Gal 1:22). The Palestinian Jewish Christian author of the Emmaus narrative describes Cleopas and his companion as such Judean followers of Jesus.

When Jesus of Nazareth spoke to the two of them on their way home to Emmaus, they noticed his Galilean accent, just as the maid of the high priest recognized Peter in Jerusalem as a Galilean (Mark 14:70 and Luke 22:59; Matt 26:73 has "your accent betrays you").[57] Assuming that Jesus is returning to Galilee after attending part of the Passover festival in Jerusalem, or much less probably that he had temporarily been in the city for some other reason, Cleopas addresses him: "Are you the only stranger in Jerusalem...?"

The Greek here is: σὺ μόνος παροικεῖς Ἰερουσαλήμ. While the verb παροικέω can simply mean to inhabit or live in a place, here the meaning is to inhabit a place as a stranger, as in the LXX.[58] I suggest that the Palestinian Jewish Christian author of the Emmaus narrative borrowed the equivalent Semitic expression from Judges 19.

B.

The account of the Levite and his concubine in Judges 19 begins by stating that "a certain Levite, 'residing' in the remote parts of the hill country of Ephraim, took to himself a concubine from Bethlehem in Judah" (v 1). Later on in the narrative, when no one befriends them in the open square of Gibeah by offering to take them in for the night, an old man came from his work in the field. "The man was from the hill country of Ephraim, and 'he was residing' in Gibeah," which was of

---

[56] Cf. John 2:13; 5:1; 7:14; and 12:1. See also the "how often" of Matt 23:37 // Luke 13:34.

[57] There is no reason whatsoever to consider Cleopas and his companion as Galileans. Against M. Goulder (*Luke, A New Paradigm, II* 781), who bases his interpretation on Jesus' statement in Mark 14:28 (see also 16:7), "But after I am raised up, I will go before you to Galilee." This means the Resurrection appearances there, not a literal "walking" to the north. For the latter reason, Goulder considers Emmaus to be located north of Jerusalem, which is wrong.

[58] The LXX usage is "mostly of strangers, who live in a place without holding citizenship..." (BAGD 628-629).

another tribe, the Benjaminites (v 16). It was he, a "stranger" in Gibeah, who then befriended the "strangers" seeking shelter for the night.[59]

The Hebrew for "residing" in both verses is the verb גּוּר. It means to sojourn or dwell as a newcomer, without any inherited rights,[60] that is, to be a real stranger. In the LXX, παροικέω usually translates גּוּר.[61] This is also the case in LXX Judg 19:1 and 16. I suggest that the Palestinian Jewish Christian author of the Emmaus narrative appropriated the term גּוּר from Judg 19:1 and 16 and described Jesus the Galilean as such a "stranger," one who had gone from Galilee to Jerusalem, and was now on his way home to Galilee via the Emmaus road. When a Hellenistic Jewish Christian translated the narrative into Greek, he used for גּוּר the standard παροικέω, as in the LXX of Judg 19:1 and 16. This accounts for the very rare occurrence of παροικέω in Luke 24:18, which except for Heb 11:9 is only found here in the NT.

2. Urging.

A.

When the three wayfarers approached the village of Emmaus, Jesus acted as if he would continue on, leaving Cleopas and his companion there. "But they urged him strongly, saying, 'Stay with us, because it is almost evening and the day is now nearly over.' So he went in to stay with them" (Luke 24:29).

The Greek of "But they urged him strongly" is: καὶ παρεβιάσαντο αὐτόν. The verb παραβιάζομαι means to *use force* to accomplish something, here to urge strongly, prevail upon.[62] Except for Acts 16:15, where Lydia "urges" Paul and his helpers to come and stay at her home in Philippi, this is the only occurrence of the verb in the NT. I suggest that the Palestinian Jewish Christian author of the Emmaus narrative borrowed the Semitic form of the verb from Judges 19.

---

[59] Cf. also *Pseudo-Philo* 45:3 on this incident, where the inhabitants of the city say: "It has never happened that 'the strangers' gave orders to the natives" (*OTP* 2.359; the Latin *advene* is in Harrington 1.306).

[60] BDB 157. The same holds true for a גֵּר (p. 158). The verb can also simply mean to abide or dwell somewhere, yet the whole context in Judges 19 argues against this meaning here. The Levite and his party are treated as if they had no rights whatsoever.

[61] Cf. Hatch-Redpath 1071.

[62] BAGD 612; LSJ 1305, here to constrain or compel.

B.

When the Levite from Ephraim went to Bethlehem to retrieve his concubine, his father-in-law first made him stay with him three days, so the man and his servant ate, drank and stayed there. When they prepared to leave on the fourth day, the father-in-law requested that they first eat together. So the "two of them" (Judg 19:6; see also v 8, 2 Kgs 2:6-8, 11, and Luke 24:13) sat down to eat and drink together. Then the concubine's father asked his son-in-law: "Why not spend the night and enjoy yourself?" After the meal, the Levite got up to go, but "his father-in-law 'kept urging him' until he stayed and spent the night there again" (v 7).

The Hebrew of "kept urging him" here is: וַיִּפְצָר-בּוֹ. The verb פָּצַר literally means to push or press, but here as in eight other cases to "urge."[63] LXX Judg 19:7 A and B both translate with the simple form ἐβιάσαντο.[64]

I suggest that the Palestinian Jewish Christian author of the Emmaus narrative borrowed the motif of "urging" in Luke 24:29 from its occurrence in Judg 19:7. There it is also found in connection with "staying" (see the next section, 3.), and with the day's declining (v 8) and its drawing to a close (v 9), also reflected in Luke 24:29. An additional reason for the author's thinking of פָּצַר in Judg 19:7 may have been its occurrence in 2 Kgs 2:17 (with "stay" in vv 2, 4 and 6), a chapter so important for his whole account.

3. *Staying.*

A.

As pointed out in section I. 10. above, Luke 24:29 has Cleopas and his companion say: " '*Stay* with us, because it is almost evening and the day is now nearly over.' So [Jesus] went in *to stay* with them." Both Greek verbs are from μένω, primarily meaning to remain, stay, but often as here in the special sense of to stay (overnight) with someone, to lodge.[65]

---

[63] BDB 823, including the better readings in 1 Sam 28:23; 2 Sam 13:25 and 27; and 2 Kgs 5:23. On the textual corruptions, cf. also BDB 829 on פרץ, 10.

[64] The Greek παραβιάζομαι renders פרץ בּ in five of the seven LXX occurrences of the verb with a Hebrew equivalent. Cf. Hatch-Redpath 1056, including 1 Kgdms 28:23 (see the previous note for the corrupt forms).

[65] BAGD 503.

Above I suggested that the twofold emphasis on "staying" here is due first of all to the repetition of the singular imperative "Stay!" in 2 Kgs 2:2, 4 and 6: שֵׁב. The Palestinian Jewish Christian author of the Emmaus narrative received his primary inspiration for the motif of staying from the account of Elijah and Elisha's walking together before the former was taken up / ascended. He based the actual formulation, however, on the episode in Judges 19.

B.

After the Levite's father-in-law made him stay at his home in Bethlehem, the former "stayed" (יֵּשֶׁב) with him three days. When they had eaten and drunk, they "spent the night" there (Judg 19:4). The latter verb is לִין, לוּן, to lodge or pass the night.[66] Here the verbs יֵשׁב, to stay, and לוּן, to spend the night, are synonyms.

Verse 7, containing the expression "urging" analyzed above in section 2., continues the narrative after the Levite spent the night at his father-in-law's. It reads: "When the man got up to go, his father-in-law kept urging him. He then 'stayed' and spent the night there."[67] The verb יֵשׁב is employed here for "stayed," and "spent the night" is לוּן, as in v 4.

I suggest that the Palestinian Jewish Christian author of the Emmaus narrative borrowed the expression "to urge" from Judg 19:7, and then continued by borrowing the term "to stay" (יֵשׁב) directly after it in the same verse. He employed יֵשׁב in the sense of "staying overnight," as in Judg 19:4. When a Hellenistic Jewish Christian translated the Emmaus account into Greek, he employed μένω, as is also found at times in the LXX.[68]

The probability of the above suggestion is increased by the next two sections, dealing with the appropriation of imagery from the nearby verses Judg 19:9 and 6.

---

[66] BDB 533.

[67] The NRSV unfortunately omits here the verb for remaining, probably considering it redundant.

[68] Cf. Gen 24:55; Ps 9:7; 101:12; and Zech 14:10. Only in several minor MSS of Judg 19:9 does μένω translate the לוּן of the MT (see Rahlfs 1.482, apparatus of A).

4. *The Day is Now Nearly Over.*

A.

Cleopas and his companion strongly urge Jesus to stay (overnight) with them in Emmaus "because it is almost evening and the day is nearly over" (Luke 24:29). This is in Greek: ὅτι πρὸς ἑσπέραν ἐστὶν καὶ κέκλικεν ἤδη ἡ ἡμέρα. It is the only occurrence in Luke of a double time reference.[69] This phenomenon alone points to a source as probably being used here.

The noun ἑσπέρα, "evening," only occurs here in the four Gospels.[70] The term κλίνω, to incline or bend, is found seven times in the NT, yet only here and in Luke 9:12 of the day's "declining" or "being far spent."[71] Except for LXX Jer 6:4 and the plural "days" as declining like a shadow in LXX Ps 101:11, the only occurrences of the day's "declining" with κλίνω in the LXX are found in Judg 19:8, 9 and 11. The incident of the Levite's concubine in this chapter also provides the background for the time references in Luke 24:29.

B.

Judges 19 is simply full of time references. In addition to "spending the night" or "staying (overnight)," they are found in vv 5, 8, 9, 11, 14, 16, 25, 26 and 27. The only verse with a multiple time reference, however, is 9. It reads:

> When the man with his concubine and his servant got up to leave, his father-in-law, the girl's father, said to him: "Look, the day has worn on until it is almost evening. Spend the night. See, the day has drawn to a close. Spend the night here and enjoy yourself. Tomorrow you can get up early in the morning for your journey, and go home."

The phrase "the day has worn on until it is almost evening" in Hebrew is: רָפָה הַיּוֹם לַעֲרֹב. The verb רָפָה means to sink or decline,[72]

---

[69] Cf. I. Marshall's remark: "it is noteworthy that Luke, who often abbreviates Mark's double time-expressions, here has one of his own" (*The Gospel of Luke*, 898).

[70] Cf. also Acts 4:3; 20:15 v. 1.; and 28:23.

[71] BAGD 436.

[72] BDB 951, 1.

the verb עָרַב to become evening.[73] The phrase could thus be translated: "The day is declining / turning towards evening." Twilight should not already be envisaged here, however, for it is still called "evening" in v 16 after the party has journeyed some 13 km (8 miles) from Bethlehem to Gibeah north of Jerusalem.

The phrase "the day has drawn to a close" in v 9 is in Hebrew: חֲנוֹת הַיּוֹם. The verb חָנָה means to decline, bend down, encamp, and here to decline in the sense of the day's drawing to its close.[74]

I suggest that the Palestinian Jewish Christian author of the Emmaus narrative appropriated the imagery of a double time reference in Judg 19:9 and slightly modified it in Luke 24:29. If his account was in Hebrew, it could have been something like the following: כִּי הָעֶרֶב קָרֵב וּכְבָר נָטָה / פָּנָה הַיּוֹם, "for evening has approached, and the day is already declining / going away."[75] When a Hellenistic Jewish Christian translated this account into Greek, he recognized the imagery as deriving from Judg 19:9. He therefore employed terms from the LXX of that verse, which, however, condensed the two Hebrew phrases into one: εἰς ἑσπέραν κέκλικεν ἡ ἡμέρα.

The final borrowing from Judges 19 has to do with reclining at dinner and derives from v 6.

5. Reclining at Dinner.

A.

After Jesus entered the home of either Cleopas or his companion in Emmaus, Luke 24:30 continues by stating: " 'When he was at the table with them,' he took bread, blessed and broke it, and gave it to them." The Greek of the first phrase is: καὶ ἐγένετο ἐν τῷ κατακλιθῆναι αὐτὸν μετ' αὐτῶν. The NRSV does not indicate whether the three were sitting

---

[73] BDB 788.

[74] BDB 333, 1., who call attention to similar expressions in vv 8 and 11.

[75] On נטה and פנה, see Jastrow 898, 2) and 1187, 2), respectively. The first verb is found in Judg 19:8. On this reconstruction, cf. also the Hebrew New Testaments of Delitzsch (p. 161) and the United Bible Societies (p. 231). The verb רפה does not seem to be employed in rabbinic Hebrew of the day's "declining" (Jastrow 1490), yet the phrase from Judg 19:9 is found in modern Hebrew (Alcalay 2478). For a first century CE paraphrase of Judg 19:9, see Josephus' retelling of the incident in *Ant.* 5.138.

or reclining here. The primary meaning of κατακλίνομαι, however, is to recline at dinner.[76]

I suggest that the Semitic original of this term was derived from Judaic tradition on Judg 19:6.

B.

On the fourth day of the Levite's stay in Bethlehem, his father-in-law encouraged him to fortify himself with some food before departing. Judg 19:6 then continues: "So they sat down, and the two of them ate together and drank." *Targum Jonathan* on this verse, however, has instead of their sitting down: "they reclined" - ואסחרו.[77] The af. form of סחר here means to recline around the table, to dine.[78] D. Harrington and A. Saldarini correctly note about this passage that the Targum "assumes one reclines to eat, according to the custom of its own time."[79] The father-in-law of the Levite is not pictured here as preparing a large banquet for the Levite, with many honored guests. It was rather a normal meal for the two of them before the son-in-law went home, a meal at which both "reclined" to eat and drink. I suggest that the Palestinian Jewish Christian author of the Emmaus narrative, who appropriated other imagery from Judg 19:1 and 16 ("stranger"), 7 ("urging" and "staying"), and 9 (the day's declining towards evening), also knew of the Judaic "reclining at dinner" interpretation of v 6 now still found in the Targum.[80] He then employed it for Jesus' reclining at table with Cleopas and his companion in Emmaus, a meal which would not have differed much from that of the Levite and his father-in-law in Judges 19. The Hellenistic Jewish Christian translator of the Emmaus account then correctly rendered the Semitic term by κατακλίνομαι.

* * *

---

[76] BAGD 411, passive; LSJ 894, passive: lie at table. See also ἀνάκειμαι in BAGD 55,2., and Str-B 2.257 on Luke 22:27.

[77] Sperber 2.86.

[78] Jastrow 971,4). He calls attention to the hiphil of סבב as used similarly.

[79] *Targum Jonathan of the Former Prophets* 94, n. 5.

[80] The *final* date of the present Targum to the Former Prophets, of course, has nothing to do with the age of individual traditions now found within it. Cf. the balanced discussion in Harrington and Saldarini 13-14.

The above five expressions can be questioned individually. The cumulative argument is strong, however, that the Palestinian Jewish Christian author of the Emmaus narrative employed imagery and a setting (a journey on the road to a place and back again) not only in regard to Elijah and his disciple Elisha, especially as developed in Judaic tradition on 2 Kings 2, but also in regard to Judges 19. As pointed out above, the incident of the Levite and his concubine was already connected at an early time with the figure of Elijah (Phinehas) and his ascension. In section V. B. below I shall describe the implications of the appropriation of this imagery and the setting for the purposes of the original Emmaus record.

III.   The Original Language, Provenance and Genre.

1.   *The Original Language.*

Throughout section I. above I cited major affinities of the Emmaus narrative to Palestinian Judaic traditions on the prophet Elijah, especially in regard to 2 Kings 2. Almost all of these sources are in Hebrew, or were originally written in Hebrew (e.g. Sirach). Hebrew was the original language of *Pseudo-Philo*, a Palestinian work from the beginning of the first century CE,[81] and most of the Dead Sea Scrolls literature is in Hebrew. It is thus quite possible that this was the original language of the Emmaus account. I list in a table below ten indications of the Semitic background of the pericope, all in Hebrew.

Elsewhere I have analyzed other materials from "Special L" in Luke 2:1-20,[82] 2:41-51a,[83] 10:25-37,[84] 15:11-32,[85] and 23:39-43.[86] Each time I ascertained a Semitic original always worked over by the gifted Greek

---

[81] Cf. *OTP* 2.298-300. The same view is held for *The Lives of the Prophets* by numerous scholars. Cf. *OTP* 2.380-382.

[82] *Weihnachten, Barmherziger Samariter, Verlorener Sohn.* Studien zu ihrem jüdischen Hintergrund (ANTZ 2; Berlin: Institut Kirche und Judentum, 1988) 11-58.

[83] *Samuel, Saul and Jesus.* Three Early Palestinian Jewish Christian Gospel Haggadoth (SFSHJ 105; Atlanta: Scholars Press, 1994) 1-64.

[84] *Weihnachten, Barmherziger Samariter, Verlorener Sohn* 59-125.

[85] *Ibid.,* 126-173.

[86] *Samuel, Saul and Jesus* 157-173.

stylist Luke, yet nevertheless still clearly visible. This is also true for Luke 24:13-35.[87] While Aramaic is possible for the original version of the Emmaus narrative,[88] (and the Hebrew would have been translated into Aramaic at a very early stage anyway in order to reach a broader audience), in light of the following table I consider Hebrew to be the original language. My main point is simply that it was originally in Semitic.

Table with Signs of the Semitic Background of Luke 24:13-35

1)	V 13: Καὶ ἰδού	וְהִנֵּה
	V 25: τοῦ πιστεύειν ἐπί	מַהֲאֲמִין בְּ'
2)	V 13: δύο ἐξ αὐτῶν	שְׁנֵיהֶם
3)	דבר both as the verb "to speak," and as the noun "word / matter / thing."	
	V 14: "and they were talking"	וְהֵם דִּבְּרוּ
	V 15: "while they were talking"	בְּדַבְּרָם
	V 17: "these words"	הַדְּבָרִים הָאֵלֶּה
	V 21: "these things"	הַדְּבָרִים הָאֵלֶּה
	V 25: "they have spoken"	דִּבְּרוּ
	V 27: "the things" about himself	אֵת הַדְּבָרִים
	V 32: "while he was talking" to us	כְּשֶׁדִּבֶּר
4)	The extensive use of αὐτός / αὐτοί, especially before the verb, for הוּא / הֵם.	
	V 14: καὶ αὐτοὶ ὡμίλουν	וְהֵם דִּבְּרוּ
	V 21: ὅτι αὐτός ἐστιν	כִּי זֶה הוּא

---

[87] Cf. section V. A. below for Lukan redaction of the original narrative.

[88] Cf. my reference to the Targum of Judg 19:6 in regard to the "reclining" of Luke 24:30 above in section II. 5.

	V 25: καὶ αὐτὸς εἶπεν	וְהוּא אָמַר
	V 28: καὶ αὐτὸς προσεποιήσατο	...וְהוּא
	V 31: καὶ αὐτὸς ἄφαντος ἐγένετο	וְהוּא נִגְנַז
	V 35: καὶ αὐτοὶ ἐξηγοῦντο	וְהֵם סִפְּרוּ
5)	V 18: μόνος	לְבַד
	V 25: καρδία	לֵבָ(ב)
	V 32: καρδία	לֵבָ(ב)
6)	V 25: καὶ βραδεῖς τῇ καρδίᾳ	וְכִבְדֵי לֵב
	V 26: τὴν δόξαν αὐτοῦ	כְּבוֹדוֹ
7)	V 27: διερμήνευσεν	באר
	V 32: καιομένη ἦν	בער
8)	שׁוּב , to return, hiphil to answer; יָשַׁב , to remain.	
	V 18: ἀποκριθείς	הֵשִׁיב
	V 19: οἱ δὲ εἶπαν αὐτῷ	הֵשִׁיבוּ לוֹ
	V 29: μεῖνον	שֵׁב
	V 29: τοῦ μεῖναι	לָשֶׁבֶת
	V 33: ὑπέστρεψαν	יָשׁוּבוּ
9)	V 31: διηνοίχθησαν	נִפְקְחוּ (פקח)
	V 32: διήνοιγεν	פָּתַח
10)	V 34: ὄντως	בֶּאֱמֶת

The Palestinian Jewish Christian author of the Emmaus narrative showed his great artistic ability by employing the same Semitic root in various ways, including assonance and wordplays. This would have been very appealing to his first hearers (and later readers). Unfortunately, this part of the narrator's art was lost when the account was later translated into Greek.

2. The Provenance.

As indicated by the original language, Hebrew or possibly Aramaic, Palestine is the most probable provenance of the Emmaus narrative. This can be narrowed down, however. The appearance of the resurrected Jesus to Cleopas and his companion is not represented as taking place in Galilee, which would speak for a Galilean Jewish Christian author. Instead, the two adherents of Jesus are depicted as returning from attending the Passover festival in Jerusalem to the village of Emmaus just to the west of the capital. It is there that they invite the "stranger" to eat and stay (overnight) at the home of one of them. That is, Cleopas and his companion stand for a Jewish Christian community in Judea, with its headquarters in Jerusalem.[89] As I have indicated before, the Apostle Paul mentions the churches of Judea in 1 Thess 2:14 and Gal 1:22 (cf. Acts 26:20), and there are some indications that Jesus may have had a more extensive ministry in Judea and Jerusalem than is generally thought.[90]

The Palestinian Jewish Christian community in Jerusalem and Judea greatly revered the figure of Elijah, as shown in the large number of references to this prophet in the materials from Special Luke which entered the Third Gospel.[91] There was even a Judaic tradition that Elijah's hometown was Jerusalem.[92] This special Judean / Jerusalem reverence for the prophet Elijah also explains why the Gospel of Luke, which clearly draws on them, is the only Gospel to have an account at the end of Jesus' "ascension." It too was modeled on that of Elijah in 2 Kings 2, a text so important for the Emmaus account.

A. Schlatter proposed that the Emmaus narrative was the Easter story of those who led not only the Christian community in Jerusalem,

---

[89] Cf. on this J. Nolland, *Luke 18:35 - 24:53*, 1200.

[90] Cf. Luke 4:44; 7:17; and 23:5, as well as 5:17 and 6:17. It is improbable that all these references are only due to Luke himself. The Evangelist John also indicates that Jesus was in Judea and Jerusalem for various festivals (2:13 – 25; 5:1; 10:22; 11:7; and 13:1).

[91] Cf. again M. Öhler, *Elia im Neuen Testament* 175-244, with the table on p. 233. Öhler, however, views Luke himself as the author of many of these pericopes, based on the LXX.

[92] Cf. 1 Chr 8:27-28, and *Exod. Rab.* Ki Thissa 40/4 on Exod 31:2 (Mirqin 6.128-129; Soncino 3.463), as well as *Gen. Rab.* Vayetze 71/9 on Gen 30:11 (Theodor and Albeck 833-834; Soncino 2.659-660), and *Eliyyahu Rabbah* 18 (Friedmann 97; Braude and Kapstein 256-257, with notes).

but also the entire church from there.[93] W. Grundmann, borrowing an idea from A. von Harnack, even contended that the Emmaus narrative was the Easter story of Jesus' own family, which belonged to the original core of the Jerusalem Christian community. It was perhaps designed to contend with, or even to take priority over, the appearances to the Twelve.[94] While both of these suggestions are purely speculative, at least the first is quite possible.[95] All that can be said with any degree of probability, however, is that the Palestinian Jewish Christian author of the Emmaus narrative was a Judean (or perhaps even a native of Jerusalem). He may have known of Jesus' Resurrection appearances to his disciples in Galilee,[96] yet he greatly wanted to have one also in Judea, his home region. Thus his choice of the road to Emmaus / Moṣa just west of Jerusalem, within Judea, for the setting of the beautiful narrative he composed.

3. The Genre.

While G. Petzke considers the Emmaus narrative to have the form of instruction given to the disciples,[97] H. D. Betz would label it a "cultic legend," dealing with teaching and proclamation in the form of a narrative.[98] On the basis of Jesus' sudden disappearing after Cleopas and his companion recognize him in 24:31, a number of commentators point to classical and Hellenistic parallels to the recognition scene in a Greek drama, or to figures such as Romulus or Apollonius of Tyana.[99]

---

[93] *Das Evangelium des Lukas*, 454. For his view that the author was definitely a Jewish Christian, cf. 453.

[94] *Das Evangelium nach Lukas* (THKNT 3; Berlin: Evangelische Verlagsanstalt, 1984[10]) 443.

[95] Cf. John 20, which also mentions Jesus' ascension in v 17, and the Jerusalem appearance of Jesus to the disciples in vv 19-29 after the narrative of the empty tomb. Chapter 21 then records an appearance in Galilee.

[96] Cf. Mark 14:28 and 16:7, as well as John 21.

[97] *Das Sondergut des Evangeliums nach Lukas* (Zurich: Theologischer Verlag, 1990) 202.

[98] "Ursprung und Wesen christlichen Glaubens nach der Emmauslegende (Lk. 24, 13-32)" in *ZTK* 66 (1969) 8. The essay is also in English as "The Origin and Nature of Christian Faith according to the Emmaus Legend" in *Int* 23 (1969) 32-46, unavailable to me.

[99] Cf. E. Klostermann in *Das Lukasevangelium* (HNT 5; Tübingen: Mohr/Siebeck, 1929[2]) 238; A. Ehrhardt, "The Disciples of Emmaus" in *NTS* 10 (1963-64) 194-196; H. D. Betz, "Ursprung und Wesen" 9, n. 8; and L. Johnson, *The Gospel of Luke* 398.

For this reason the term ἀναγνωρισμός has been suggested, a narrative aiming at recognition and reunification.[100]

Since Cleopas and his companion finally "recognize" Jesus in Emmaus, the Greek term ἀναγνωρισμός could be employed for the account. However, it should rather be called an "appearance narrative," for in it Jesus appears to his followers after his Resurrection. Its structure is based on the appearances the angel Elijah was thought to make to human beings after he ascended or was taken up to heaven in 2 Kings 2. There he is often represented as suddenly appearing to someone, posing a question, answering it himself, providing the proper interpretation of Scripture, and then leaving for elsewhere, as Jesus also does in the Emmaus account. Gentile Christians or interested pagan readers of the Greek version of Luke 24:13-35 may have thought of similar classical and Hellenistic figures who appeared to humans after their own death. The first hearers of the Semitic Emmaus narrative, however, rather recalled the very popular prophet Elijah's appearing to, and disappearing from, human beings on earth. Such Elijah stories are also "appearance narratives," and in many of them the prophet appears without a disguise and is recognized immediately. The latter is not the case, however, for Cleopas and his companion in regard to Jesus because their eyes are first (divinely) kept from recognizing Jesus until he interprets the Scriptures to apply to himself as the Messiah, and he breaks bread with them (24:31-32), as he had done so often before during his earthly life.

Especially in light of the Elijah background of the pericope, the original and present Emmaus account can thus best be described as an "appearance narrative."

IV. The Historicity of the Narrative.

In regard to its historicity, the Emmaus account is usually either considered to be completely genuine, pure legend, or based on a distant original experience.

---

[100] Cf. for example W. Grundmann, *Das Evangelium nach Lukas* 442, citing K. Kerenyi, *Die griechisch-orientalische Romanliteratur in religionsgeschichtlicher Beleuchtung* (Tübingen, 1927) 87 ff.

A strong representative of the first category is N. Geldenhuys, who maintains: "The Emmaus story in these verses bears throughout the stamp of genuineness, and every unprejudiced reader of it feels that it has been taken from actual life."[1] M.-J. Lagrange at the end of his analysis of the narrative also calls it "un fait réel et historique."[2] In regard to the name Cleopas, A. Plummer notes: "The mention of the name is a mark of reality."[3] Since the name of Cleopas' companion is not mentioned, however, various suggestions have been made as to his identity, also as a warrant for the narrative's historicity: a) St Luke.[4] b) Peter.[5] c) Sim(e)on, the son of Cleopas.[6] d) Philip.[7] Finally, the early church historian Eusebius of Caesarea thought that originally the Emmaus narrative was handed down by Jesus' own family.[8] All of the above maintain that the Emmaus narrative is completely historical.

The opposite opinion is maintained, for example, by R. Bultmann, who wrote that the account "has the character of a true legend."[9] C. Montefiore agreed, calling the story in its present form "surely sheer legend."[10]

---

[1] *Commentary on the Gospel of Luke* (NICNT 3; Grand Rapids, Michigan: Eerdmans, 1966) 636.

[2] *Évangile selon Saint Luc* (EB; Paris: Gabalda, 1921²) 610.

[3] *The Gospel According to S. Luke* (ICC 33; Edinburgh: Clark, 1956⁵) 553. Cf. also I. Marshall, *The Gospel of Luke* 894: "it is likely that the person was known to Luke's readers...."

[4] Cf. the remarks by A. Edersheim in *The Life and Times of Jesus the Messiah* 2.638.

[5] J. Lightfoot, *A Commentary on the New Testament from the Talmud and Hebraica* (Oxford: Oxford University, 1859; reprint 1989) 3.218.

[6] So apparently A. Schlatter in *Das Evangelium des Lukas* 454, who believes Cleopas' son led the church in Jerusalem up to the time of Trajan. Cf. also T. Zahn as cited by E. Klostermann in *Das Lukasevangelium* 233. He also notes earlier opinions.

[7] L. Sabourin, *L'Évangile de Luc* (Rome: Editrice Pontificia Università Gregorìana, 1985) 379-380.

[8] Cf. E. Ellis, *The Gospel of Luke* (NCB; London: Oliphants, 1977) 277. See also n. 94 above.

[9] *The History of the Synoptic Tradition* 286.

[10] *The Synoptic Gospels*, 2.641. Cf. also M. Dibelius, *From Tradition to Gospel* 191, who maintains that the legend "has been preserved in an almost pure form." Interestingly, A. Loisy in *L'Évangile selon Luc* (Paris: 1924; reprint Frankfurt am Main: Minerva, 1971) 584 says the Emmaus narrative is from a vision which came spontaneously to a Christian prophet.

Between these two extremes there is the view that although the Emmaus story in its present form is very much amplified, there is probably an historical basis to it. W. Manson believes, for example, it is probable that "the Emmaus-narrative represents a certain elaboration of some original experience...."[11]

As I have shown in section I. above, however, even the latter attempt to rescue a small historical core for the account is in vain. There is very good reason for its not being found in the other three Gospels, and for Cleopas and his companion not appearing in the early list at 1 Cor 15:5-8. The Evangelist Luke appropriated it already in Greek from one of his own sources, "Special Luke." That in turn had appropriated it from the Judean or even Jerusalem Jewish Christian community in which Elijah (and Elisha) were very highly revered. This explains the abundance of such Elijah materials in Luke's Gospel, in contrast to the other three.

A member of the Palestinian Judean (or Jerusalem) Jewish Christian community composed the Emmaus narrative with Jesus represented as Elijah. Jesus is described as unexpectedly appearing to Cleopas and his companion on the road, and then disappearing again. As noted above, the author took over this scheme from Judaic traditions on the "angel" Elijah, especially as developed in regard to 2 Kings 2. He also was thought to unexpectedly appear and disappear among mortals, and even to provide them with the proper interpretation of a Scriptural passage, as Jesus does. None of these appearance / disappearance episodes with Elijah in Judaic tradition is historical, nor were they originally intended to be considered as such. They had other purposes, for example to indicate the correct interpretation of a Scriptural passage, to encourage the persecuted, or to entertain while making a point in a synagogue sermon.

The Emmaus narrative is a typical Palestinian Jewish Christian haggadah. As J. Goldin states, "imaginative dramatization" is typical of this genre.[12] M. Herr is also certainly correct when he maintains: "the *aggadah* does contain truth which is greater than that of historical and

---

[11] Cf. *The Gospel of Luke* (Moffatt; London: Hodder and Stoughton, 1963) 268, where he points primarily to vv 28-31.

[12] *The Song at the Sea* 27. While the Emmaus account is in part dependent on Judaic traditions on 2 Kings 2 and Judges 19, it is not a "midrash" on these passages. That term should be employed more narrowly only to describe specific comment, haggadic or halakhic, on a definite Scriptural passage.

philological reality, and more important than that of the natural sciences."[13] While the Emmaus narrative is not historical, it does have its own religious truths. To these I now turn.

V. The Extent and Purposes of the Original Emmaus Narrative.

1. *The Extent of the Original Narrative.*

In regard to the Emmaus account, I. Marshall has written: "It is difficult to assess the validity of attempts to differentiate tradition from Lucan redaction."[14]   D. Tiede agrees when he asserts: "It is futile to attempt to identify Luke's source(s) for this account or to separate the verses into possible pre-Lukan documents."[15] On the basis of vocabulary analysis, J. Wanke concludes that one cannot get back to pre-Lukan tradition on the basis of language alone.[16] Nevertheless, he attempted to differentiate between Lukan, non-Lukan and Special Luke terminology,[17] and J. Jeremias later examined the pericope extensively in this regard.[18] J. Fitzmyer even finds twenty-four points in the narrative which betray Lukan redaction or composition.[19] J. Nolland correctly concludes in regard to the question of Lukan source(s) that there is "no consensus in sight."[20] Yet he can also contend: "Luke is rarely an innovator, and most of his motifs are given him from the tradition...."[21]

---

[13] Art. "Aggadah" in *EJ* (1971) 2.355.

[14] *The Gospel of Luke* 890.

[15] *Luke* (Augsburg Commentary on the New Testament; Minneapolis: Augsburg, 1988) 433. He also states: "This story is a literary whole and not evidently a compilation of sources."

[16] *Die Emmauserzählung* 114.

[17] *Ibid.,* 110-114.

[18] *Die Sprache des Lukasevangeliums.*   Redaktion und Tradition im Nicht-Markusstoff des 3. Evangeliums (Göttingen: Vandenhoeck & Ruprecht, 1980) 313-320.

[19] *The Gospel According to Luke X-XXIV*, 1555-1556.

[20] *Luke 18:35 – 24:53*, 1198, where he lists four views.

[21] *Ibid.,* 1199. Nolland maintains, however, that "two" in v 13 is a Lukan substitution for an originally larger group (1200), and vv 22-24 and 28b-30 are also Lukan (1198-1199).

I agree with the latter statement by Nolland and would maintain that in spite of Luke's covering over the entire narrative with his own style, he has not changed the substance of the Emmaus account he borrowed from tradition (already in Greek) in any major way. This is especially true at two points.

Many scholars attribute 24:22-24 to the Third Evangelist. Yet these verses are integral to the original account, which is in part designed to *complement* the already present tradition of the empty tomb on Easter Sunday morning (see section VI. below on the dating of the narrative). The short résumé of the latter was therefore helpful as a foil for the Palestinian Jewish Christian who composed the original account. He intentionally alluded to the Jerusalem tradition of the empty tomb in order to indicate to his hearers how his own narrative complemented it. An empty tomb alone could not prove the validity of Jesus' Resurrection (cf. for example Matt 27:64). Yet Jesus' personal appearing to Cleopas and his companion on the road to Emmaus and their recognizing him at the breaking of bread there had precisely such a function, just as the other Resurrection appearances had (v 34; 1 Cor 15:5-8). In addition, I maintained above in section I. 15. that the phrase "he is alive" in 24:23 is strongly influenced by early Judaic tradition on Elijah. It emphasizes that after his ascension he too was "alive."[22] For the above reasons[23] it is very probable that, in spite of Lukan stylistic redaction, vv 22-24 were already a part of the original Emmaus narrative.

Other scholars maintain that 24:33-35 can also be attributed to the Evangelist Luke, perhaps as a redactional connection of v 32 to v 36. Yet if v 32 formed the conclusion of the narrative, Cleopas and his companion would remain in Emmaus. Just as the Palestinian Jewish Christian author of the account began it by describing Cleopas and his companion as coming from Jerusalem (v 13), so it is a part of his literary artistry also to end it there.[24] In addition, it was also his intention as a Judean or Jerusalem Jewish Christian to have his narrative end in Jerusalem, where Jesus is represented as in the meantime having also appeared to Simon (Peter, v 34), and not in Galilee, as in the earliest

---

[22] From a different perspective, cf. also J. Ernst, *Das Evangelium nach Lukas* 661: "Das Stichwort 'er lebt' (V. 23) ist Kennzeichen für SLk (24,5), nicht aber für lk Mk-Redaktion (gegen J. Wanke)."

[23] Cf. in addition the statement by J. Creed in *The Gospel According to St. Luke* (New York: St Martin's Press, 1969; original London: Macmillan, 1930) 296: "without vv. 22-24 the rebuke of v. 25 loses its point."

[24] J. Green in *The Gospel of Luke* 842 calls this a part of the "inverted parallelism" of the account.

appearance traditions. He wanted to emphasize the capital city as the site where the Church was soon to be founded, and from which Christian missionary work proceeded. Jerusalem was the center of his own home church, and he wanted to emphasize its significance by composing an appearance narrative which took place close to the city. From a nearby Judean village two adherents of Jesus thus return to the eleven (disciples) and those with them in Jerusalem (v 33). Verses 33-35 thus form a very appropriate conclusion to the original Emmaus narrative.

Finally, the original account may have begun something like this: "On the first day of the week two of them were going...."[25] When the Evangelist Luke appropriated the narrative, which mentions "this morning" in v 22 and the day's declining toward evening in v 29, he logically placed it in his Gospel after the story of the empty grave, which took place "at early dawn" (24:1). He himself then connected the Emmaus narrative with the following appearance of Jesus to the disciples in Jerusalem (vv 36b-49) with the words: "While they were talking about this" (v 36a). At the very end of his Gospel Luke then had Jesus carried up into heaven at Bethany on the very same Easter evening (vv 50-51). The latter was another influence, however, from the "Special Luke" materials of Palestinian Jewish Christians, who modeled Jesus' being carried up into heaven (his ascension) on that of the prophet they so revered, Elijah (2 Kings 2).

For the above reasons, in spite of some Lukan stylistic changes, the original Emmaus narrative should be thought of as basically that which is still found in 24:13-35.

2. The Purposes of the Original Emmaus Narrative

The original Emmaus story had not only one purpose. It expressed at least six religious truths.

1)
The account is an additional affirmation or proof of Jesus' Resurrection. It is in part designed to confirm that the Lord has "truly / in fact" risen (v 34), and not only appeared to Simon (*ibid.*; 1 Cor 15:5). He is now "alive" (v 23). He also appeared to other adherents, Cleopas and his companion, who did not belong to the eleven (v 33) or to the twelve (1 Cor 15:5; cf. Acts 1:26).

---

[25] The original may have even begun with וְהִנֵּה, "Behold," as in the present v 13. Luke, however, himself may have added Καὶ ἰδού as part of his antiquating, LXX style.

2)

After his Resurrection Jesus appeared not only to his first followers in Galilee, to which, out of fear for their own lives, they had all fled when he was arrested in the Garden of Gethsemane (Mark 14:50 par.). Mark 14:28 par. and 16:7 par. confirm that the first Resurrection appearances to Peter and the other (10) disciples took place in Galilee (see also John 21). The Emmaus narrative was composed by a Palestinian Jewish Christian from Judea (or even Jerusalem) in part in order to emphasize that Jesus also appeared in Judea. To this extent it resembles the traditions found in Luke 24:36-49 and John 20:11-29, which emphasize Jerusalem as the site of Jesus' appearances. The Emmaus narrative was thus at least in part designed to put Judean Christians on the same level as Jesus' adherents in Galilee in regard to an appearance of the risen Lord. Cleopas and his companion are described as returning from the Judean village of Emmaus to Jerusalem. Everyone later knew that the capital, Jerusalem, soon became the center of the Church, to which Peter returned from Galilee, and where Jesus' brother James (1 Cor 15:7) also provided leadership (Acts 12:17; 15:13; 21:18; 1:14, and Gal 1:19; 2:9 and 12). In the Emmaus account, Judean / Jerusalem Christians obtained their own post-Resurrection appearance narrative.

3)

The Emmaus account also emphasizes that Jesus is the long awaited Messiah (24:26), who will someday redeem Israel completely (v 21). If Christians contemporary with the author only search *all* the Scriptures (vv 27 and 32), even in Jesus' absence they can recognize that it is indeed he who truly fulfills them. The Scriptures, now read privately or within the Christian community in light of the Easter event, confirm Jesus as the Messiah.

4)

Although no longer physically present, Jesus can still be "recognized" in the breaking of bread (24:30) at the Christian community's common meals. This table fellowship now provides a regular opportunity for his adherents to experience his true presence among them. The Emmaus narrative thus also encourages them both to pursue such table fellowship, and to invite "strangers" to join them in it as their guests (the motif of hospitality).

5)

As he did with Cleopas and his companion, Jesus now wishes to accompany his followers on their path or way in life, especially when they begin to have doubts as to whether he is truly the Redeemer (24:21), the Messiah (v 26). Christianity as "the Way" (see also Acts 9:2; 18:25; 19:9, 23; 22:4; 24:14, 22) means that one's journey of faith is always an ongoing process, open to new revelations as to the manner and significance of Christ's presence. In addition, this road should be walked with at least one other person, with whom one can discuss the christological or messianic meaning of the Scriptures and experience Christ's presence in table fellowship along the way.

6)
         Finally, at least one segment of early Palestinian Judaism so revered the prophet Elijah that it considered him to be the final redeemer of Israel and to assume messianic tasks (see section I. 12. above). The Judean and Jerusalem Jewish Christians, to whom the composer of the Emmaus narrative belonged, shared this reverence for Elijah, as shown in other materials from "Special L" which entered the Third Gospel. While Jesus is portrayed in the Emmaus account in terms of the angel Elijah who appears and disappears among humans when he wants to, the clear statement is made in the narrative that *all* of Scripture (even motifs from the "ugly story" of Judges 19) points to Jesus as the true Messiah (24:26), who will one day redeem Israel, fulfilling his adherents' hopes (v 21). Jesus is thus described as much more than the extremely popular prophet Elijah, who also ascended to heaven at the end of his earthly life (2 Kings 2).

*   *   *

The sixth religious truth expressed in the original Semitic Emmaus narrative may still have been recognized and appreciated by Hellenistic Jewish Christians when the account was translated into Greek. Gentile readers, like those today, however, no longer recognized the background of the story in Judaic traditions on Elijah and 2 Kings 2. Otherwise, the first five purposes or religious truths intended by the original composer of the Emmaus narrative are still valid for its present form in the Gospel of Luke.

VI. The Dating of the Original Narrative.

Elsewhere I have argued that the earliest Palestinian Jewish Christians believed Jesus' soul ascended directly to God at his death on the Cross, a common view in early Judaism especially in regard to the death of a martyr.[26] This is still reflected, for example, in Luke 23:43, where Jesus tells one of the criminals crucified with him: "Truly I tell you, today you will be with me in Paradise." Here no mention is made of the events three days later, on Easter Sunday. Numerous commentators also see an indication of this early view in the Emmaus narrative, where Jesus scolds Cleopas and his companion with the words: "Oh, how foolish you are, and slow of heart to believe all that the prophets have declared! Was it not necessary that the Messiah should suffer these things and then enter his glory?" (24:25-26). Here "entering his glory" appears to refer to the Crucifixion.[27]

The influence of Hos 6:2 ("After two days He will revive us; on the third day He will raise us up, that we may live before Him"), however, made itself felt in regard to Jesus' Resurrection at a very early time. This is because early Judaic tradition also interpreted the verse of the resurrection, especially in regard to imperiled Israelites.[28] For this reason Paul in 1 Cor 15:4, only some 25 years after the death of Jesus (thus ca. 55 CE), could state that Jesus "was raised on the third day in accordance with the Scriptures." It was a tradition which Paul himself had received from earlier Christians (v 3). Yet neither at this point, where one would most expect it, nor elsewhere does the Jewish Apostle to the Gentiles refer to the story of the empty tomb, although it would greatly have strengthened his argument for Jesus' Resurrection. It is probable that the tradition had not yet developed, but did so very soon on the basis of Judaic interpretation of Hos 6:2.

As indicated in section V. A) above, I consider Luke 24:22-24 on the empty tomb to belong to the original Semitic account. The Emmaus narrative from the very outset was designed to present an appearance of Jesus to two of his followers on Easter Sunday (v 13), not on Good Friday.[29] Also as indicated in section V. A) above, the Emmaus account not only presupposes the Palestinian Jewish Christian haggadah of the empty tomb, it is in part intended to complement it. This is important for the dating of the Emmaus narrative.

---

[26] Cf. *Samuel, Saul and Jesus* 173-187.

[27] Cf. A. Loisy, *L'Évangile selon Luc* 573; E. Klostermann, *Das Lukasevangelium* 237; S. Gilmour, "The Gospel According to St. Luke" in *IB* (1952) 8.424-425; C. Montefiore, *The Synoptic Gospels* 2.636 as a question; and R. Bultmann, *The History* 290.

[28] See the texts I cite in *Samuel, Saul and Jesus* 183-187.

[29] This is true although "entering into his glory" in v 26 may indeed be a remnant of an earlier Christology, which was reworked into the present context.

Jesus' appearance to Cleopas and his companion on the road to Emmaus is not included in the early list of appearances in 1 Cor 15:5-8, beginning with Cephas / Peter (cf. Luke 24:34) and ending with Paul himself. The former presupposes the narrative of the empty tomb, already taken over by Luke in 24:1-12 from Mark 16:1-8, but purposely omitting the reference in v 7 to Jesus' preceding his disciples to Galilee, where they will "see" him. The Gospel of Mark is usually thought to have reached completion shortly before or after the end of the Jewish-Roman War, from 66-70 CE,[30] and the Third Gospel somewhere between 85-90 CE.[31] The Palestinian Jewish Christian author of the Emmaus narrative may thus have composed his account with knowledge of an earlier, Semitic form of the empty tomb story which, when translated into Greek, was later appropriated by Mark for the end of his Gospel.

Yet the empty tomb story itself was most probably from after ca. 55 CE (1 Cor 15:4). Dependent on the empty tomb story and complementing it, the Emmaus narrative thus appears to have been composed sometime between 55 and 85-90 CE. An earlier dating within this range is more probable, however, since the narrative, part of "Special Luke" like the Christmas story in 2:1-20 and the account of Jesus as a twelve-year-old in the Jerusalem Temple in 2:41-52, first had to be translated from the Semitic original into Greek, from which language Luke later appropriated it for his Gospel. Emmaus / Moṣa just west of Jerusalem is also still represented in the Emmaus narrative as a well-known Jewish village, as in *m. Sukk.* 4:5, which mentions obtaining large willow branches from there for the altar of the Temple at the festival of Booths, thus before the destruction of the Temple in 70 CE (see section VII. below on the location of Emmaus). When 800 Roman veterans of the recent war were settled there just afterwards (Josephus, *Bell.* 7.217), the original Jewish inhabitants most likely had to move elsewhere, perhaps 1.5 km or 1 mile NW up the Soreq Valley to Beit Mizza, which probably preserves the name Moṣa.[32]

When all of the above factors are considered, a date between 55-66 CE is most probable for the original Semitic Emmaus narrative.

---

[30] Cf. J. Marcus, "The Jewish War and the Sitz im Leben of Mark" in *JBL* 111 (1992) 460;   D. Lührmann, *Das Markus-Evangelium* 6; and J. Gnilka, *Das Evangelium nach Markus* (Mk 1 - 8,26) 34.

[31] Cf. W. Wiefel, *Das Evangelium nach Lukas* 5 for the double work Luke-Acts; J. Fitzmyer, *The Gospel According to Luke I-IX,* 57 (80-85 CE); and W. Kümmel, *Introduction to the New Testament* (Nashville and New York: Abingdon, 1966[14]) 106 ("between 70 and 90").

[32] Cf. Fischer, Isaac and Roll, *Roman Roads in Judaea,* II. 223 and 227.

VII.   The Location of Emmaus.

The Emmaus narrative begins in Luke 24:13 by stating: "And behold, two of them on the same day were walking to a village sixty stadia from Jerusalem, the name of which was Emmaus." All important MSS read here for the place-name: Ἐμμαοῦς. Nevertheless, in spite of a long monograph by L.-H. Vincent and F.-M. Abel,[33] encyclopedia articles, and other special studies,[34] and the remarks of commentators on the Gospel of Luke, up to now there has been no general consensus in regard to which of the five sites called Emmaus at different periods of time is meant.[35] The distance of sixty stadia complicates the matter. One στάδιον is 185 meters, or 600 Greek feet, which are 625 Roman and ca. 607 English feet.[36] This would mean Emmaus was 11.1 km or 6.9 English miles from Jerusalem. Yet no well-attested site proposed for Emmaus fits this distance. For this reason several much less significant MSS read 160 stadia. Nor is the problem solved by proposing that 60 stadia mean the round-trip Jerusalem / Emmaus / Jerusalem,[37] for which there is no indication in the text.

Here I will first propose significant reasons for excluding four possible locations for Emmaus, and then substantiate the suggestion made above in I. 19. for the village מוֹצָא near Jerusalem as meant by Emmaus in Luke 24:13.

---

[33] *Emmaüs. Sa Basilique et son Histoire* (Paris: Leroux, 1932).

[34] Cf. the art. "Emmaus" by M. Seligsohn in *JE* (1903) 5.153; "Emmaus" by M. Avi-Yonah in *EJ* (1971) 6.726-727; "Ammaus" by I. Benziger in PW (1894) 1.1843; "Emmaus" by K. Clark in *IDB* (1962) 2.97-98; A. Neubauer, *La Géographie du Talmud* (Amsterdam: Meridian, 1965; original 1868) 100-102; P. Thomsen, *Loca Sancta* (Halle: Haupt, 1907) 20-21; G. Dalman, *Orte und Wege Jesu* 241-246; P. Billerbeck in Str-B 2.270-271; M. Avi-Yonah, *Gazeteer of Roman Palestine* (Qedem 5; Jerusalem: Hebrew University, 1976) 55; E. Schürer, *The History of the Jewish People* 1.512-513; G. Reeg, *Die Ortsnamen Israels nach der rabbinischen Literatur* (Beihefte zum Tübinger Atlas des Vorderen Orients, B 51; Wiesbaden: Reichert, 1989) 45-47 with sixteen different spellings for Emmaus (p. 46); and M. Fischer, B. Isaac and I. Roll, *Roman Roads in Judaea, II.* 151-159. See also the "Bibliography on the Site of Emmaus" in Fitzmyer, *The Gospel According to Luke X-XXIV*, 1571-1572.

[35] Cf. the remark by J. Fitzmyer in *The Gospel According to Luke X-XXIV*, 1562: "Emmaus is in the vicinity of Jerusalem, and that is all that matters."

[36] BAGD 764; LSJ 1631.

[37] Against J. Nolland, *Luke 18:35 – 24:53*, 1207. He may have this from J. Fitzmyer, *The Gospel According to Luke X-XXIV*, 1562.

1. *Ammathus.*

Josephus calls the village with a hot spring (θέρμα) just south of Tiberias on the Sea of Galilee Ἀμμαθοῦς (*Ant.* 18. 36). It is labeled Ἀμμαοῦς or Emmaus in one MS.[38] In *Bell.* 4.11 the Jewish historian explains the name as stemming from a "spring of warm / hot water" (πηγὴ θερμῶν ὑδάτων) with curative properties.[39] In Aramaic the site is called חַמְּתָא, Ḥammetha, "Hot [Springs],"[40] and even today is visited because of these waters, especially in the winter.[41]

This location in Galilee is obviously excluded as a candidate for the Emmaus of Luke 24:13 because of its great distance from Jerusalem. I note it, however, to point out that if the Semitic form of the Lukan Ἐμμαοῦς were חַמְּתָא because of there being hot spring(s) at the site, one might expect the Greek form Ἀμμαθοῦς, as above.[42] Nevertheless, caution is appropriate at this point, as shown in the variant reading Ἀμμαοῦς, also cited above, and because Emmaus / Nicopolis may instead be derived from חמה and not חמת(א) (see 4. below).

2. *Abu Ghosh.*

Located exactly halfway or 9 Roman miles between Emmaus / Nicopolis (see 4. below) and Jerusalem, Abu Ghosh is most probably the Kiriath-jearim of the OT. It had a fine spring and was called by the Crusaders "Fontenoid." Theodoric in 1172 CE and John Phocas in 1177 CE referred to it as the Emmaus of Luke 24:13. Yet already in the thirteenth century it was supplanted by el-Qubeibeh (see 3. below) as Emmaus because the main pilgrim route from the west to Jerusalem then passed through el-Qubeibeh.[43] There is no early attestation for Abu Ghosh as Emmaus.

---

[38] Cf. MS "W" cited in the LCL edition apparatus, as well as in B. Niese, *Flavii Iosephi Opera* 4.146.

[39] Cf. the English translations by L. Feldman and H. Thackeray in the LCL edition.

[40] Jastrow 481. Cf. already Josh 19:35 (חַמַּת) and BDB 329.

[41] Cf. Z. Vilnay, *Israel Guide* (Jerusalem, 1979²¹) 484, and the map on p. 481.

[42] Cf. also A. Schlatter, *Zur Topographie und Geschichte Palästinas* (Calw and Stuttgart: Verlag der Vereinsbuchhandlung, 1893) 5 on this issue.

[43] Cf. the relevant texts in Fischer, Isaac and Roll, *Roman Roads in Judaea*, II. 114-115; as well as O. Keel and M. Küchler, *Orte und Landschaften der Bibel* 2.793-802.

3. El-Qubeibeh.

Ever since the fifteenth century CE Franciscans have maintained that this site is Emmaus. It is located 11½ km, almost 7 miles, or 75 stadia NW of Jerusalem. When the Crusaders were forced out of Jerusalem and the hills of Judea in 1244 CE, pilgrims primarily employed the road from the west passing through el-Qubeibeh. Emmaus was then no longer sought in Abu Ghosh or in 'Imwas / Nicopolis (see 4. below), but in el-Qubeibeh. It is identified as Emmaus by travelers as of 1280 CE. Since el-Qubeibeh has neither a spring nor a hot spring, and never is referred to as Emmaus in ancient sources, it must also be excluded as a possibility for the Emmaus of Luke 24:13.[44]

4. Emmaus / Nicopolis.

Located north of Latrun on the modern road from Jerusalem to Tel-Aviv, and before 1967 called 'Imwas or 'Amwas because of the name of the Arab village there, this site was favored as Emmaus by Eusebius (d. ca. 339 CE),[45] who noted that "this significant city is now Nicopolis of Palestine." He was followed by Jerome[46] and many others.[47]

Ca. 43 BCE the Roman general Cassius reduced the "city" (πόλις) Emmaus ('Αμμαοῦς) to servitude.[48] This was later revoked by Antony.[49] It was then made into the capital of a toparchy, which Josephus speaks of as valid at the time of the Jewish-Roman War in 66-70 CE,[50] although the Roman governor of Syria, Varus, out of revenge for a revolt had had it

---

[44] Cf. Fischer, Isaac and Roll, *Roman Roads in Judaea*, II. 237-241; Dalman, *Orte und Wege* 241-242; and the secondary literature cited by J. Fitzmyer, *The Gospel According to Luke X-XXIV*, 1562. See also C. Kopp, *Die heiligen Stätten der Evangelien* (Regensburg: Pustet, 1959) 449-450 on el-Qubeibeh. The modern Qubeiba can be reached from Jerusalem via Nabi Samwil and Biddu. A. Edersheim in *The Life and Times of Jesus the Messiah* 2.639, n. 3, attempts to connect el-Qubeibeh via Beit Mizza to Colonia / Moṣa, which is pure harmonization.

[45] Cf. the LCL edition of his *Ecclesiastical History*, trans. K. Lake (1.xiii).

[46] Cf. for both the *Onomastikon* (Klostermann 90-91).

[47] Cf. the discussion in Schürer, *The history* 1.512-513, including Sozomen and Julius Africanus. For the third century renaming of the city as Nicopolis, see also Fischer, Isaac and Roll, *Roman Roads in Judaea*, II. 153.

[48] Cf. Josephus, *Ant.* 14.275 and *Bell.* 1.222.

[49] *Ant.* 14.304.

[50] *Bell.* 3.54-55 ('Αμμαοῦς).

burnt to the ground in ca. 4 BCE after its inhabitants fled.[51] They clearly returned and reoccupied it, as Josephus indicates elsewhere (see B. below). Rabbinic sources also speak, for example, of R. Eleazar b. Arakh, a second generation Tanna,[52] who after the fall of Jerusalem and the founding of a new academy in Yabneh by his teacher Yoḥanan b. Zakkai, did not follow him there. Instead, he preferred to join his wife in Emmaus (מאוס), "a location of good water and good climate."[53]

Christian sources relate that there was a spring in Emmaus with healing qualities.[54] Public baths erected there led to a variant of the Eleazer b. Arakh anecdote above as having דמסית instead of Emmaus.[55] This loanword derives from (βαλανεῖον) δημόσιον, " 'public' bath."[56] In *b. Šabb.* 147b the "heat" (חמים) of Diomsith (Emmaus) is mentioned, which H. Freedman explains as "the heat of its springs."[57] The passage also refers to the (healing) "mud" of the site, and people staying there for three weeks (for the healing benefits).[58] *Cant. Zuta* on 6:9 speaks of "Ḥammat (חַמַּת) in Judea,"[59] and *Lam. Rab.* 1:16 § 46 has Hadrian set up a garrison of soldiers (between 132-135 CE) in חַמְתָא, the Aramaic form of the Hebrew.[60] Both of the latter certainly refer to Emmaus.

The above passages in Hebrew and Aramaic point to the Semitic background of Emmaus / Nicopolis, for חַם means warm or hot.[61] M. Jastrow for example maintains that עמאוס אימאוס, אמָּאוס and other

---

[51] *Bell.* 2.71 (Ἀμμαοῦς). See also *Ant.* 17.291. On this, cf. Schürer, *The history* 1.331-332.

[52] Strack and Stemberger, *Introduction* 78.

[53] *'Avot R. Nat.* B 29 (Schechter 59; Saldarini 168-169); *Eccl. Rab.* 7:7 §2 (Vilna 19a or p. 37 with אמאוס; Soncino 8.180). *Mek. Baḥodesh* 1 on Exod 19:1 (Lauterbach 2.193) relates an account of Yoḥanan's going up to Emmaus (מאוס) in Judea after the Jewish-Roman War.

[54] Cf. Fischer, Isaac and Roll, *Roman Roads in Judaea*, II. 155, with n. 238.

[55] *'Avot R. Nat.* A 14 (Schechter 59; Goldin 77).

[56] Jastrow 300 on דימוסין and דימוסיא, 4). If λουτρόν was employed of the bathing place, it would have been in the pl. (LSJ 1061).

[57] Soncino 750, n. 2.

[58] Soncino 749, with notes 9-10.

[59] Buber 17a or p. 33.

[60] Cf. Vilna 17a or p. 33; Soncino 7.125, with notes 3-4.

[61] BDB 328; Jastrow 475. Why Fischer, Isaac and Roll, *Roman Roads in Judaea*, II. 151 only speak of an "alleged presence of baths or hot springs" is strange.

variants of this place-name are the Hellenized form of חמה, אתָמָח.[62]
The first, vocalized as חַמָּה, means "heat."[63] While it is not attested as
such in rabbinic sources, it may well provide the Semitic background to
'Αμμαοῦς, with two "a"s: 'Ammaous. As usual, the ḥet was
transformed into 'A, and *ous* was added at the end. The noun חמה,
however, can also be vocalized as חֵמָה, also meaning "heat."[64] The
ṣere (..) may account for the variant Greek spelling 'Ẹmmaous, found in
five of the nineteen occurrences in Josephus.[65]

This derivation of 'Αμμαοῦς / 'Εμμαοῦς from the Hebrew חמה for
"heat," vocalized in two different ways, is more probable than from the
Hebrew חַמַּת or the Aramaic חַמְתָא. As noted in section 1., Josephus for
example calls the place with the latter name just south of Tiberias
'Αμμαθοῦς (*Bell.* 4.11 and *Ant.* 18.36), the Greek θ reflecting the ת of the
Semitic.[66]

I emphasize this point here because the *Semitic* original of Emmaus /
Nicopolis is very different from that of מוֹצָא, which Josephus also labels
'Αμμαοῦς and I identify with the Emmaus of Luke 24:13 in section 5.
below. The latter derives rather from מוֹצָא, "spring," and not from חמה,
"heat" (or possibly חמת, חמתא: "warm / hot [springs])."

There are, however, two main reasons why Emmaus / Nicopolis
cannot be the Emmaus of Luke 24:13.

A. The Distance.

Emmaus / Nicopolis is exactly 18 Roman miles from Jerusalem,[67]
equivalent to 17.5 English miles or 27.1 km.[68] Unless one were a
marathon runner, it would be extremely difficult to reach Jerusalem the
same evening after eating a meal when it was already towards evening
and the day had declined (Luke 24:29 - 35).[69] Nor should one speculate

---

[62] Jastrow 74.

[63] BDB 328, 1.

[64] Jastrow 475.

[65] Cf. *Ant.* 12.298, 306-307; 17.282 and 291 (text of the LCL edition).

[66] Cf. also the Transjordanian city of 'Αμαθοῦς (v.1. 'Αμμαθοῦς) in *Bell.* 1.86, 89,
170, and *Ant.* 13.356, 374, and 14.91.

[67] Fischer, Isaac and Roll, *Roman Roads in Judaea*, II. 296 and 154.

[68] Cf. M. Avi-Yonah, art. "Emmaus" in *EJ* (1971) 6. 726.

[69] Against R. Riesner in *Dictionary of Jesus and the Gospels*, ed. J. Green and S.
McKnight (Downers Grove, Illinois: Intervarsity Press, 1992) 43: Going from
Jerusalem to Emmaus / Nicopolis and back the same day "does not seem to have

222   Stilling the Storm, Calling First Disciples, and the Road to Emmaus

on whether one of the city gates would have allowed Cleopas and his companion to enter at such a late hour.[70]   The Emmaus narrative is simply not concerned with such a question.   The great distance from Jerusalem by itself excludes Emmaus / Nicopolis as a candidate for the Emmaus of Luke 24:13.

B.   Emmaus as a Village, not a City.

Luke 24:13 and 28 call Emmaus a "village" (κώμη),[71] which in Greek usually means an "unwalled village, opp. fortified city."[72]   It would be כְּפָר in Hebrew.[73]   This excludes Emmaus / Nicopolis, which was clearly labeled a "city" (πόλις, עִיר) from the second century BCE to the period when Josephus wrote at the end of the first century CE.   The following examples show this.

First Maccabees, originally written in Hebrew at the beginning of the first century BCE,[74] relates in 9:50 that Bacchides built strong "cities" (πόλεις) in Judea, including Emmaus, with high walls, gates and bars. That is, Emmaus / Nicopolis already at the time reported (second century BCE) was a fortified city.[75]   Above I already called attention to Cassius' reducing Emmaus to servitude ca. 4 BCE.   Josephus in *Ant.* 14.275 states that together with Gophna it was the most important of four "cities" the Roman general conquered.

Vespasian in 68 CE first moved south from Caesarea to Emmaus. Then he "occupied the approaches to the capital of the province," fortified a camp, left the fifth legion there, and advanced towards Jerusalem.   Here in *Bell.* 4.444 Josephus even calls Emmaus a

---

been an impossible feat in that day and culture."   See also C. Kopp, *Die heiligen Stätten der Evangelien* 448: "Einer solchen Leistung [55 km] sind rüstige Araber auch in der heißen Zeit noch fähig."   Kopp speculates that Cleopas and his companion may have ridden back.

[70] Against A. Ehrhardt, "The Disciples of Emmaus" 182.   Ehrhardt thus believes the narrative ended at v 32.

[71] BAGD 461.   Luke differentiates between a village and a city in 8:1 and 13:22.

[72] LSJ 1017.

[73] Jastrow 662: village, country town.   It is contrasted to an עִיר, town, city (p. 1075), and קִרְיָה, town, settlement, fort (p. 1419).   See also P. Alexander in Schürer, *The history* 2.188-189.   Both the Hebrew New Testaments of Delitzsch (pp. 160-161) and the United Bible Societies (pp. 230-231) have כפר in Luke 24:13 and 28.

[74] Nickelsburg, *Jewish Literature* 117.

[75] Cf. Josephus, *Ant.* 13.15-16 with cities, towers and very high strong walls.

μητρόπολις, the region's major city or "capital." This agrees with his labeling it a "toparchy" in Judea, also at the time of the Jewish-Roman War (*Bell.* 3.54-55). Varus' burning of the walled, fortified city ca. 4 BCE thus had no lasting effect.[76]

One rabbinic source also calls Emmaus / Nicopolis a "city" and not a village. In *'Avot R. Nat.* B 29, R. Eleazar b. Arakh proposes that the disciples of Yoḥanan b. Zakkai, forced to leave Jerusalem, should go to Emmaus, a pleasant "city" (עִיר) with pleasant waters.[77]

The very well documented designation of Emmaus / Nicopolis as a "city" (πόλις, עִיר) precludes consideration of the site as the "village" Emmaus precisely labeled so in Luke 24:13 and 28. That is the case, however, for מוֹצָא, Emmaus, a small settlement just west of Jerusalem.

5. Emmaus / Moṣa.

A. The Distance to Jerusalem.

The site Moṣa (מוֹצָא) lies on the ancient Roman road leading west from Jerusalem via Abu Ghosh to Emmaus / Nicopolis. It is ca. 38 stadia or 7 km (4.2 English miles) from the Jaffa Gate of Jerusalem.[78] While Luke 24:13 says Emmaus is 60 stadia distant from Jerusalem, Josephus in *Bell.* 7.217 notes that 'Aμμαοῦς (which I identify with Moṣa / Emmaus below) is 30 stadia from Jerusalem. Since there is "no ancient site ... exactly 30 stades from Jerusalem,"[79] Josephus, a native of Jerusalem, is

---

[76] Since Emmaus / Nicopolis was never a "village" from the second century BCE at least to the end of the first century CE, it seems quite strained when Vincent and Abel maintain this for the time of Cleopas and his companion and for when Luke "sojourned" in Palestine (*Emmaüs* 311). They cannot cite one relevant source for their assertion.

[77] Schechter 59; Saldarini 168-169. The statement is then repeated.

[78] Cf. Fischer, Isaac and Roll, *Roman Roads in Judaea*, II. 223, and for Moṣa the whole section 222-229. See also G. Reeg, *Die Ortsnamen* 402-403, with secondary literature on p. 403, as well as 569; G. Dalman, *Orte und Wege Jesu* 244-245, who cites 6½ km; A. Neubauer, *La Géographie du Talmud* 152-153; F.-M. Abel, *Géographie de la Palestine*, II. 392-393; S. Cohen, art. "Mozah" in *IDB* 3.455; O. Keel and M. Küchler, *Orte und Landschaften der Bibel* 2.790-793; M. Avi-Yonah, art. "Moza" in *EJ* (1971) 12.494; and "Modern Times" by E. Orni, 494-495; G. Schmitt and C. Möller, *Siedlungen Palästinas nach Flavius Josephus* (Beihefte zum Tübinger Atlas des Vorderen Orients, B14; Wiesbaden: Reichert, 1976) 16-17: slightly less than 7 km to the Jaffa Gate of Jerusalem; L.-H. Vincent and F.-M. Abel, *Emmaüs* 284 and 321.

[79] Fischer, Isaac and Roll, *Roman Roads in Judaea*, II. 223.

clearly guilty of an approximation at this point. No milestones had been erected by the Romans yet, and to estimate 30 instead of 38 stadia was not a great blunder. Elsewhere for example Josephus by mistake gives two different numbers for the same distance,[80] and at least once he cites 30 for what should have been ca. 60.[81] The Jewish historian also frequently employs 30 as a round number.[82] A passage such as *Vita* 349 with 30, 60 and 120 stadia indicates that Josephus probably meant an hour's walk to be 30 stadia.[83] If so, he thought one could walk from Jerusalem to Emmaus in about an hour. The Palestinian Jewish Christian author of the Emmaus account may have intentionally had the number 60 not in order to indicate the actual distance (ca. 38 stadia), but to accentuate the two hours' time (2 x 30) it took Cleopas and his companion to walk from Jerusalem to Emmaus. They were so engaged in "talking and discussing" (Luke 24:15) that their "stopping" when Jesus addressed a question to them (v 17) was probably not their first halt or pause. Listening attentively to Jesus' interpretation of the things about himself "in all the Scriptures" (v 27) would also not have allowed a normal pace.

The above suggestion makes more sense then to presuppose that the number 60 was the round-trip distance (see n. 37), or that the Evangelist Luke later inserted the number into the narrative himself. Some critics maintain his knowledge of Palestinian geography was poor.[84] Rather, Josephus himself erred by ca. 8 stadia (the actual 38 and not his 30), and the Palestinian Jewish Christian author of the Emmaus narrative probably intentionally wanted to emphasize a two hours' walk. The way back to Jerusalem (24:33) may then have only taken Cleopas and his

---

[80] Cf. *Bell.* 2.516 with 50, and *Ant.* 7.283 with 40; *Ant.* 5.139 with 30, and 7.312 with 20; *Ant.* 7.283 with 40, and *Bell.* 2.516 with 50; and *Ant.* 18.60 with 200, and *Bell.* 2.175 with 400.

[81] Cf. *Ant.* 12.408 and n. "c."

[82] Cf. *Bell.* 2.386, 551; 3.447, 521; 4.55, 615; 5.51; 7.101, 284; *Ant.* 12.408; 19.6; and *Vita* 157, 281.

[83] Cf. also *Bell.* 4.3 with 30 and 60 for the breadth and length of the Sea of Galilee, and the distance 60 stadia in *Bell.* 7.168; *Ant.* 5.4; 13.359; 15.324; and *Vita* 115, 214. Fischer, Isaac and Roll in *Roman Roads in Judaea*, II. 223 state: "Thirty stades (3.75 miles, or about 5.5 km.) would have represented roughly one hour's walk." G. Schmitt and C. Möller, *Siedlungen Palästinas nach Flavius Josephus* 16, note that 30 and 60 are often used, approximate standards "which stand for 1 or 2 hours of walking."

[84] Cf. W. Wiefel, *Das Evangelium nach Lukas* 410; W. Schmithals, *Das Evangelium nach Lukas* (Zürcher Bibelkommentare 3.1; Zurich: Theologischer Verlag, 1980) 233; and J. Fitzmyer, *The Gospel According to Luke X-XXIV*, 1562.

companion somewhat over an hour, which would have been the usual time.

B. *The Place-Name Moṣa as Colonia and Emmaus.*

As I suggested in section I. 19. above, the Palestinian Jewish Christian author of the Emmaus narrative borrowed the term מוֹצָא from v 21 of 2 Kings 2, a chapter which, especially in Judaic tradition, greatly influenced his account. The occurrence of מוֹצָא there caused him to think of the site מוֹצָא just west of Jerusalem and to make it the goal of Cleopas and his companion's walk.

The above village מוֹצָא, with exactly this spelling, is attested for the Second Temple period, i.e. up to 70 CE, including the time when the Palestinian Jewish Christian author of the Emmaus narrative created his account in a Semitic language (see section III. above).

In regard to the festival of Booths (Sukkoth), Lev 23:40 states: "On the first day you shall take the fruit of majestic trees, branches of palm trees, boughs of leafy trees, and 'willows of the brook'; and you shall rejoice before the Lord your God for seven days." These "willows of the brook" are עַרְבֵי-נָחַל in Hebrew. The passages *m. Sukk.* 3:3-4 and *t. Sukk.* 2:7 deal with these willow branches.[85]   Abba Saul, a third generation Tanna,[86] then maintains in 3:1 of the latter tractate that while others think "the law of the willow-branch is a law revealed to Moses at Sinai" which is not in Scripture, it is found in Lev 23:40, including a willow branch for the lulab, and "a willow branch for the altar."[87] The latter are meant in *m. Sukk.* 4:5, which states:

> How was the rite of the willow branch fulfilled? There was a place below Jerusalem called Moṣa. They went down there and cut themselves young willow branches.   They came [back to Jerusalem] and set these up at the sides of the altar so that their tops were bent over the altar.[88]

---

[85] Cf. Albeck 2.266-267; Danby 176; Neusner 284; and Zuckermandel / Liebermann 194-195, and Neusner 2.216-217, respectively. The latter refers to Lev 23:40.

[86] Strack and Stemberger, *Introduction* 86.

[87] Zuckermandel / Liebermann 195; Neusner 2.218, where Lev 23:4 is a mistake for 23:40. Cf. also *Sifra* 'Emor 16, par. 238 on Lev 23:40 (Neusner 3.266), and *y. Sukk.* 4:1, 54b (Neusner 17.93-94).

[88] Albeck 2.271; Neusner 287. I slightly modify the translation of Danby 178.

While the making of the *lulab* was a concern of each individual person, *b. Sukk.* 43b states that "in the case of the willow-branch the emissaries of the Beth din would bring [them]" for the altar.[89] That is, only a small number of official representatives went to Moṣa and cut down willow branches for the Temple altar in Jerusalem. Regarding these a Tanna taught in *b. Sukk.* 45a: "They were large and long and eleven cubits high, so that they might bend over the altar one cubit."[90] Eleven cubits are more than 5 m (16½ feet).[91] Such large willow branches could only be found where there was much water, for example near the spring of Moṣa, itself meaning "spring."[92]

The Mishnah states that there was a "place" (מָקוֹם) called Moṣa "below" Jerusalem, to which (the emissaries of the Beth din) "went down." This agrees with the known difference in elevation between Jerusalem and Moṣa, ca. 205 meters (673 feet).[93] In fact, part of the ancient road leading from there to Jerusalem was known as the "Ascent of the Romans" (Ma'aleh ha-Roma'im).[94]

A Tannaitic tradition found in *b. Sukk.* 45a in regard to the Mishnah's Moṣa states: "It was the place called Colonia" (קְלֹנִיא).[95] In *y. Sukk.* 4:3, 54b it is R. Tanḥuma who reports that it was called Colonia (קלוניא).[96] There is no reason to doubt this Tannaitic, Palestinian identification of

---

[89] Soncino 198.

[90] Soncino 207. The Jerusalem Talmud identifies the Tanna as Bar Qappara (*y. Sukk.* 4:3, 54b in Neusner 17.98).

[91] Cf. O. Sellers, art. "Weights and Measures" in IDB 4.836-837, D.4.a.

[92] This also excludes Khirbet ("the ruins of") Beit Mizza, 1½ km (.9 mile) north of Moṣa's spring, as a possibility for Emmaus. It was on a hill, without a spring, and thus not capable of producing such willows. Cf. Fischer, Isaac and Roll, *Roman Roads in Judaea*, II. 227 on this site, as well as Dalman, *Orte und Wege Jesu* 244, n. 7.

[93] Here I employ 560 meters for the spring of Moṣa (based on a map of modern Jerusalem on a scale of 1:50,000 kindly consulted for me by M. Krupp, who himself lives at the nearby Mevasseret Zion), and 765 m for the Tower of David (Phasael Tower) at Jerusalem. On the latter, see the *Encyclopedia of Archaeological Investigations in the Holy Land*, ed. M. Avi-Yonah (London: Oxford University Press, 1976) 2.559. Fischer, Isaac and Roll, *Roman Roads in Judaea*, II. 222, say there is an ascent of ca. 300 m (984 feet) from Wadi Qaluniya (Naḥal Soreq) to "the plateau on which Jerusalem lies."

[94] *Roman Roads in Judaea*, II. 97, n. 104. Cf. also n. 78 here.

[95] Soncino 207.

[96] Neusner 17.98. He was a fifth generation Palestinian Amora (Strack and Stemberger, *Introduction* 106). For the noun קְלַנְיָא, as *colonia*, see Jastrow 1379. Both Talmuds also include the wordplay of Moṣa as "exempt" from taxes.

Moṣa and Colonia.[97]   Up until 1948 the Arab village of "Qaluniya" occupied the slope of the hill above the spring of Moṣa. It retained the earlier name of the site.

In *Bell.* 7.216-217 the Jerusalem native Josephus wrote the following about the period directly after the end of the Jewish-Roman War in 70 CE:

> About the same time Caesar sent instructions to Bassus and Laberius Maximus, the procurator, to farm out [or "lease"] all Jewish territory. For he founded no city there, reserving the country as his private property, except that he did assign to eight hundred veterans discharged from the army a place for habitation called Emmaus, distant thirty furlongs from Jerusalem.[98]

The Greek for "place for habitation" here is χωρίον...εἰς κατοίκησιν.[99] It is intentionally contrasted to a "city" (πόλις), so it was either a (small) town or village, the latter found for Emmaus in Luke 24:13 and 28. Josephus' Greek for Emmaus here is Ἀμμαοῦς. Of priestly descent and a native of Jerusalem, he was certainly a regular general participant in the annual week-long Sukkoth (Booths) festival. He will have known that the willow branches for the Temple altar were procured from Moṣa by official representatives.

The Greek form in Josephus cannot be fully explained, yet there are several indications of its origin. The ancient name of Moṣa in Josh 18:26 was הַמֹּצָה, for which the Targum has מוֹצָה,[100] LXX A Αμωσα, the Vulgate Ammosa, Eusebius in his *Onomastikon* Ἀμσα, and Jerome in his translation of the latter Amsa.[101] All four of the latter sources preface the

---

[97] Against Schürer, *The history* 1.513, end of n. 142. See also Fischer, Isaac and Roll, *Roman Roads in Judaea*, II. 222, n. 770: "the Jerusalem Talmud in particular was produced by scholars living in Palestine, and nothing is gained by assuming that they would have invented geography." Cyrill of Scythopolis (Bethshan) in the middle of the fifth century CE also wrote in his "Life of the Holy Father Saba" 67 that during a long-standing drought, "the springs of Colonia and Nephtoah" (Lifta, just to the east) ceased to flow (Schwartz 168). This shows the site was still called Colonia in the fifth century CE.

[98] LCL translation by H. Thackeray. On the "farming out / leasing," cf. B. Isaac, "Judaea after AD 70" in *JJS* 35 (1984) 44-50.

[99] Cf. LSJ 2016,1. for χωρίον as place, spot, district.

[100] Sperber 2.32. For the מֹצָא of 1 Chr 8:36-37, the Targum has the same (Déaut and Robert, 2.32), the LXX Μαισα, and the Vulgate Mosa.

[101] Cf. Klostermann 28 for the last two.

place-name with an "A," as does Josephus. When translated into Greek, ṣade (צ) also typically became "s." More, unfortunately, cannot be said. Since Moṣa lay at the beginning of the very frequently traveled Roman road to Emmaus / Nicopolis, called 'Αμμαοῦς, the latter may have influenced the spelling of Moṣa also as 'Αμμαοῦς.

The Palestinian Jewish Christian author of Luke 24:13-35 employed מֹוצָא in v 13, the same form of the name found in his source, 2 Kgs 2:21, and *m. Sukk.* 4:5. At this stage it was impossible for hearers to confuse the site with Emmaus / Nicopolis. When a Hellenistic Jewish Christian later translated the narrative into Greek, he employed 'Εμμαοῦς, very similar to Josephus' 'Αμμαοῦς. As pointed out above, Josephus employs for Emmaus / Nicopolis 'Εμμαοῦς five times, and 'Αμμαοῦς fourteen times. The 'Ε and 'Α were variants.

Only at the Jewish Christian Greek stage of the name Moṣa, 'Εμμαοῦς, could it be confused with Emmaus / Nicopolis. Unfortunately, this confusion has prevailed for centuries. Now, however, there is no good reason to retain and repeat it.

C. The Site Moṣa, and the Route to Jerusalem.

1) The Site.

Moṣa's spring, after which the locality was named, can still be viewed next to a Crusader tower. During his 1973 excavations there, E. Eisenberg also found a richly decorated house from the Second Temple period,[102] the same time at which very tall willow branches were cut and brought from Moṣa for the Temple altar in Jerusalem. Until it collapsed because of heavy winter rains in 1877-1878, there used to be a stone bridge over the brook Naḥal Soreq (meaning "choice vine")[103] at its narrowest point. Its base may have been Roman.[104] Moṣa is now just within the western city limits of Jerusalem, with the suburb Mevasseret Yerushalaim (Zion) at the top of the hill to the northwest.

Directly north of Second Temple Moṣa[105] the Soreq Valley widens, and the good soil there is cultivated. While G. Dalman only noted its

---

[102] Fischer, Isaac and Roll, *Roman Roads in Judaea*, II. 225-226.

[103] BDB 977 on שֶׂרֶק.

[104] Fischer, Isaac and Roll, *Roman Roads in Judaea*, II. 227. See also the nineteenth century steel engraving of the bridge: plate 23, p. 396.

[105] It was north of the present bridge on the modern highway from Jerusalem to Tel-Aviv. Modern Moṣa lies to the south and east of the bridge.

many olive trees,[106] A. Edersheim also spoke of its "scented orange- and lemon-gardens, olive-groves, [and] luscious fruit trees...."[107] A traveler in 1483, Hans Werli von Zimber, described it as "a valley which is very fertile with olive and fig trees and grapes, but particularly numerous are the Terebinths, big trees that carry tasteful berries from which oil is pressed."[108] Jewish families from the Old City of Jerusalem farmed the land already in 1859, yet they did not stay at Moṣa permanently. The modern Israeli village of Moṣa, now south and east of the highway to Tel Aviv, was founded at the beginning of the 1890's, and Moṣa Illit (Upper Moṣa) further to the west was added in 1933. Moṣa is now basically a garden suburb of Jerusalem.[109]

2) The Route to Jerusalem.

From the former ancient bridge that crossed the Naḥal Soreq not far from the spring of Moṣa, the ancient road leading east proceeded ca. 1800 meters (through what is now part of the Jerusalem Forest) before reaching the winding "Ascent of the Romans."[110] After that it is only ca. 500 meters to the modern site Giv'at Sha'ul. Departing from there, the ancient Roman road most probably followed the modern Jerusalem streets Ketav Sofer, Giv'at Sha'ul and Weizmann Boulevard. "Then it may have followed Jaffa Street for 1.5 km till Herut Square," ending more probably at the Jaffa Gate, less probably at the Damascus Gate.[111]

Cleopas and his companion are represented in Luke 24 as walking approximately this stretch of road (7 km or 4.2 miles) twice, on Easter Sunday afternoon and evening, once joined by the resurrected Jesus.

---

[106] *Orte und Wege Jesu* 244.

[107] *The Life and Times of Jesus the Messiah* 2.639. On p. 640, n. 1, he remarks: "Even today [before the first edition of 1883] this seems a favourite resort of the inhabitants of Jerusalem for an afternoon...." Another nineteenth century scholar noted "figs, pomegranates, quinces, pears, etc." (Fischer, Isaac and Roll, *Roman Roads in Judaea*, II. 225, with n. 794).

[108] Quoted in *ibid.*, 224, with n. 789.

[109] Cf. E. Orni, art. "Moza," "Modern Times" in *EJ* (1971) 12.494-495, and E. Orni and E. Efrat, *Geography of Israel* (Jerusalem: Israel Program for Scientific Translations, 1964) 158.

[110] On an official Jerusalem city map from before 1967 (M. Gabrieli for the Israel Government Tourist Corporation), the street from Moṣa to Giv'at Sha'ul, including the winding "Via Romanorum," is still clearly shown.

[111] Fischer, Isaac and Roll, *Roman Roads in Judaea*, II. 97.

Sources and Reference Works

I. The Bible

Kittel, *Biblia Hebraica*, ed. R. Kittel et al. (Stuttgart: Privilegierte Württembergische Bibelanstalt, 1951⁷).

Rahlfs, *Septuaginta*, ed. A. Rahlfs (Stuttgart: Württembergische Bibelanstalt, 1962⁷).

Wewers, *Genesis*, Septuaginta, Vetus Testamentum Graecum 1, ed. J. Wewers (Göttingen: Vandenhoeck & Ruprecht, 1974).

Ziegler, *Sapientia Iesu Filii Sirach*, Septuaginta, Vetus Testamentum Graecum 12:2, ed. J. Ziegler (Göttingen: Vandenhoeck & Ruprecht, 1980²).

Hatch-Redpath, *A Concordance to the Septuagint*, ed. E. Hatch and H. Redpath (Oxford: Clarendon, 1897; corrected reprint Grand Rapids, Michigan: Baker Book House, 1983), 2 vols.

Ben Ḥayyim, *The Book of Ben Sira*. Text, Concordance and an Analysis of the Vocabulary, ed. Z. Ben Ḥayyim (The Historical Dictionary of the Hebrew Language; Jerusalem: The Academy of the Hebrew Language and the Shrine of the Book, 1973).

Lévi, *The Hebrew Text of the Book of Ecclesiasticus*, ed. I. Lévi (SSS 3; Leiden: Brill, 1951; original 1904).

Weber, *Biblia Sacra*. Iuxta Vulgatam Versionem, Tomus I, ed. R. Weber (Stuttgart: Württembergische Bibelanstalt, 1975²).

Nestle / Aland, *Novum Testamentum Graece*, ed. E. Nestle, K. Aland, et al. (Stuttgart: Deutsche Bibelgesellschaft, 1990²⁶).

Hebrew New Testament, by F. Delitzsch (Berlin: Trowitzsch and Son, 1885).

Hebrew New Testament (Jerusalem: The United Bible Societies, 1979).

II.   *The Targums*

Sperber, *The Bible in Aramaic,* ed. A. Sperber (Leiden: Brill, 1959), 4 vols.

Rieder, *Targum Jonathan ben Uziel on the Pentateuch,* ed. with a Hebrew translation by D. Rieder (Jerusalem, 1984), 2 vols.

Etheridge, *The Targums of Onkelos and Jonathan Ben Uzziel on the Pentateuch with the Fragments of the Jerusalem Targum,* trans. J. Etheridge (New York: KTAV, 1968; original 1862).

Clarke, *Targum Pseudo-Jonathan: Deuteronomy,* ed. E. Clarke (The Aramaic Bible 5 B; Edinburgh: Clark, 1998).

Harrington and Saldarini, *Targum Jonathan of the Former Prophets,* trans. D. Harrington and A. Saldarini (The Aramaic Bible 10; Edinburgh: Clark, 1987).

Stenning, *The Targum of Isaiah,* ed. and trans. J. Stenning (Oxford: Clarendon, 1949).

Levine, *The Aramaic Version of Jonah,* ed. E. Levine (New York: Sepher-Hermon Press, 1981³).

Merino, *Targum de Salmos.* Edición Príncipe del Ms. Villa-Amil n.5 de Alfonso de Zamora, ed. L. Merino (Madrid: Consejo Superior de Investigaciones Científicas, 1982).

Levine, *The Aramaic Version of Qohelet,* ed. E. Levine (New York: Sepher-Hermon Press, 1981).

Déaut and Robert, *Targum des Chroniques,* II., ed. R. Le Déaut and J. Robert (AnBib 51; Rome: Biblical Institute, 1971).

III.   *The Mishnah and Tosefta*

Albeck, *Shisha Sidre Mishna,* ed. Ch. Albeck (Jerusalem and Tel Aviv: Bialik Institute and Dvir, 1975), 6 vols.

Danby, *The Mishnah,* trans. H. Danby (London: Oxford University, 1933).

Neusner, *The Mishnah,* trans. J. Neusner (New Haven: Yale University, 1988).

Bornhäuser, *Die Mischna*, II. Seder, Mo'ed. 6. Traktat, Sukka, ed. H. Bornhäuser (Berlin: Töpelmann, 1935).

Zuckermandel, *Tosephta*, ed. M. Zuckermandel, with a supplement by S. Liebermann (Jerusalem: Wahrmann, 1970).

Neusner, *The Tosefta*, trans. J. Neusner et al. (Hoboken, New Jersey: KTAV, 1977-1986), 6 vols.

IV. *The Talmuds*

Soncino, *The Babylonian Talmud*, ed. I. Epstein, various translators (London: Soncino, 1952), 18 volumes and index.

Soncino, *The Minor Tractates of the Talmud*, ed. A. Cohen, various translators (London: Soncino, 1965), 2 vols.

Goldschmidt, *Der Babylonische Talmud*, ed. with a German translation by L. Goldschmidt (Haag: Nijoff, 1933), 9 vols.

Krotoshin, *Talmud Yerushalmi*, Krotoshin edition (Jerusalem: Shilah, 1969).

Neusner, *The Talmud of the Land of Israel*, trans. J. Neusner et al. (Chicago: University of Chicago, 1982-1995), 34 vols.

Horowitz, *Berakhoth*, German of the Talmud Yerushalmi by C. Horowitz (Tübingen: Mohr, 1975).

Wewers, *Sanhedrin*, German of the Talmud Yerushalmi by G. Wewers (Tübingen: Mohr / Siebeck, 1981).

V. *Halakhic Midrashim*

Lauterbach, *Mekilta de-Rabbi Ishmael*, ed. and trans. J. Lauterbach (Philadelphia: The Jewish Publication Society of America, 1976), 3 vols.

Neusner, *Sifra. An Analytical Translation*, trans. J. Neusner (BJS 138-140; Atlanta: Scholars Press, 1988), 3 vols.

Horowitz, *Siphre ad Numeros adjecto Siphre zutta*, ed. H. Horowitz (Jerusalem: Wahrmann, 1976).

Neusner, *Sifre to Numbers*, trans. J. Neusner (BJS 118-119; Atlanta: Scholars Press, 1986), 2 vols.

Kuhn, *Der tannaitische Midrasch Sifre zu Numeri*, German by K. Kuhn (Stuttgart: Kohlhammer, 1959).

Finkelstein, *Sifre on Deuteronomy*, ed. L. Finkelstein (New York: The Jewish Theological Seminary of America, 1969).

Hammer, *Sifre*. A Tannaitic Commentary on the Book of Deuteronomy, trans. R. Hammer (YJS 24; New Haven: Yale University, 1986).

Neusner, *Sifre to Deuteronomy*. An Analytical Translation, trans. J. Neusner (BJS 98 and 101; Atlanta: Scholars Press, 1987), 2 vols.

Hoffmann, *Midrasch Tannaim zum Deuteronomium*, ed. D. Hoffmann (Berlin, 1908-1909).

VI. *Haggadic Midrashim*

Soncino, *Midrash Rabbah*, ed. H. Freedman and M. Simon (London: Soncino, 1939), 9 volumes and index.

Midrash Rabbah (Vilna: Romm, 1887).

Mirqin, *Midrash Rabbah*, Pentateuch. Ed. and vocalized by M. Mirqin (Tel Aviv: Yavneh, 1981), 11 vols.

Theodor and Albeck, *Midrash Bereshit Rabba*, ed. J. Theodor and Ch. Albeck (Jerusalem: Wahrmann, 1965), 3 vols.

Margulies, *Leviticus Rabbah*: Midrash Wayyikra Rabbah, ed. M. Margulies (Jerusalem: Ministry of Education and Culture of Israel, American Academy for Jewish Research, 1953–1960).

Margulies, *Midrash Haggadol on the Pentateuch*, Genesis, ed. M. Margulies (Jerusalem: Mosad Harav Kook, 1975).

Midrash Tanḥuma, Eshkol edition (Jerusalem: Eshkol, no date).

Buber, *Midrasch Tanḥuma*: Ein agadischer Commentar zum Pentateuch, ed. S. Buber (Vilna: Romm, 1885).

Bietenhard, *Midrasch Tanḥuma B*, German by H. Bietenhard (Judaica et Christiana 5-6; Bern: Peter Lang, 1980–1982), 2 vols.

Schechter, *Aboth de Rabbi Nathan* (A and B), ed. S. Schechter (Vienna, 1887; reprinted New York: Feldheim, 1945).

Goldin, *The Fathers According to Rabbi Nathan* (A), trans. J. Goldin (YJS 10; New Haven: Yale University, 1955).

Neusner, *The Fathers According to Rabbi Nathan. An Analytical Translation and Explanation*, trans. J. Neusner (BJS 114; Atlanta: Scholars Press, 1986).

Saldarini, *The Fathers According to Rabbi Nathan* (B), trans. A. Saldarini (SJLA 11; Leiden: Brill, 1975).

Mandelbaum, *Pesikta de Rav Kahana*, ed. B. Mandelbaum (New York: The Jewish Theological Seminary of America, 1962), 2 vols.

Braude and Kapstein, *Pesikta de-Rab Kahana*, trans. W. Braude and I. Kapstein (Philadelphia: The Jewish Publication Society of America, 1975).

Neusner, *Pesiqta de Rab Kahana. An Analytical Translation*, trans. J. Neusner (BJS 122–123; Atlanta: Scholars Press, 1987).

Friedmann, *Pesikta Rabbati*, ed. M. Friedmann (Vienna, 1880; reprint Tel Aviv, 1962–1963).

Braude, *Pesikta Rabbati*, trans. W. Braude (YJS 18; New Haven: Yale University, 1968), 2 vols.

Friedmann, *Seder Eliahu rabba und Seder Eliahu zuta*, ed. M. Friedmann (Vienna, 1902–1904; reprint Jerusalem, 1969).

Braude and Kapstein, *Tanna debe Eliyyahu*, trans. W. Braude and I. Kapstein (Philadelphia: The Jewish Publication Society of America, 1981).

Buber, *Midrasch Tehillim*, ed. S. Buber (Vilna: Romm, 1891).

Braude, *The Midrash on Psalms*, trans. W. Braude (YJS 13, 1–2; New Haven: Yale University, 1959), 2 vols.

Buber, *Midrasch Mischle*, ed. S. Buber (Vilna, 1893; reprint Jerusalem, 1965).

Visotzky, *The Midrash on Proverbs*, trans. B. Visotzky (YJS 27; New Haven: Yale University, 1992).

Donsqi, *Midrash Rabbah. Shir ha-Shirim*, ed. S. Donsqi (Jerusalem: Dvir, 1980).

Eshkol, *Pirqe Rabbi Eliezer*, Eshkol edition (Jerusalem: Eshkol, 1973).

Higger, *Pirqe R. Eliezer*, ed. M. Higger in *Horeb* 8 (1944) 82–119; 9 (1946) 94–116; and 10 (1948) 185–294.

Friedlander, *Pirke de Rabbi Eliezer*, trans. G. Friedlander (New York: Hermon, 1970; original London, 1916).

Buber, *Aggadat Bereshit*, ed. S. Buber (Cracow: Fischer, 1902; reprint Vilna: Romm, 1925).

Milikowsky, *Seder Olam*. A Rabbinic Chronography, ed. and trans. Ch. Milikowsky (1981 Yale University Ph.D. dissertation).

Jellinek, *Bet ha-Midrasch*, ed. A. Jellinek (Jerusalem: Wahrmann Books, 1967³), 6 volumes in 2.

Eisenstein, *Ozar Midrashim*, ed. J. Eisenstein (New York: E. Grossman's Hebrew Book Store, 1915).

Horowitz, *Sammlung kleiner Midraschim*, ed. Ch. Horowitz (Berlin, 1881; reprint Jerusalem, 1966–1967).

Wünsche, *Aus Israels Lehrhallen*. German by A. Wünsche (Leipzig: Pfeiffer, 1907–1909; reprint Hildesheim: Olms, 1967), 5 vols.

Wünsche, "Der Prophet Jona in der agadischen Deutung des Jalkut Schimoni," Hebrew and German by A. Wünsche in *Vierteljahrschrift für Bibelkunde* 1 (1905) 235–255.

Greenup, *The Yalkut of R. Machbir bar Abba Mari*, ed. A. Greenup (London, 1909).

*   *   *

Siegert, *Drei hellenistische Predigten*. Ps-Philon, "Über Jona," etc. German by F. Siegert (WUNT 20; Tübingen: Mohr / Siebeck, 1980).

VII. *Apocrypha, Pseudepigrapha, Philo, Josephus, Qumran*

Apocrypha: see Rahlfs, *Septuaginta*.

OTP. The Old Testament Pseudepigrapha, ed. J. Charlesworth (Garden City, New York: Doubleday, 1983-1985), 2 vols.

Harrington, *Les Antiquités Bibliques*, ed. D. Harrington, French by J. Cazeaux (SC 229–230; Paris: du Cerf, 1976), 2 vols.

LCL, *Philo*, Greek and English translation by F. Colson, G. Whitaker, J. Earp and R. Marcus (Cambridge, Massachusetts: Harvard University, 1971), 10 volumes with 2 supplements.

Niese, *Flavii Iosephi Opera*, ed. B. Niese (Berlin: Weidmann, 1952).

LCL, *Josephus*, Greek and English translation by H. Thackeray, R. Marcus and A. Wikgren (Cambridge, Massachusetts: Harvard University, 1969), 9 vols.

Martínez and Tigchelaar, *The Dead Sea Scrolls Study Edition*, ed. F. Martínez and E. Tigchelaar, Vol. One (Leiden: Brill, 1997).

Charlesworth, *Graphic Concordance to the Dead Sea Scrolls*, ed. J. Charlesworth (Tübingen: Mohr; Louisville: Westminster, John Knox, 1991).

VIII. *Greek and Roman Writers*

Strabo, *The Geography of Strabo*, trans. H. Jones (LCL; Cambridge, MA: Harvard University Press, 1932 / 1959).

Plutarch's Lives, trans. B. Perrin (LCL; Cambridge, MA: Harvard University Press, 1914 / 1982), 11 vols.

Appian's Roman History, trans. H. White (LCL; Cambridge, MA: Harvard University Press, 1912 / 1982), 4 vols.

Dio Cassius, *Dio's Roman History*, trans. E. Cary (LCL; Cambridge, MA: Harvard University Press, 1914–1927 / 1954–1955), 9 vols.

Aristaenetus, *Aristaeneti Epistularum libri II*, ed. O. Mazal (Stuttgart: Teubner, 1971).

Aristainetos: Erotische Briefe, German by A. Lesky (Zurich: Artemis-Verlag, 1951).

Diogenes Laertius, *Lives of Eminent Philosophers*, trans. R. Hicks (LCL; Cambridge, MS: Harvard University Press, 1925 / 1958), 2 vols.

Diogenes Laertii, Vitae Philosophorum, ed. H. Long (Oxford: Oxford University Press, 1964), 2 vols.

Ammianus Marcellius, trans. J. Rolfe (LCL; Cambridge, MA: Harvard University Press, 1935–1939 / 1956–1958), 3 vols.

Caesar, Gaius Julius, *The Civil Wars*, trans. A. Peskett (LCL; Cambridge, MA: Harvard University Press, 1914 / 1966).

Cicero. The Speeches, "Pro Lege Manilia," etc., trans. H. Grose (LCL; Cambridge, MA: Harvard University Press, 1927 / 1966).

Suetonius, *The Lives of the Caesars*, trans. J. Rolfe (LCL; Cambridge, MA: Harvard University Press, 1913 / 1989), 2 vols.

Lucan, *The Civil War, Books I–X (Pharsalia)*, trans. J. Duff (LCL; Cambridge, MA: Harvard University Press, 1928 / 1962).

IX.   *Church Fathers*

Origen, "Contra Celsum" in *Origenes Werke*, ed. P. Koetschau (GCS 3; Leipzig: Hinrichs, 1899).

Klostermann, *Eusebius, Das Onomastikon der biblischen Ortsnamen*, ed. E. Klostermann (Leipzig: Hinrichs, 1904; reprint Hildesheim: Olms, 1966).

Jérôme. Commentaire sur Jonas, ed. Y.-M. Duval (SC 323; Paris: du Cerf, 1985).

Jerome, *S. Hieronymi Presbyteri Opera*. Pars I, Exegetica, 7: Commentariorum in Matheum, Liber IV (CChr, Series Latina LXXVII; Turnhout: Brepols, 1969).

Schwartz, *Kyrillos von Skythopolis*, ed. E. Schwartz (Texte und Untersuchungen zur Geschichte der altchristlichen Literatur 49.2; Leipzig: Hinrichs, 1939).

X.   *Dictionaries and Reference Works*

BDB, *A Hebrew and English Lexicon of the Old Testament*, by F. Brown, S. Driver and C. Briggs (Oxford: Clarendon, 1962).

Jastrow, *A Dictionary of the Targumim*, the Talmud Babli and Yerushalmi, and the Midrashic Literature, by M. Jastrow (New York: Pardes, 1950), 2 vols.

Alcalay, *The Complete Hebrew-English Dictionary*, by R. Alcalay (Tel Aviv and Jerusalem: Massadah, 1965).

Krauss, *Griechische und Lateinische Lehnwörter in Talmud, Midrasch und Targum*, by S. Krauss (Berlin: Calvary, 1898–1899).

Krauss, *Talmudische Archäologie*, by S. Krauss (Leipzig: Fock, 1911; reprint Hildesheim: Olms, 1966).

Hyman, *Torah Hakethubah Vehamessurah*. A Reference Book of the Scriptural Passages Quoted in Talmudic, Midrashic and Early Rabbinic Literature, by Aaron Hyman, second edition by Arthur Hyman (Tel Aviv: Dvir, 1979), 3 vols.

Schürer, *The history of the Jewish people in the age of Jesus Christ (175 B.C. – A.D. 135)*, by E. Schürer, ed. G. Vermes, F. Millar and M. Black (Edinburgh: Clark, 1973–1986), 3 vols.

Strack and Stemberger, *Introduction to the Talmud and Midrash*, by H. Strack and G. Stemberger (Minneapolis: Fortress, 1992). At times I refer to the German edition, *Einleitung in Talmud und Midrasch* (Munich: Beck, 1982[7]).

Ginzberg, *The Legends of the Jews*, by L. Ginzberg (Philadelphia: The Jewish Publication Society of America, 1968), 6 volumes and index.

JE, *The Jewish Encyclopedia* (New York: Funk and Wagnalls, 1905), 12 vols.

EncJud, *Encyclopaedia Judaica* (Jerusalem: Keter, 1971), 16 vols.

LSJ, *A Greek-English Lexicon*, by H. Liddell, R. Scott and H. Jones (Oxford: Clarendon, 1966[9]).

BAGD, *A Greek-English Lexicon of the New Testament and Other Early Christian Literature*, by W. Bauer, W. Arndt, F. Gingrich and F. Danker (Chicago: University of Chicago, 1979[2]).

BDF, *A Greek Grammar of the New Testament and Other Christian Literature*, by F. Blass, A. Debrunner and R. Funk (Chicago: University of Chicago Press, 1962).

Chambers Murray latin-english Dictionary, ed. W. Smith and J. Lockwood (Edinburgh: Chambers; London: Murray, 1986).

TDNT, *Theological Dictionary of the New Testament*, ed. G. Kittel and G. Friedrich (Grand Rapids, Michigan: Eerdmans, 1964–1976), 9 volumes and index.

Str-B, *Kommentar zum Neuen Testament aus Talmud und Midrasch,* by (H. Strack and) P. Billerbeck (Munich: Beck, 1924–1961), 6 vols.

Nickelsburg, *Jewish Literature Between the Bible and the Mishnah,* by G. Nickelsburg (Philadelphia: Fortress, 1981).

Index of Modern Authors

About the Author

Roger David Aus, b. 1940, studied English and German at St. Olaf College, and theology at Harvard Divinity School, Luther Theological Seminary, and Yale University, from which he received the Ph.D. degree in New Testament Studies in 1971. He is an ordained clergyman of the Evangelical Lutheran Church in America, currently serving the German-speaking Luthergemeinde in Berlin-Reinickendorf, Germany. The Protestant Church of Berlin-Brandenburg (Berlin West) kindly granted him a short study leave in Jerusalem, Israel, in 1981. His study of New Testament topics always reflects his great interest in, and deep appreciation of, the Jewish roots of the Christian faith.

WITHDRAWN